The Agentic Revolution

Build, Optimize, Deploy AI That Acts!

Amrita Panjwani

Table of Contents

First Edition, 2026

Author: Amrita Panjwani

1. From Prompts to Practical AI Agents

Key Objectives

- Shift from Prompts to Systems
- Real-World Problems That Necessitated Agents
- What Is an AI Agent?
- Core Components of an Agent System
- Agent vs Workflow vs Automation
- The Spectrum of Agent Capabilities
- Trade-Offs and Engineering Realities
- When Not to Use Agents
- Common Failure Modes in Agent Systems
- From Understanding to Building

1.1 The Shift from Prompts to Systems

When large language models became widely accessible, they felt transformative. For the first time, software could generate coherent text, write functional code, summarize documents, and perform reasoning tasks simply by responding to natural language instructions. It seemed as though programming itself had changed. Instead of writing logic, we could describe intent.

This gave rise to what many called the era of prompt engineering. Developers experimented with clearer instructions, structured outputs, role-based prompting, and chain-of-thought reasoning. With careful wording, the same model could produce dramatically different results. For many early applications, this approach was more than sufficient.

But as use cases expanded beyond simple generation tasks, limitations began to surface.

Consider a realistic requirement: - analyze a dataset - detect anomalies - query related records from a database - validate the findings - produce a structured report.

A single prompt cannot reliably execute such a workflow. It cannot access external tools directly, verify intermediate results, retry failed steps, or maintain structured state across multiple operations. Attempting to compress all logic into one large prompt introduces new problems — token explosion, fragile reasoning paths, lack of execution validation, and absence of persistence.

The limitation here is not intelligence. It is structure. A prompt produces an output. A system requires orchestration.

Orchestration involves deciding what happens next, selecting appropriate tools, executing actions, observing results, updating internal state, and continuing until a goal is achieved. Traditional software systems handle this deterministically through predefined control flow. In modern AI systems, part of this decision-making can be delegated to a language model — but it still requires an architecture around it.

This is the fundamental shift. We move from asking a model for an answer to building a system that uses the model as a reasoning component inside a control loop.

The difference is profound. Prompt-based systems optimize for response quality. Agentic systems must optimize for reliability, traceability, cost control, safety, and scalability. Once we introduce iterative reasoning and tool interaction, we are no longer simply generating text — we are engineering behavior.

Understanding this shift is essential before building practical AI agents. Without recognizing the difference between generation and orchestration, it is easy to mistake a powerful demo for a production-ready system.

1.2 Real-World Problems That Necessitated Agents

As organizations began integrating large language models into production systems, it became clear that generation alone was insufficient for many real-world tasks.

Early applications focused on summarization, drafting content, and answering questions within a bounded context. These use cases were largely stateless and single-step. A prompt was issued, and a response was returned. While impressive, this interaction model proved limiting when tasks required structure, verification, or interaction with external systems.

Consider the problem of automated financial analysis. A system may be required to retrieve structured financial data, compute derived metrics, compare multiple entities, validate inconsistencies, and produce a reasoned report. Each of these steps requires not only reasoning but execution and validation. A language model cannot independently access databases, perform guaranteed numerical computations, or confirm the correctness of intermediate steps. These capabilities must be provided by the surrounding system.

Similarly, in software development automation, a model may generate code that appears correct but fails during execution. A practical system must be able to run the code, capture errors, revise the implementation, and re-test until correctness criteria are satisfied. This requires iteration and feedback loops — capabilities beyond single-response prompting.

Another example arises in document intelligence. Suppose an organization needs to analyze hundreds of documents, extract structured information, reconcile conflicting statements, and produce a consolidated summary. The task requires retrieval, cross-verification, context tracking, and structured reasoning across multiple steps. Attempting to compress such logic into a single prompt results in fragile outputs and unpredictable reasoning paths.

Across domains — finance, healthcare, legal analysis, research automation, data engineering — similar patterns emerged. These tasks required systems that could reason across multiple steps, make decisions based on intermediate results, invoke external tools when necessary, retain contextual information between steps, verify outputs before proceeding, and refine their results through iteration.

These requirements exposed a structural gap. While LLMs could reason about text, they could not autonomously manage multi-step execution.

This gap led to the development of agentic architectures — systems that embed language models inside controlled loops capable of planning, acting, observing, and updating state.

Agents did not emerge because models became smarter.
They emerged because real-world tasks demanded structured orchestration.

1.3 What is an AI Agent?

Having examined the limitations of prompt-only systems and the real-world problems that exposed those limitations, we can now define what an AI agent is in practical terms. An AI agent is a system that uses a language model within a structured control loop to pursue a goal through reasoning, action, and observation. It uses that model as one component inside a broader architecture that governs how decisions are made and how actions are executed.

At a minimum, an agentic system involves the following elements:

- A defined objective or goal
- A mechanism for reasoning about the next step
- The ability to execute actions, often via tools
- A way to observe outcomes of those actions
- A method to update internal state
- A loop that continues until the goal is satisfied

This structure can be conceptualized as a control loop:

1. Evaluate the current state relative to the goal.
2. Determine the next action.
3. Execute the action.
4. Observe the result.
5. Update state and repeat.

Without this loop, the system remains a single-step generator. With this loop, the system becomes capable of iterative problem-solving. It is important to note that autonomy exists on a spectrum. Some agents require frequent human oversight. Others operate semi-independently within predefined constraints. Fully autonomous systems are rare and introduce significant reliability challenges.

Therefore, we define an AI agent operationally: **An AI agent is a goal-driven system that uses a language model to dynamically determine and execute actions within a structured control loop.**

This definition emphasizes architecture rather than intelligence. The defining characteristic of an agent is not that it is "smart", but that it participates in a decision–action–observation cycle.

AI Agent – Flow of Thinking and Action

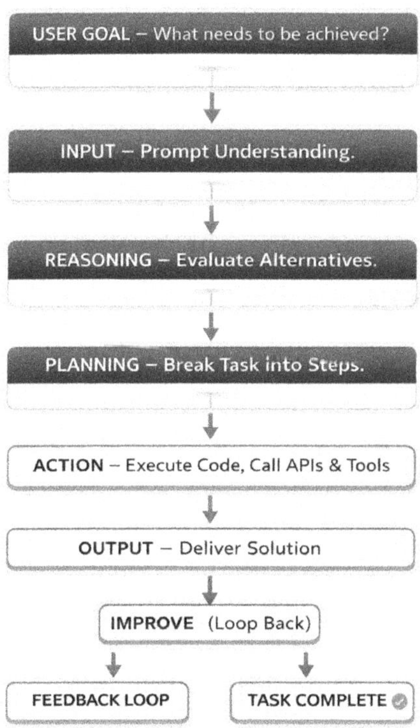

1.4 Core Components of an Agent System

An agentic system is not a single construct but a composition of interacting components. Understanding these components individually is essential before attempting to design or implement practical AI agents.

At a high level, every agent system can be decomposed into five architectural layers: - the model layer - the orchestration layer - the tool layer - the memory layer - the evaluation layer.

While implementations may vary, these layers consistently appear in production-grade systems.

1. The Model Layer

At the center of the system lies the language model. The model provides reasoning capability, pattern recognition, and language understanding. It does not manage execution, enforce correctness, or maintain structured state beyond its input context.

In an agent system, the model serves as a decision-making engine. It interprets the current state and proposes the next action. However, it does not execute that action directly. The model reasons; the system acts. Recognizing this separation prevents a common design mistake: overloading the model with responsibilities that belong in orchestration logic.

2. The Orchestration Layer

The orchestration layer governs control flow. It determines when the model is invoked, how its output is interpreted, and what happens next. This layer implements the control loop described earlier:

- evaluating the goal
- selecting actions
- executing tools
- observing outcomes
- and determining whether iteration should continue.

In practical systems, orchestration includes safeguards such as maximum step limits, structured output parsing, error handling, and termination conditions. Without this layer, the agent lacks structure and reliability.

3. The Tool Layer

Agents become powerful when they extend beyond text generation. The tool layer enables interaction with external systems such as databases, APIs, file systems, search engines, or computational engines.

Tools must be explicitly defined and safely invoked. The agent does not inherently "know" how to execute SQL queries or perform arithmetic reliably; it must delegate these tasks to deterministic tools.

This separation ensures correctness where precision is required and preserves the model's role as a reasoning component rather than an execution engine.

4. The Memory Layer

Unlike prompt-only systems, agentic systems often require persistence. The memory layer manages information across steps or sessions. This may include short-term state within a single reasoning loop, long-term storage of prior interactions, or structured representations of intermediate results.

Without memory, agents cannot refine their outputs effectively or maintain coherence across multi-step tasks. Designing memory carefully is critical. Excessive memory increases cost and complexity, while insufficient memory limits reasoning depth.

5. The Evaluation Layer

An often-overlooked component of agent systems is evaluation. Generation alone does not guarantee correctness. Practical systems must measure:

- task completion success
- accuracy of outputs
- tool invocation validity
- cost per execution

- and latency

Evaluation mechanisms allow the system to detect failure conditions and, in more advanced designs, trigger corrective loops or escalation to human oversight.

These components do not operate independently. They form an integrated architecture in which reasoning, action, memory, and validation work together within a controlled loop. Understanding this decomposition shifts the perspective from "using a model" to engineering a structured system.

1.5 Agent vs Workflow vs Automation

As agent-based systems gained popularity, the term "agent" began to be used loosely. Not every automated system is an agent, and not every workflow involving a language model qualifies as agentic.

To design practical systems responsibly, we must distinguish clearly between automation, workflows, and AI agents.

Automation

Automation refers to a fixed sequence of predefined steps executed deterministically.
The logic is fully specified in advance, and no dynamic reasoning occurs during execution.

For example, a data pipeline that extracts records, transforms fields, and loads them into a database operates through deterministic logic. The sequence does not change based on contextual interpretation by a model.

Automation optimizes for predictability and reliability. It does not introduce uncertainty.

Workflow Systems

Workflow systems introduce conditional branching but remain structurally predefined. In a workflow system, the possible execution paths are known ahead of time. Conditional logic determines which path is taken, but the system does not invent new steps at runtime.

For example, a customer service system may route tickets based on predefined categories: - If billing issue → send to billing pipeline. - If technical issue → send to support pipeline.

Even when a language model is used within a workflow, the overarching structure remains fixed. Workflow systems increase flexibility compared to automation but remain fundamentally deterministic in structure.

Agentic Systems

An agentic system differs in a critical way: it determines its own next action dynamically. Rather than selecting from predefined execution branches, the agent reasons about the current state and proposes the next step based on context. The control loop allows the system to adapt its sequence of actions at runtime.

This introduces non-determinism. The exact path taken may vary across runs, even for similar inputs.

For example, a research agent tasked with preparing a report may:

- Decide which documents to retrieve
- Choose which tools to invoke
- Revise intermediate findings
- And iterate until a goal is met.

The execution path is not fully predetermined. It emerges through reasoning within the control loop.

The distinction can be summarized conceptually:

- Automation executes predefined steps.
- Workflows choose among predefined branches.
- Agents dynamically determine new steps within a goal-driven loop.

This distinction is not merely semantic. It determines how systems are tested, monitored, and governed. Automation emphasizes correctness and repeatability. Workflow systems emphasize structured branching. Agentic systems emphasize adaptive reasoning within constraints.

Understanding these boundaries prevents both over-engineering and misuse. Not every problem requires agency. In many cases, deterministic workflows remain superior due to simplicity and reliability.

The decision to build an agent should be deliberate, not trend-driven.

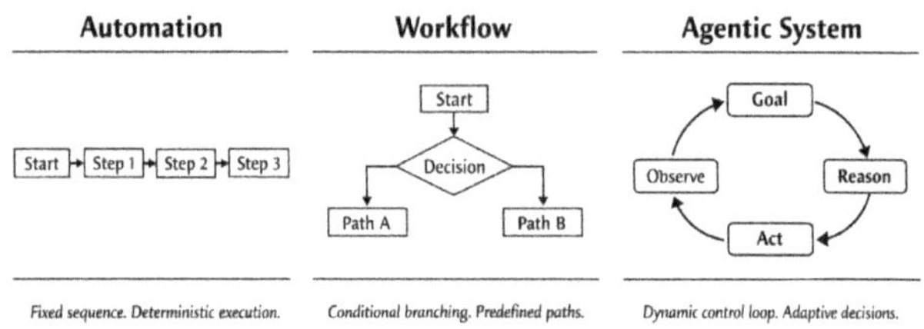

1.6 The Spectrum of Agent Capabilities

Not all agents are equal in capability or complexity. The term "AI agent" encompasses a wide range of systems — from simple tool-using assistants to sophisticated multi-agent orchestration frameworks. Treating all of them as equivalent obscures important architectural differences. Agent capability exists on a spectrum. At one end of the spectrum are lightweight, reactive systems. These agents typically operate within a constrained control loop. They may interpret user input, select from a small set of tools, and return structured outputs. Their reasoning depth is limited, and their execution path remains relatively simple. Moving along the spectrum, we encounter planning agents. These systems do not merely react; they decompose goals into subtasks. A planning agent might first outline required steps, then execute them sequentially, adapting based on intermediate outcomes. This introduces hierarchical reasoning and greater state management complexity. Further along are reflective agents. These systems incorporate evaluation mechanisms within their own loop. After producing an intermediate output, they critique or verify it before proceeding. This internal feedback loop improves reliability but increases computational cost and orchestration complexity.

At a higher level of sophistication, multi-agent systems emerge. Rather than relying on a single reasoning entity, these architectures assign specialized roles to multiple agents. One agent may retrieve information, another may analyze it, and a third may review or validate conclusions. Coordination mechanisms become central in such designs, and shared state management grows more complex.

At the far end of the spectrum lie autonomous workflow systems. These systems pursue complex goals with minimal human intervention, dynamically selecting tools, revising plans, and managing long-running tasks. While powerful, they demand rigorous monitoring, cost controls, and safety mechanisms.

Understanding this spectrum is essential for practical engineering decisions. Not every task requires a multi-agent architecture. In many cases, a constrained reactive agent is sufficient and preferable due to simplicity and reliability.

As we progress through this book, we will move deliberately across this spectrum. We will begin with foundational agent patterns and gradually increase complexity, building toward production-grade systems.

The goal is not to build the most complex agent possible.
The goal is to build the right level of agency for the problem at hand.

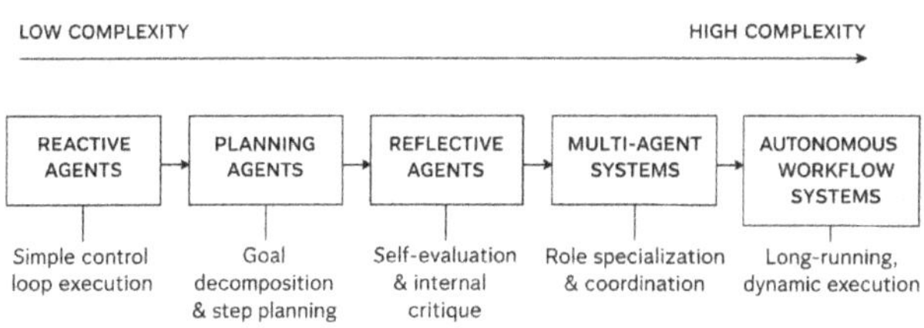

1.7 Trade-Offs and Engineering Realities

Agentic systems expand capability, but they also introduce complexity. Understanding this trade-off is essential before adopting agents in production environments.

The appeal of agents lies in their flexibility. They can reason dynamically, invoke tools, revise their outputs, and adapt execution paths at runtime. However, this flexibility comes at measurable cost — both computational and architectural. One of the most immediate trade-offs is increased resource consumption. Iterative reasoning loops require multiple model invocations. Planning steps, tool calls, validation passes, and reflection cycles all consume tokens and computational time. Compared to a single-prompt system, an agentic loop may multiply inference cost significantly.

Latency is another critical consideration. Each iteration introduces delay. In systems where responsiveness is essential — such as real-time user interfaces or low-latency decision engines — additional reasoning cycles can degrade user experience.

Debugging complexity also increases. In deterministic systems, execution paths are predefined. When behavior is dynamic, tracing the source of failure becomes more challenging. An incorrect output may result from flawed reasoning, improper tool invocation, insufficient memory context, or orchestration logic errors. Observability and logging become mandatory rather than optional.

Evaluation presents an additional challenge. Traditional software systems can often be validated through deterministic test cases. Agentic systems, by contrast, may produce varying outputs across runs. This non-determinism complicates benchmarking and regression testing. Success metrics must be carefully defined and monitored over time.

Reliability becomes a central engineering concern. Agents may:

- Over-rely on tools
- Hallucinate tool parameters
- Enter unintended reasoning loops
- Or generate plausible but incorrect conclusions

Without guardrails and termination controls, such systems can escalate cost or produce misleading results.

Finally, governance and safety considerations cannot be ignored. Systems capable of dynamic decision-making must operate within clearly defined constraints. Permissions, access controls, and escalation pathways should be explicitly engineered.

These realities do not diminish the value of agents. Instead, they reinforce the need for disciplined design. Practical AI agents are not built by maximizing autonomy. They are built by balancing flexibility with control.

1.8 When Not to Use Agents

The growing enthusiasm around agentic systems can create the impression that agents are the solution to every problem. In practice, this is rarely true. Engineering discipline requires knowing when not to introduce additional complexity. Agents are most valuable when dynamic reasoning and adaptive execution are necessary. When those characteristics are absent, simpler architectures are often superior.

If a task can be solved deterministically through predefined logic, introducing an agent may increase cost and reduce reliability without adding meaningful benefit. Data transformations, rule-based validations, scheduled batch processing, and fixed API pipelines are often better served by traditional automation.

Latency-sensitive systems are another domain where caution is warranted. Each agent iteration introduces model invocation overhead. In applications such as high-frequency decision engines or real-time transactional systems, even small delays may be unacceptable.

Regulated or safety-critical environments also demand careful consideration. Where outcomes must be strictly reproducible and auditable, deterministic workflows may provide stronger guarantees than dynamic reasoning systems.

Cost constraints further influence architectural choice. Multi-step reasoning, reflection loops, and tool invocation can significantly increase token usage and infrastructure demands. For high-volume workloads, these costs accumulate rapidly.

There is also a maintainability dimension. Agentic systems introduce orchestration logic, memory management, and monitoring requirements that increase operational complexity. Teams without adequate observability infrastructure may struggle to manage such systems effectively.

In many cases, a hybrid approach proves most practical: deterministic workflows handle structured tasks, while agents are invoked selectively for problems requiring adaptive reasoning.

Choosing not to use an agent is not a limitation. It is an architectural decision grounded in context. Practical AI engineering is not about maximizing autonomy. It is about selecting the appropriate level of agency for the problem at hand.

1.9 Common Failure Modes in Agentic Systems

Agentic systems introduce dynamic reasoning into software execution.
With that flexibility comes a distinct class of failure modes that differ from traditional deterministic systems.

Understanding these failure patterns early prevents unrealistic expectations and encourages disciplined design.

One common issue is uncontrolled iteration. Because agents operate within a reasoning loop, poorly defined termination conditions can result in repeated tool calls or extended reflection cycles. Without explicit step limits or convergence checks, cost and latency can escalate rapidly.

Tool misuse is another frequent problem. A model may hallucinate tool parameters, invoke inappropriate tools, or misinterpret tool outputs. Since tools often interact with external systems, such errors can propagate beyond the agent itself. Defensive validation and structured interfaces are therefore essential.

Memory drift presents a more subtle challenge. As agents accumulate context across iterations, irrelevant or outdated information may influence subsequent reasoning. Excessive memory retention increases noise and cost, while insufficient memory limits reasoning depth. Striking the correct balance requires careful architectural design.

Overconfidence in incorrect outputs is also characteristic of language-model-driven systems. Agents may produce plausible reasoning chains that are logically flawed or based on inaccurate assumptions. Without evaluation mechanisms or verification steps, these errors may go undetected.

Another failure pattern involves compounding uncertainty. When agents depend on outputs from prior reasoning steps, small inaccuracies can accumulate across iterations. This cascading effect makes intermediate validation critical.

Finally, observability gaps can obscure root causes. Dynamic execution paths make it difficult to reproduce issues without comprehensive logging and step tracing. In production environments, lack of transparency is itself a risk.

These failure modes are not exceptional cases. They are inherent characteristics of dynamic reasoning systems. The purpose of studying them is not to discourage the use of agents, but to emphasize the need for structured orchestration, monitoring, and evaluation.

Table: Core Failure Modes in Agentic Systems

Failure Mode	Core Pattern	Design Safeguard
Uncontrolled Iteration	Open-ended reasoning loop without proper termination.	Step limits and convergence checks.
Tool Misuse	Incorrect tool selection or invalid parameter usage.	Strict schemas and validated tool interfaces.
Memory Drift	Irrelevant or outdated context influencing decisions.	Controlled memory retention and pruning.
Overconfidence	Fluent but logically incorrect reasoning.	Verification and evaluation mechanisms.
Compounding Uncertainty	Small intermediate errors amplifying downstream.	Step-wise validation and checkpoints.

Failure Mode	Core Pattern	Design Safeguard
Observability Gaps	Lack of traceability in dynamic execution paths.	Structured logging and step tracing.

1.10 From Understanding to Building

We began by examining the limits of prompt-only systems and the structural gap between text generation and engineered systems. We then defined what constitutes an agent, decomposed its architectural layers, and clarified how it differs from workflows and automation. Finally, we examined trade-offs and common failure patterns that emerge when dynamic reasoning is introduced into software systems.

The objective was deliberate. Before building practical AI agents, one must understand that agency is not a feature added to a model. It is an architectural decision that introduces flexibility alongside complexity.

An agent is not defined by intelligence alone. It is defined by structure. It is a system in which a model participates in a controlled loop of reasoning, action, observation, and state update. That loop must be designed, constrained, monitored, and evaluated.

Throughout this book, we will approach agents not as experimental constructs but as engineered systems. Each pattern we build will be analyzed in terms of reliability, cost, observability, and scalability. Complexity will be introduced gradually, and autonomy will be earned through structure.

The goal is not to build the most autonomous system possible. The goal is to build systems that are appropriate, controlled, and dependable.

2. Core Agent Architectures

Key Objectives:

- Why Architecture Matters in Agent Design
- The ReAct Architecture
- The Planner–Executor Architecture
- The Reflective (Critic) Architecture
- Multi-Agent Architectures
- Comparing Agent Architectures
- Choosing the Right Architecture
- Common Architectural Pitfalls and Anti-Patterns|

2.1 Why Architecture Matters in Agent Design

The effectiveness of an AI agent is determined less by the model it uses and more by the architecture that governs it.

In practice, many early agent implementations focused heavily on model capability. Developers experimented with larger models, more detailed prompts, and increasingly complex instructions. While these changes sometimes improved performance, they did not address the deeper structural question: how should the system reason, act, and iterate?

Architecture defines how an agent behaves under uncertainty.

A language model generates outputs probabilistically. Without structured orchestration, this probabilistic behavior can lead to inconsistent reasoning paths, unbounded iteration, or fragile tool interactions. Architecture introduces control — not by restricting intelligence, but by channeling it through defined patterns.

Consider two agent systems using the same model. One may rely on a simple reasoning loop without task planning or validation. The other may decompose goals, execute subtasks sequentially, validate intermediate results, and enforce termination conditions. Although the underlying model is identical, the reliability and cost profile of the two systems will differ significantly.

This distinction highlights an essential principle:

Model capability influences potential.

Architecture determines outcome.

In traditional software engineering, architecture separates concerns and enforces boundaries. In agent systems, this separation becomes even more critical. The model should reason, but it should not manage execution directly. Tools should execute deterministically, but they should not decide when to act. Orchestration logic should control flow, but it should not be entangled with reasoning prompts.

When these boundaries blur, systems become difficult to debug and expensive to maintain.

Architecture also determines scalability. A reactive agent may suffice for simple tool invocation, but complex goals often require task decomposition, reflection mechanisms, or coordination between multiple specialized agents. Without recognizing these patterns, developers may attempt to solve increasingly complex tasks using an insufficient structural design.

Another reason architecture matters is observability. Structured architectures allow for clear logging, step tracing, and evaluation. Unstructured loops obscure execution paths and complicate performance analysis.

Throughout this chapter, we will examine core architectural patterns that recur across practical implementations. These patterns are not framework-specific. They represent structural approaches to organizing reasoning and execution.

Understanding these patterns is essential before writing code. Once architecture is clear, implementation becomes systematic rather than experimental.

2.2 The ReAct Architecture

The ReAct (Reason + Act) architecture is one of the foundational patterns in modern agent design. It integrates reasoning with tool execution inside a simple iterative loop.

Unlike single-prompt systems, ReAct agents do not attempt to solve a task in one response. Instead, they alternate between generating a reasoning step and executing an action based on that reasoning. Each action produces an observation, which informs the next reasoning step.

This creates a structured cycle:

Reason → Act → Observe → Update → Repeat

The loop continues until a termination condition is satisfied.

Structural Overview

At its core, the ReAct architecture consists of:

- A goal
- A reasoning step (often called "thought")
- A tool invocation step (action)
- An observation step (feedback from environment)
- A state update mechanism
- A termination condition

The language model generates the reasoning step. The orchestration layer interprets that reasoning and invokes the appropriate tool. The result of the tool is fed back into the model as context for the next iteration. The model does not execute tools directly. It proposes actions. The system executes them. This separation preserves reliability and control.

Conceptual Control Flow

The execution flow can be described as:

1. Initialize state with goal and context.
2. Generate a reasoning step.
3. Determine and execute a tool action.

4. Capture the observation.
5. Update state.
6. Check termination.
7. Repeat if necessary.

This loop introduces dynamic behavior while remaining structurally simple.

Minimal Pseudo-Code Representation

```
def react_agent(goal, environment):
    state = initialize(goal)

    while not termination_condition(state):
        # Reason
        thought = model.generate_reasoning(state)

        # Act
        action = parse_action(thought)
        observation = environment.execute(action)

        # Update
        state = update_state(state, thought, observation)

    return generate_final_output(state)
```

This pseudo-code highlights the separation between reasoning and execution. The model proposes; the system enforces.

Strengths of the ReAct Architecture

The ReAct pattern offers several advantages:

- Simplicity of implementation
- Clear reasoning traceability
- Tool extensibility
- Low architectural overhead
- Strong fit for short multi-step tasks

Because the loop is lightweight, it is often used as a baseline architecture for tool-using agents.

Limitations of ReAct

Despite its simplicity, ReAct has structural constraints.

- It does not perform explicit task planning.
- It reasons step-by-step without constructing a global plan. As tasks grow more complex, this can lead to inefficient execution or redundant tool calls.
- It also lacks built-in reflection. If an intermediate reasoning step is flawed, the loop may continue propagating that error.
- Termination control must be carefully enforced. Without strict iteration limits, cost and latency can escalate.

When to Use ReAct

The ReAct architecture is well-suited for:

- Question answering with tool usage
- Short research tasks
- Database lookup and explanation workflows
- Structured tool invocation scenarios

It is often the first practical architecture implemented in agent systems. More complex architectures build upon this foundational loop.

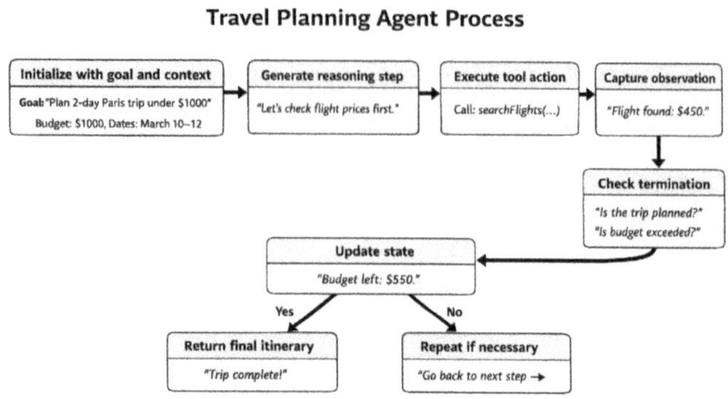

2.3 The Planner–Executor Architecture

As tasks grow in complexity, reactive step-by-step reasoning can become inefficient. The ReAct pattern determines the next action dynamically without constructing a broader strategy. While effective for short tasks, this approach may struggle when goals require coordinated multi-step execution.

The Planner–Executor architecture addresses this limitation by separating strategic planning from operational execution. Instead of deciding each action incrementally, the agent first constructs a plan — a structured decomposition of the goal into subtasks. Once the plan is generated, an executor component carries out each step sequentially, updating state along the way. This separation introduces hierarchy into the control loop.

Structural Overview

The Planner–Executor architecture typically consists of: - A goal definition
- A planning phase
- A structured task list
- An execution phase
- State updates and progress tracking
- A termination condition

The planner is responsible for reasoning about *what* needs to be done. The executor is responsible for determining *how* each step is carried out.

This reduces ambiguity during execution and improves task coordination.

Conceptual Flow

The high-level execution pattern can be described as:

1. Receive goal.
2. Generate structured plan.
3. Decompose goal into ordered subtasks.
4. Execute each subtask sequentially.
5. Update state after each step.
6. Optionally revise plan if failure occurs.
7. Terminate when all tasks are complete.

Unlike ReAct, which reasons continuously at each step, Planner–Executor introduces a dedicated planning phase before execution begins.

Minimal Pseudo-Code Representation

```
def planner_executor_agent(goal, environment):
    # Planning phase
    plan = model.generate_plan(goal)

    state = initialize(goal, plan)

    # Execution phase
    for step in plan:
        result = environment.execute(step)
        state = update_state(state, step, result)

        if failure_detected(state):
            plan = model.revise_plan(state)
            return planner_executor_agent(goal, environment)

    return generate_final_output(state)
```

This structure emphasizes hierarchy.
Planning and execution are conceptually distinct responsibilities.

Strengths of the Planner–Executor Architecture

The Planner–Executor pattern offers several advantages: - Clear task decomposition
- Improved execution coordination
- Reduced redundant tool calls
- Better scalability for complex goals
- Easier monitoring of progress

By separating strategy from action, the architecture improves transparency and control.

Limitations of the Planner–Executor Architecture

With levelling up the architecture comes a different set of challenges.

- The architecture introduces additional computational overhead during the planning phase.
- Plans may be imperfect. If the initial plan is flawed, execution may follow an inefficient or incomplete path.
- Dynamic environments pose challenges. If conditions change during execution, the agent may need to re-plan, increasing cost and latency.
- In some cases, the separation between planning and execution may reduce adaptability compared to fully reactive systems.

When to Use the Planner–Executor Architecture

This architecture is well-suited for:

- Complex multi-step tasks
- Structured report generation
- Research workflows
- Code generation and testing pipelines
- Goal-driven automation with clear decomposition

It is particularly effective when tasks can be meaningfully broken into ordered steps. The Planner–Executor pattern introduces structure beyond reactive reasoning. It represents a move toward hierarchical agent design.

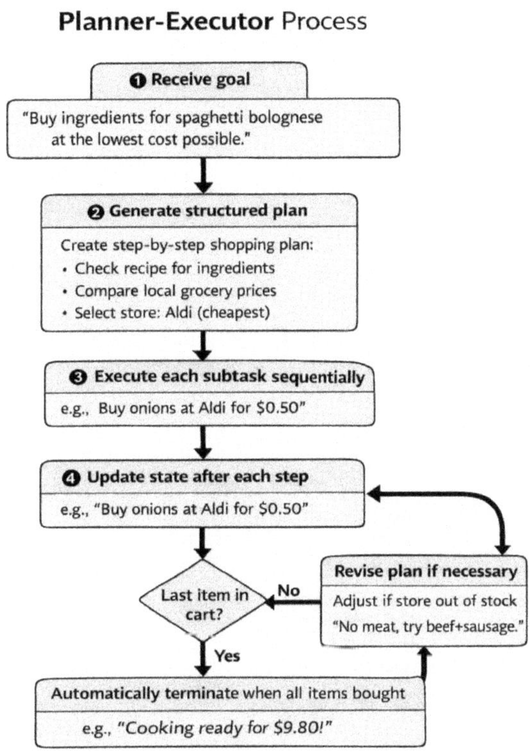

2.4 The Reflective (Critic) Architecture

As agent systems scale in complexity, a recurring challenge emerges:
how to detect and correct reasoning errors before producing a final output.

The Reflective architecture addresses this challenge by introducing a structured evaluation step within the agent loop. Instead of accepting the first generated solution, the system generates, critiques, and refines its output before finalization.

This pattern is often referred to as a "critic loop" or self-reflection mechanism.

Where ReAct focuses on reasoning and action, and Planner–Executor focuses on task structure, Reflective architectures focus on output quality and error correction.

Structural Overview

The Reflective architecture typically consists of:

- A goal definition
- An initial generation phase
- A critique or evaluation phase
- A refinement phase
- A termination condition

The system alternates between generating a candidate output and evaluating its correctness or completeness.

This evaluation may be performed:

- By the same model with a different prompt
- By a separate evaluation model
- Or by rule-based validation logic

The key principle is separation between creation and assessment.

Conceptual Flow

The high-level execution pattern can be described as:

1. Generate initial solution.
2. Evaluate the solution against defined criteria.
3. Identify weaknesses or inconsistencies.
4. Revise the solution.

5. Repeat until convergence or termination limit.

This introduces a feedback loop inside the agent.

Minimal Pseudo-Code Representation

```
def reflective_agent(goal):
    state = initialize(goal)

    while not termination_condition(state):
        # Generate
        candidate = model.generate_solution(state)

        # Critique
        feedback = model.evaluate(candidate)

        if is_satisfactory(feedback):
            return candidate

        # Refine
        state = update_state_with_feedback(state, feedback)

    return candidate
```

This architecture separates generation from evaluation, reducing blind acceptance of intermediate reasoning.

Strengths of the Reflective Architecture

The Reflective pattern offers several advantages:

- Improved output quality
- Built-in error detection
- Reduced propagation of flawed reasoning
- Better alignment with defined criteria
- Increased reliability in complex tasks

By introducing critique, the architecture compensates for probabilistic uncertainty.

Limitations of the Reflective Architecture

Reflection increases computational cost. Each refinement cycle requires additional model invocations.

Over-reflection can lead to diminishing returns. Excessive iterations may increase latency without meaningful improvement.

Critique quality depends on evaluation strength. If the evaluation mechanism is weak or poorly defined, refinement may not correct underlying errors.

Termination must be carefully controlled to prevent infinite revision loops.

When to Use the Reflective Architecture

This architecture is well-suited for:

- Code generation and validation
- Analytical reasoning tasks
- Structured report writing
- High-stakes content generation
- Any scenario where correctness is prioritized over speed

The Reflective pattern introduces self-correction into agent systems. It represents a move toward reliability through structured evaluation.

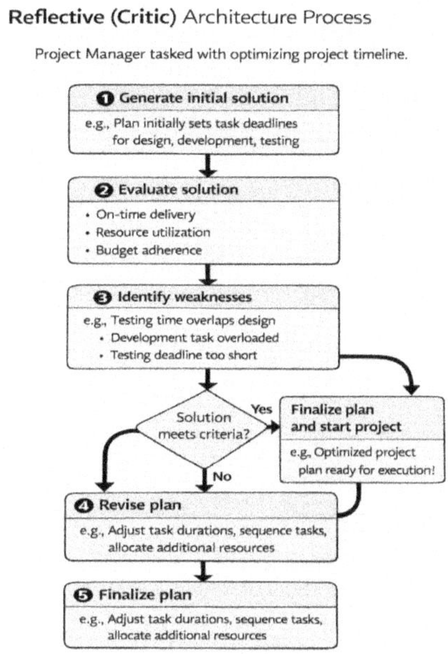

2.5 Multi-Agent Architectures

As tasks grow in complexity, a single-agent system may begin to exhibit structural strain. The agent is expected to reason, plan, critique, coordinate tools, and manage state simultaneously. While feasible for moderate tasks, this concentration of responsibilities can reduce clarity, scalability, and reliability.

Multi-agent architectures address this limitation by distributing responsibilities across specialized agents.

Rather than relying on a single reasoning entity, the system introduces multiple agents, each assigned a distinct role. These agents collaborate, exchange information, and collectively pursue a shared goal.

The defining principle of multi-agent design is specialization.

Why Single-Agent Systems Reach Limits

In single-agent architectures, the reasoning model must:

- Interpret the goal
- Decide the next action
- Manage intermediate state
- Validate outputs
- Potentially revise decisions

As complexity increases, these responsibilities become entangled. This can lead to inefficient reasoning, unclear execution paths, and higher error propagation.

Multi-agent systems reduce cognitive overload by separating concerns.

Core Concept of Multi-Agent Systems

A multi-agent system typically involves:

- Role definition
- Communication channels
- Shared or distributed state
- Coordination logic
- Termination control

Each agent focuses on a specific responsibility. For example:

- A Research Agent retrieves information.
- An Analyst Agent interprets findings.
- A Reviewer Agent critiques the output.
- A Coordinator Agent aggregates results.

This structure mirrors organizational workflows in human systems.

Common Multi-Agent Coordination Patterns

Multi-agent systems can be structured in several ways.

Sequential Collaboration

Agents operate in a pipeline.

Output from one agent becomes input to the next.

Agent A → Agent B → Agent C

This pattern is simple and controlled.

Hierarchical Supervision

A manager agent decomposes the goal and assigns tasks to worker agents. Workers execute subtasks and return results to the manager.

Manager → Workers → Manager

This structure resembles the Planner–Executor pattern but distributed across multiple agents.

Peer-to-Peer Collaboration

Agents exchange information directly and coordinate dynamically. This model increases flexibility but requires stronger communication control.

Debate-Based Systems

Multiple agents propose competing solutions. A moderator agent evaluates and selects or synthesizes the best output.

This approach increases robustness but also increases cost.

Conceptual Execution Flow

A simplified hierarchical multi-agent flow may look like:

1. Manager receives goal.
2. Manager decomposes goal into subtasks.
3. Worker agents execute subtasks.
4. Results are returned to manager.
5. Manager synthesizes final output.

Each agent operates within its own control loop, but coordination logic governs interaction.

Minimal Pseudo-Code Representation

```
def multi_agent_system(goal):
    manager = ManagerAgent()
    workers = [WorkerAgent() for _ in range(n)]

    plan = manager.create_plan(goal)
```

```
results = []
for step, worker in zip(plan, workers):
    result = worker.execute(step)
    results.append(result)

final_output = manager.aggregate(results)
return final_output
```

This structure emphasizes delegation and coordination.

Strengths of Multi-Agent Architectures

Multi-agent systems offer several advantages:

- Clear role specialization
- Improved scalability
- Parallel execution potential
- Reduced cognitive overload per agent
- Enhanced modularity

By distributing responsibility, the system becomes more adaptable for complex tasks.

Limitations of Multi-Agent Architectures

However, this architecture introduces new challenges.

- Communication overhead increases.
- State synchronization becomes more complex.
- Conflicting outputs may require arbitration.
- Monitoring multiple agents demands stronger observability.
- Cost grows as model invocations multiply.

Multi-agent systems must be designed carefully to avoid coordination chaos.

When to Use Multi-Agent Architectures

Multi-agent architectures are well-suited for:

- Complex research workflows
- Large-scale analytical tasks
- Enterprise automation systems
- Multi-domain reasoning
- Long-running autonomous processes

They are most appropriate when tasks can be meaningfully decomposed into specialized responsibilities. Multi-agent systems represent a shift from single-loop reasoning to distributed orchestration. They are powerful — but require disciplined design.

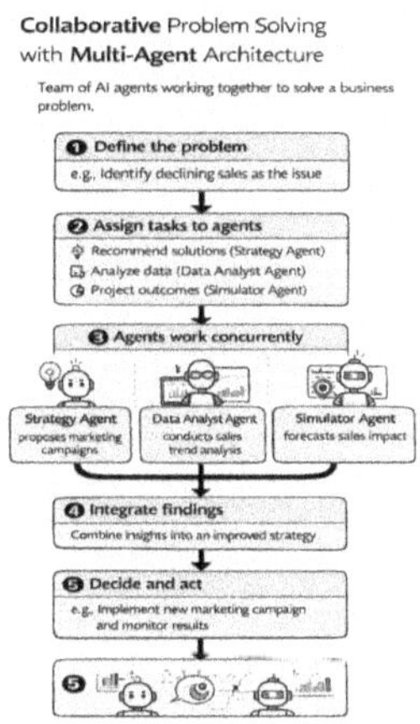

2.6 Comparing Agent Architectures

Each architecture introduced in this chapter represents a different way of structuring reasoning, execution, and control. None is universally superior. The effectiveness of an architecture depends on the nature of the task, performance constraints, and system requirements.

A structured comparison helps clarify their trade-offs.

Architectural Comparison Overview

Architecture	Complexity	Cost Impact	Reliability	Best Suited For
ReAct	Low	Low–Medium	Moderate	Short multi-step tasks, tool usage
Planner–Executor	Medium	Medium	High for structured goals	Complex multi-step tasks
Reflective (Critic)	Medium–High	Medium–High	High	Quality-sensitive outputs
Multi-Agent	High	High	High (if well-coordinated)	Large, decomposable workflows

This comparison reflects structural tendencies rather than fixed outcomes.

Structural Differences

ReAct relies on a single reasoning loop that alternates between thinking and acting. It is lightweight and flexible but lacks explicit long-term planning.

Planner–Executor introduces hierarchy by separating planning from execution. This improves task coordination but adds computational overhead.

Reflective architectures incorporate evaluation into the control loop. They improve output quality but increase iteration cost.

Multi-Agent systems distribute responsibilities across specialized agents. They scale well for complex workflows but require coordination mechanisms and stronger monitoring.

Reliability Considerations

Reliability increases as structure increases — but so does cost and orchestration complexity.

ReAct systems may produce acceptable results quickly, but they rely heavily on incremental reasoning accuracy.

Planner–Executor systems reduce redundant actions but depend on the quality of the initial plan.

Reflective systems reduce propagation of reasoning errors but require well-defined evaluation criteria.

Multi-Agent systems can improve robustness through specialization but introduce coordination risks.

No architecture eliminates uncertainty. Each manages it differently.

Cost and Latency Implications

As architectural complexity increases:

- Model invocation count increases
- Control logic becomes more elaborate
- State management becomes heavier
- Monitoring requirements grow

Architectural sophistication must be justified by task complexity.

Choosing the Right Architecture

Selecting an architecture should begin with three questions:

1. How complex is the goal?
2. Is task decomposition required?
3. Is correctness more important than speed?

For simple, tool-driven tasks, ReAct is often sufficient. For structured multi-step workflows, Planner–Executor may be more appropriate. For quality-critical outputs, Reflective mechanisms provide added reliability. For large-scale or decomposable goals, Multi-Agent systems offer scalability.

Architectural decisions should be deliberate. The simplest architecture that satisfies requirements is usually the most practical.

2.7 Choosing the Right Architecture

Architectural selection is an engineering decision shaped by constraints, objectives, and trade-offs. The purpose of understanding multiple agent architectures is not to maximize sophistication, but to apply the appropriate level of structure for a given problem.

A Practical Decision Framework

Before selecting an architecture, consider the following questions:

1. How complex is the task?
2. Can the goal be decomposed into clear substeps?
3. Is output correctness more important than speed?
4. Does the task require role specialization?
5. Are cost and latency tightly constrained?

These questions guide architectural choice.

If the Task Is Simple and Tool-Oriented

When the task involves short reasoning chains and limited tool interaction, a ReAct architecture is often sufficient. It provides dynamic reasoning without introducing unnecessary hierarchy.

Over-structuring such tasks may increase latency and cost without improving outcomes.

If the Task Requires Structured Decomposition

When goals can be clearly broken into ordered subtasks, the Planner–Executor architecture offers greater control. Planning introduces clarity and reduces redundant reasoning.

This pattern is particularly useful for workflows such as structured reporting, code generation with multiple stages, and goal-driven automation.

If Output Quality Is Critical

When correctness is prioritized over speed — for example, in analytical reasoning or code validation — incorporating a Reflective architecture improves reliability.

Reflection introduces self-correction. However, this added reliability must be balanced against increased computational cost.

If the Task Is Large and Decomposable Across Roles

For complex systems requiring specialization, Multi-Agent architectures become appropriate. Delegation improves modularity and scalability but demands disciplined coordination.

This pattern is best suited for enterprise-scale systems or workflows spanning multiple domains.

The Principle of Architectural Minimalism

In practical engineering, simplicity is an advantage. The simplest architecture that satisfies task requirements is usually preferable. Additional layers should be introduced only when justified by complexity, reliability needs, or scalability demands. Excessive architectural sophistication can introduce unnecessary cost, coordination burden, and debugging difficulty.

2.8 Common Architectural Pitfalls and Anti-Patterns

Understanding architectural patterns is only part of designing effective agent systems. Equally important is recognizing common design mistakes that lead to instability, inefficiency, or unnecessary complexity. Many agent systems fail not because of model limitations, but because of structural misalignment.

Overusing Complex Architectures

One frequent mistake is introducing hierarchical or multi-agent architectures for tasks that could be solved using a simpler loop. Complexity increases coordination overhead, cost, and debugging difficulty. If a ReAct architecture can solve the task reliably, introducing planning layers or multiple agents may reduce clarity without improving outcomes. Architectural sophistication should be justified by task complexity — not by novelty.

Misusing ReAct for Deeply Structured Tasks

ReAct works well for short, adaptive workflows. However, applying it to deeply decomposable tasks can result in inefficient reasoning paths and redundant tool invocations. Without explicit planning, the system may repeatedly re-evaluate the same subproblems. Structured tasks often benefit from Planner–Executor architectures instead of purely reactive loops.

Entangling Orchestration with Prompting

Another common anti-pattern is embedding control logic directly inside prompts. For example, instructing the model to simulate planning, execution, and validation entirely within a single prompt reduces transparency and observability. While this may produce plausible outputs, it eliminates structural control and makes debugging difficult. Orchestration should exist outside the model wherever possible.

Models reason. Systems control.

Ignoring Termination Conditions

Agent loops without clearly defined stopping criteria can escalate cost and latency. Reflection loops without iteration limits may fail to converge. Multi-agent systems without coordination guards may enter cyclical communication patterns. Every architecture must include explicit termination logic.

Neglecting Evaluation and Observability

Dynamic systems require monitoring. Without logging, step tracing, and evaluation metrics, diagnosing failure becomes nearly impossible. Agent architectures must include structured state tracking and transparent execution logs from the outset.

Overlooking Cost and Latency Implications

Each architectural layer increases model invocations. Planning phases, critique cycles, and multi-agent coordination all add overhead.

Architectural decisions should consider:

- Expected iteration depth
- Tool invocation frequency
- Monitoring infrastructure
- Budget constraints

Engineering trade-offs must remain visible. Architectural discipline requires balance. The most practical agent system is rarely the most complex one. It is the one whose structure aligns precisely with task requirements.

3. Designing Agents as Systems

Key Objectives

- What Is State in an Agent System?
- Designing Control Flow Around State.
- Tool Abstraction Layers
- Memory Design (Short-Term vs Long-Term)
- Termination and Guardrails
- Cost, Latency, and Token Awareness
- Engineering for Failure and Resilience

3.1 What Is State in an Agent System?

Before designing control flow, memory, or tools, we must understand a foundational concept: state. In software systems, state refers to the current condition of a system at a given point in time. It captures everything the system knows about itself and its environment that influences its next decision.

In agent systems, state determines how the agent reasons, what it has already done, and what remains to be completed. Without state, an agent cannot operate coherently across multiple steps.

State in Traditional Systems

Consider a simple example: a banking application. At any moment, the system maintains state such as account balance, transaction history, authentication status and pending operations. Each action modifies that state. The next action depends on it. Agent systems operate similarly — but their state includes reasoning context.

Why Agents Require Explicit State

Unlike single-prompt interactions, agents operate iteratively. Each reasoning step produces intermediate outputs. Each tool invocation generates results. Each update influences future decisions. If these intermediate results are not captured in structured state, the system loses coherence. Appending prior messages to a prompt is not sufficient state management. It is an implicit and fragile form of memory.

Explicit state modeling allows:

- Controlled reasoning progression
- Structured task tracking
- Transparent debugging
- Reliable termination conditions

What Constitutes State in an Agent?

At a minimum, agent state may include:

- The original goal
- Intermediate reasoning steps
- Tool invocation history
- Tool outputs
- Progress indicators
- Error signals
- Memory references
- Budget usage (tokens, time, cost)

State answers the question:

What does the agent currently know, and what has it already done?

A Concrete Example

Consider a research agent tasked with preparing a report.

At iteration 1, it retrieves documents.

At iteration 2, it extracts key metrics.

At iteration 3, it drafts a section.

If state is not structured, the agent may:

- Re-fetch the same documents
- Lose track of completed sections
- Repeat analysis
- Miss termination criteria

Explicit state tracking prevents these failures.

State as the Backbone of Control

State is not an optional implementation detail. It is the backbone of agent control.

Every architectural pattern introduced in Chapter 2 — ReAct, Planner–Executor, Reflective, Multi-Agent — relies on state. The difference lies not in whether state exists, but in how it is structured and updated.

Before designing control loops, we must first decide: What does the agent need to remember in order to act intelligently?

3.2 Designing Control Flow Around State

If state represents what an agent knows, control flow determines what the agent does next.

In agent systems, control flow is the mechanism that governs how reasoning, action, and observation are sequenced over time. It defines the order of operations, the conditions under which decisions are made, and the rules that determine when execution should continue or stop.

Without explicit control flow, an agent becomes unpredictable.

Control Flow in Traditional Software vs Agent Systems

In traditional software, control flow is typically explicit and deterministic. Developers define loops, conditionals, and function calls that execute in a known order.

Agent systems differ in one important way:
the reasoning step is probabilistic.

This means the system must combine: - probabilistic reasoning (from the model), and - deterministic control (from the orchestration layer).

The responsibility of control flow is to ensure that probabilistic reasoning does not lead to unbounded or unsafe execution.

The Agent Control Loop

Most agent systems follow a variant of a control loop. At a high level, the loop performs the following actions:

1. Read the current state.
2. Invoke the model to reason about the next step.
3. Interpret the model's output.
4. Execute an action, often via a tool.
5. Observe the result.
6. Update state.
7. Check termination conditions.

This loop repeats until a stopping criterion is met.

Crucially, the loop itself must be deterministic, even if the reasoning within it is not.

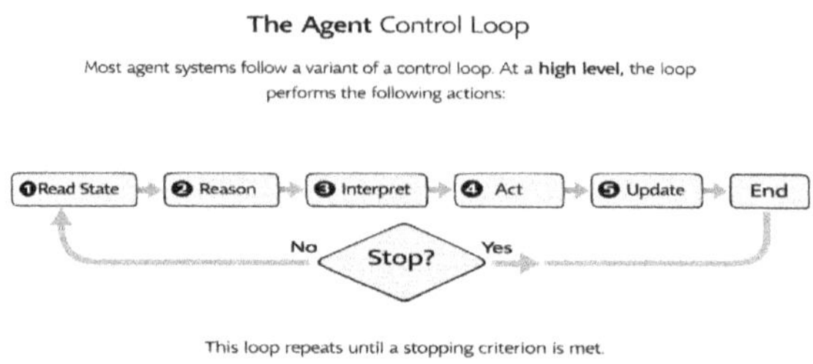

Making Control Flow Explicit

A common mistake in early agent implementations is embedding control logic inside prompts. For example, instructing the model to “decide when to stop” or “loop until satisfied” shifts responsibility from the system to the model.

This approach reduces transparency and makes behavior difficult to debug.

Instead, control flow should be implemented explicitly in code. The model should propose actions; the system should decide whether and how those actions are executed.

A simplified control loop may look like:

```
while True:
    reasoning = model.generate(state)
    action = parse_action(reasoning)

    if not is_valid(action):
        handle_error()
        break

    observation = execute(action)
    state = update_state(state, reasoning, observation)

    if termination_condition(state):
        break
```

Here, the loop structure, validation, and termination are controlled by the system.

Control Flow and Safety

Explicit control flow enables safeguards that are essential in practical systems:

- Maximum iteration limits
- Tool invocation constraints
- Budget enforcement (time, tokens, cost)
- Error handling and retries
- Escalation to human oversight

Without these safeguards, agent systems may enter infinite loops, misuse tools, or exceed operational budgets.

Control Flow as a Design Decision

Control flow is not an implementation detail. It is a design decision that determines reliability, cost, and predictability. Different architectures impose different control flow structures:

- ReAct uses a simple iterative loop.
- Planner–Executor introduces phased execution.
- Reflective systems add evaluation cycles.
- Multi-agent systems coordinate multiple loops.

In all cases, the quality of the system depends on how clearly control flow is defined and constrained. With state and control flow in place, we can now examine how agents interact with the external world through tools.

3.3 Tool Abstraction Layers

An agent without tools is limited to reasoning about information. An agent with tools can act upon the world. This distinction is fundamental. A language model can analyze text, generate explanations, and suggest strategies. However, it cannot directly execute database queries, perform guaranteed numerical calculations, retrieve real-time data, or interact with external systems. These operations require deterministic execution outside the model. Tools provide that capability.

But introducing tools into an agent system is not merely a matter of connecting APIs. It is a design decision that determines safety, reliability, and control.

From Reasoning to Action

In earlier chapters, we emphasized the separation between reasoning and execution.

The model proposes.
The system enforces.

Tools are the mechanism through which enforcement occurs.

When an agent needs to retrieve sales data, compute statistics, execute code, or fetch documents, it must delegate that task to a controlled function. The model should not execute arbitrary operations. Instead, it should produce a structured action request that the system validates and executes through a defined interface. This separation protects both correctness and security.

What Is a Tool, Precisely?

In a practical agent system, a tool is a deterministic function with a well-defined contract.

A tool should:

- Accept structured inputs.
- Perform a specific operation.
- Return structured outputs.
- Handle errors predictably.

Examples include:

- Querying a database for structured records.
- Calling a financial API.
- Executing a Python function for numerical analysis.
- Performing web search.
- Retrieving files from storage.

The key characteristic is determinism. Given the same input, a properly designed tool should produce consistent results. This property compensates for the probabilistic nature of language models.

Why Abstraction Is Necessary

A common mistake in early agent implementations is exposing raw functions directly to the model without validation or control.

This creates several risks:

- The model may hallucinate tool names.
- Parameters may be malformed.
- Sensitive operations may be invoked unintentionally.
- Execution errors may cascade silently.

Tool abstraction introduces a controlled boundary between reasoning and action. Instead of giving the model unrestricted execution ability, we define an interface layer that governs how tools are discovered, validated, and executed.

This abstraction layer serves several purposes:

- It validates inputs before execution.
- It enforces permissions.
- It standardizes output formatting.
- It logs execution history.
- It isolates failures from reasoning logic.

Without this layer, agent systems become fragile and difficult to audit.

Designing a Tool Interface

Every tool in a production-grade agent system should be explicitly defined.

A well-designed tool interface includes:

- A clear name.
- A description of its purpose.
- A structured input schema.
- A structured output format.
- Validation rules.

- Error-handling logic.

For example:

```
class Tool:
    def __init__(self, name, description, input_schema):
        self.name = name
        self.description = description
        self.input_schema = input_schema

    def execute(self, parameters):
        validate(parameters, self.input_schema)
        result = perform_operation(parameters)
        return result
```

The language model does not execute `perform_operation` directly. It generates a structured action request, which the system parses and routes to the appropriate tool. This design keeps reasoning separate from execution.

The Tool Registry Pattern

As the number of tools increases, managing them individually becomes impractical. A tool registry provides structured access.

The registry:

- Maintains a list of approved tools.
- Maps tool names to implementations.
- Enforces access constraints.
- Tracks usage for monitoring.

Conceptually, the system operates as follows:

1. The model proposes an action.
2. The system parses the action.
3. The registry verifies that the tool exists.
4. Input parameters are validated.
5. The tool executes.
6. The result is returned to the agent state.
7. The execution is logged.

This controlled pipeline prevents arbitrary execution and ensures observability.

Isolation as a Design Principle

One of the most important engineering principles in agent systems is isolation. The model should not have direct access to system-level operations.

Instead:

- The model proposes intent.
- The orchestration layer interprets that intent.
- The tool layer executes under constraints.

This separation enables:

- Deterministic execution.
- Structured error handling.
- Safer deployment.
- Easier debugging.

When isolation is ignored, agents become unpredictable and difficult to control.

Reliability and Testability

Well-designed tools are independently testable. Before integrating tools into an agent loop, each tool should be validated in isolation. Its inputs and outputs should be predictable. Failure cases should be explicitly handled.

An agent system built on unstable tools will inherit instability regardless of architectural elegance. Tools expand an agent's capability. Tool abstraction preserves its reliability.

Controlled Tool Invocation

```
+---------------------------+
|          Model            |
|  (Proposes Action Intent) |
```

```
+-------------+-------------+
              |
              v
+---------------------------+
|   TOOL ABSTRACTION        |
|   BOUNDARY                |
|                           |
| Parse -> Validate -> Check |
| Registry -> Enforce Policy |
+-------------+-------------+
              |
              v
+---------------------------+
|  Deterministic Tool       |
|  Execution Environment    |
+-------------+-------------+
              |
              v
       Result -> Logged -> State
```

3.4 Memory Design (Short-Term vs Long-Term)

Memory determines how information persists beyond a single reasoning step. Without memory, an agent can reason only within the immediate context of the current iteration. With memory, it can accumulate knowledge, track progress, and refine decisions over time.

However, memory in agent systems is often misunderstood. Appending conversation history to a prompt is not a memory architecture. It is merely context extension. True memory design requires deliberate structuring.

What Is Memory in an Agent System?

Memory refers to information retained across iterations or sessions that influences future reasoning. Memory differs from state.

- **State** represents the current working context of the agent.

- **Memory** represents retained information beyond immediate execution.

State changes rapidly during execution. Memory persists and accumulates over time. A well-designed agent system distinguishes clearly between the two.

Short-Term Memory

Short-term memory exists within a single execution cycle or task session.

It includes:

- Recent reasoning steps
- Tool outputs
- Intermediate conclusions
- Temporary variables
- Progress tracking

Short-term memory is typically stored in structured state objects and passed through the control loop.

It enables the agent to:

- Avoid repeating actions
- Build upon intermediate results
- Maintain logical coherence

However, short-term memory should be bounded. Unrestricted accumulation increases token cost and reasoning noise.

Long-Term Memory

Long-term memory persists beyond a single task.

It may include:

- Historical interactions
- Prior task outcomes
- Stored documents
- User preferences
- Learned patterns
- Domain knowledge embeddings

Long-term memory enables continuity across sessions. For example, a research agent that stores prior analysis can avoid reprocessing identical documents in future tasks.

Unlike short-term memory, long-term memory often requires storage mechanisms such as:

- Databases
- Vector stores
- Structured knowledge graphs
- Document repositories

Retrieval from long-term memory must be selective. Retrieving everything introduces noise and degrades reasoning quality.

Retrieval as a Memory Operation

Memory is not useful unless it can be accessed effectively.

Retrieval mechanisms determine:

- What information is relevant
- When it should be injected into context
- How much should be included
- In what format it should appear

Poor retrieval design leads to:

- Context overload
- Increased token cost
- Conflicting information
- Reduced reasoning precision

Memory design must therefore consider both storage and retrieval.

Memory Boundaries

One of the most important design decisions is defining memory boundaries.

Ask:

- What information should persist?

- For how long?
- Under what conditions should it be updated?
- When should it be pruned?

Unbounded memory growth leads to inefficiency and instability. Practical systems often implement:

- Time-based expiration
- Task-scoped memory
- Relevance-based pruning
- Size constraints

Memory and Agent Reliability

Improper memory design can degrade performance in subtle ways. Excess memory introduces distraction. Insufficient memory causes repetition. Poorly structured memory leads to contradictions. Memory should support reasoning, not overwhelm it.

Agents do not become intelligent by remembering everything. They become effective by remembering the right things.

Agent Memory Architecture

```
+-----------------------------+
|      Long-Term Memory       |
|  (DB / Vector Store / KG)   |
+--------------+--------------+
               ^
         Retrieval
               |
+-------------+   +-------------+   +-------------+
| Input /     |-->| Short-Term  |-->| Execution   |
| Perception  |   |   Memory    |   |   Loop      |
+-------------+   +-------------+   +-------------+
               |
               v
         State Updates
```

3.5 Termination and Guardrails

An agent without termination logic is not autonomous — it is unstable.

In iterative systems, execution must be bounded. Every agent loop must have clearly defined stopping conditions and safety constraints. Without them, systems may enter infinite loops, overuse tools, exceed budget limits, or produce cascading errors.

Termination and guardrails transform an experimental agent into a production-ready system.

Why Termination Is Critical

In traditional software, loops are explicitly bounded by conditions defined by the developer. In agent systems, however, part of the reasoning is probabilistic. This introduces uncertainty in how long an agent may continue reasoning or revising.

If termination is delegated entirely to the model, behavior becomes unpredictable. A robust agent system must enforce termination at the orchestration level.

Types of Termination Conditions

Termination may occur under several conditions:

- Task completion detected
- Maximum iteration count reached
- Budget limit exceeded (tokens, cost, or time)
- Confidence threshold satisfied
- External interruption or user input

Each architecture introduced earlier depends on termination design. For example:

- ReAct systems require iteration limits.
- Reflective systems require revision caps.
- Multi-agent systems require coordination completion checks.

Termination must be deterministic, even if reasoning is not.

Guardrails as System Constraints

Guardrails are constraints that limit unsafe or undesired behavior.

They may include:

- Tool invocation limits
- Access control policies
- Output validation checks
- Domain restrictions
- Budget ceilings
- Execution timeouts

Guardrails operate alongside termination conditions but serve a different purpose.

Termination answers:

"When should the system stop?"

Guardrails answer:

"What is the system allowed to do while running?"

Budget Awareness and Enforcement

One of the most overlooked aspects of agent design is budget awareness.

Every reasoning step consumes:

- Tokens
- Latency
- Compute resources
- Monetary cost

Guardrails may enforce:

- Maximum tokens per loop
- Maximum tool calls per task
- Total cost thresholds
- Maximum session duration

These constraints prevent runaway systems.

Human-in-the-Loop Safeguards

In sensitive applications, additional safeguards may include:

- Approval checkpoints
- Escalation triggers
- Manual override mechanisms

These mechanisms ensure that autonomy does not eliminate accountability.

Designing for Predictable Termination

A practical termination structure might include:

```
if iterations >= MAX_ITERATIONS:
    stop()

if total_tokens > TOKEN_LIMIT:
    stop()

if task_complete(state):
    stop()
```

Termination logic should be transparent, testable, and observable.

Guardrails as Architectural Discipline

Guardrails are not optional features added later. They are core architectural components. As agent systems become more autonomous, guardrails become more important — not less.

Intelligence without constraints leads to instability. Autonomy without boundaries leads to risk.

Agent Loop with Termination and Guardrails

```
+----------------------------------------+
|            Guardrails Layer            |
| - Token Limits                         |
| - Tool Restrictions                    |
```

```
| - Output Validation                    |
| - Access Policies                      |
+-------------------+--------------------+
                    |
                    v
+----------------------------------------+
|         Agent Execution Loop           |
|                                        |
|     Think -> Act -> Observe -> Reflect|
|                                        |
+-------------------+--------------------+
                    |
                    v
+----------------------------------------+
|           Termination Check            |
| - Max Iterations                       |
| - Budget Exceeded                      |
| - Task Complete                        |
+----------------------------------------+
```

3.6 Cost, Latency, and Token Awareness

Agent systems are not only architectural constructs. They are economic systems. Every reasoning step, tool invocation, reflection cycle, and memory retrieval consumes resources. These resources translate directly into latency, infrastructure load, and financial cost. Ignoring these factors may not affect small experiments. In production systems, however, cost and latency determine viability.

The Hidden Cost of Iteration

Single-prompt systems incur a single inference cost. Agent systems rarely do.

A ReAct loop may invoke the model multiple times.

A Reflective architecture may double those calls.

A Multi-Agent system may multiply them further.

If a single model invocation costs C, and an agent executes n iterations, total cost approximates:

$$\text{Total Cost} \approx n \times C + \text{Tool Costs}$$

As architectural complexity increases, n increases. Cost scales with iteration depth.

Token Accumulation

Every iteration typically includes:

- The original goal
- Updated state
- Tool outputs
- Prior reasoning

This increases token count over time. Token growth affects cost, latency, model performance and context window limits. Unbounded state accumulation leads to exponential token growth in poorly designed systems. Token awareness must therefore be built into memory and state design.

Latency Compounding

Latency accumulates sequentially.

For example:

- Model reasoning: 1.2 seconds
- Tool execution: 0.8 seconds
- Reflection step: 1.1 seconds

If these occur sequentially, total latency becomes sum of each step. As steps increase, user experience degrades. Parallelization in multi-agent systems may reduce wall-clock time, but coordination overhead introduces its own cost. Latency is not merely a technical metric. It shapes usability.

Budget-Conscious Design

Practical agent systems often include explicit budget tracking within state:

- Current token usage

- Estimated remaining budget
- Tool invocation count
- Execution duration

For example:

```
if state.token_usage > MAX_TOKENS:
    terminate("Token limit exceeded")

if state.iterations > MAX_STEPS:
    terminate("Iteration limit reached")
```

Budget awareness transforms cost from an afterthought into a design parameter.

Cost vs Reliability Trade-Off

Increasing reliability often increases cost.

- Reflection improves quality but doubles calls.
- Planning improves structure but adds overhead.
- Multi-agent specialization increases modularity but multiplies invocations.

Architectural decisions must weigh:

- Accuracy requirements
- Latency tolerance
- Financial constraints
- User expectations

There is no universally optimal balance.

Designing for Sustainable Execution

Sustainable agent design involves:

- Bounded iteration
- Controlled memory growth
- Selective retrieval

- Structured tool invocation
- Monitoring and logging

Without these controls, agent systems may become economically infeasible. Practical AI agents are not only intelligent. They are efficient.

3.7 Engineering for Failure and Resilience

No agent system operates in a perfectly controlled environment.

Even if the reasoning architecture is sound and the tools are well-designed, real-world execution introduces uncertainty. Tool calls fail. APIs timeout. Models return malformed outputs. Memory retrieval surfaces irrelevant documents. Termination conditions trigger prematurely or too late.

Failure is not exceptional in agent systems — it is expected. The difference between an experimental agent and a production-ready system lies not in eliminating failure, but in engineering for it. Designing for resilience means anticipating failure modes before deployment and building mechanisms that contain, trace, and recover from them.

Failure as a Multi-Layered Phenomenon

Agent systems fail at multiple layers. At the model level, failures may include malformed structured outputs, hallucinated tool names, incomplete parameter sets, or reasoning inconsistencies.

At the tool layer, failures may manifest as execution exceptions, API errors, timeouts, or invalid data responses.

Memory systems may retrieve irrelevant context or fail to retrieve relevant data, degrading reasoning quality without triggering explicit errors.

Control flow may break due to improper loop management, misconfigured termination conditions, or incorrect state updates.

Budget constraints may be exceeded, resulting in token overflows, cost overruns, or unacceptable latency.

Each of these layers requires explicit handling. Ignoring one weakens the entire system. Resilience begins by acknowledging that failure is structural, not accidental.

Observability as a Foundational Requirement

Dynamic systems require transparency. Unlike deterministic pipelines, agent systems make decisions step-by-step. Without visibility into those decisions, debugging becomes guesswork.

A production-grade agent system should log:

- Each reasoning step
- Each tool invocation
- The parameters passed to tools
- Tool outputs and errors
- State transitions
- Token usage and cost metrics
- The reason for termination

These logs should be structured, timestamped, and searchable. Observability transforms unpredictable behavior into traceable execution. It enables engineers to reconstruct what happened, identify weak points, and refine the system. Without observability, resilience is impossible.

Designing Retry Strategies

Not all failures are permanent. Some failures are transient — temporary network interruptions, rate limits, or recoverable formatting errors. Retry mechanisms can improve robustness, but they must be bounded and deliberate.

A practical retry strategy may include:

- A limited number of retry attempts
- Exponential backoff delays
- Validation of corrected parameters
- Fallback to alternative tools when appropriate

However, unbounded retries create infinite recovery loops. Resilience requires balance. Recovery logic must include its own termination conditions. Retries should recover from instability, not amplify it.

Fallback and Graceful Degradation

Some failures cannot be automatically resolved. In such cases, the system must degrade gracefully rather than collapse unpredictably.

Fallback mechanisms may include:

- Returning partial results with a structured explanation
- Switching to a simpler reasoning strategy
- Escalating the task for human review
- Providing diagnostic output for corrective action

Graceful degradation preserves user trust and system stability. A resilient agent system does not conceal failure. It manages it transparently.

Defensive Parsing and Validation

Because model outputs are probabilistic, parsing must be defensive. It is unsafe to assume that a model will always produce valid JSON, correct tool names, or complete parameter sets. Structured outputs must be validated rigorously before execution.

Defensive validation includes:

- Schema enforcement
- Required field checks
- Type validation
- Range validation
- Explicit rejection of malformed data
- Comprehensive logging of anomalies

Validation is not a minor implementation detail. It is a core safety mechanism. Resilience begins at the boundary between reasoning and execution.

Controlled Failure as an Engineering Objective

A resilient agent system is not one that never fails. It is one that fails predictably and safely.

Predictable failure includes:

- Clear and structured error messages

- Bounded execution loops
- Preserved state integrity
- Logged execution traces
- Explicit termination reasons

The objective is not perfection.
The objective is control.

When failure is controlled, it becomes manageable. When it is unmanaged, it becomes systemic risk.

With state, control flow, tools, memory, guardrails, economic awareness, and resilience mechanisms defined, we now have a complete systems-level understanding of agent design.

Summary: From Concept to Engineered Systems

Across the first three chapters, we have moved deliberately from understanding to structure, and from structure to discipline.

In Chapter 1, we examined why prompt-based interactions are insufficient for complex tasks and introduced the concept of AI agents as goal-driven systems operating within controlled loops. We clarified that agents are not defined by intelligence alone, but by architecture.

In Chapter 2, we studied the core architectural patterns that govern agent behavior — ReAct, Planner–Executor, Reflective, and Multi-Agent systems. We analyzed how each pattern structures reasoning, action, coordination, and evaluation. Architecture, we established, determines reliability.

In this chapter, we shifted focus from patterns to engineering principles. We examined state as the backbone of coherent reasoning, control flow as the mechanism of deterministic governance, and tool abstraction as the boundary between probabilistic reasoning and deterministic execution. We explored memory design, distinguishing short-term working context from long-term persistence. We defined termination logic and guardrails as necessary constraints, not optional enhancements. We confronted the economic realities of cost, latency, and token growth. Finally, we addressed resilience, recognizing that production systems must be designed to anticipate and contain failure.

Together, these foundations transform the idea of an agent from a conceptual construct into a structured, controllable system.

An effective agent is not one that simply reasons.
It is one that reasons within boundaries, acts through validated interfaces, remembers selectively, terminates predictably, and fails safely.

With these principles in place, we are now prepared to transition from design to implementation.

In the next chapter, we begin building practical agent systems — not as experiments, but as engineered architectures grounded in the discipline established so far.

Project 1: The ReAct Reasoning Agent

Key Objectives

- Why This Task Requires an Agent
- Define problem statement & data
- Build and Test the Tools (Before the Agent)
- Define the Agent State (Minimal but Explicit)
- Implement the ReAct Loop (First Version: Deterministic Reasoning)
- Walking Through the ReAct Execution step
- Adding an Execution Trace (Making the Loop Visible)
- From Scripted Actions to Model-Driven Reasoning
- Introducing LLMs: Enabling Natural Language Reasoning
- Conclusion: Building a Controlled, LLM-Driven Agent

4.1 Problem Statement: Why This Task Requires an Agent

In this project, we aim to build a system capable of answering the following question:

> "What were the top three selling products last quarter, and what trend explains their performance?"

At first glance, this may appear to be a simple analytical query. One might argue that this can be solved using a straightforward Python function:

- Filter the dataset by quarter.
- Group by product.
- Sort by sales.
- Return the top three entries.
- Print a summary.

If the question were always fixed, the dataset structure never changed, and the interpretation logic remained static, then a deterministic script would indeed suffice.

However, real-world analytical queries are rarely this rigid.

Why Simple Automation Is Not Enough

Consider how such questions typically appear in practice:

- "What were the best performers last quarter, and why?"
- "Which product improved the most compared to Q2?"
- "Are there seasonal effects in the data?"
- "Which items are trending upward despite lower absolute sales?"
- "Can you compare current performance with historical trends?"

These queries are not identical. They require interpretation.

A simple function cannot generalize across open-ended, natural language requests without being explicitly programmed for every variation. Traditional automation requires predefined logic paths for each scenario.

The moment variability enters the problem, static scripts become insufficient.

The Need for Iterative Reasoning

To answer analytical questions in a flexible manner, a system must:

1. Interpret the user's intent.
2. Determine what data is required.
3. Decide which tool to call.

4. Observe the returned results.
5. Possibly refine the analysis.
6. Synthesize a coherent explanation.
7. Decide when it is finished.

This is not a single-step computation.

It is a sequence of reasoning and action cycles.

A standard Python function executes a fixed set of instructions.

An agent decides which instructions to execute based on intermediate observations.

That difference is fundamental.

Why This Necessitates an Agent Architecture

An agent architecture becomes necessary when:

- The task requires dynamic decision-making.
- The required sequence of operations cannot be fully predetermined.
- The user input is variable and expressed in natural language.
- The system must choose among multiple tools.
- The number of reasoning steps is not fixed in advance.

In this project, we deliberately structure the problem to require:

- A retrieval step (querying data).
- An analytical step (computing summaries).
- A synthesis step (generating explanation).
- Controlled termination.

The sequence is not hard-coded as a single pipeline. Instead, it emerges from a reasoning loop.

An agent architecture allows the system to:

- Reason about what to do next.
- Invoke tools when necessary.
- Update its state.
- Continue iterating until a completion condition is satisfied.

This flexibility is precisely what distinguishes an agent from a static script.

Automation Executes. Agents Decide.

We begin with deterministic tools.

Then we embed them inside a controlled reasoning loop.

Finally, we enforce bounded execution to ensure safety and predictability.

4.2 Problem statement & data

We will build an agent that answers a simple business question using external tools. The question we will use throughout this project is:

> "What were the top three selling products last quarter, and what trend explains their performance?"

A single prompt is often insufficient for such tasks because the system must retrieve data, compute summaries, and then synthesize an explanation. This is a good fit for a ReAct agent because the agent can reason, call tools, observe results, and iterate toward an answer.

To keep this project self-contained and reproducible, we will create a small sales dataset directly in the notebook. In real systems, the same logic would apply to data pulled from a database, API, or files.

The data created contains three columns product name , quarter and sales generated in that quarter for that specific project. With the intent to focus on the agent, the data is small and simple.

Execution of the code:

```
import pandas as pd
import warnings
warnings.filterwarnings("ignore")

# Create sample sales data
data = pd.DataFrame({
    "product": ["A", "B", "C", "A", "B", "C", "A", "B", "C"],
    "quarter": ["Q1", "Q1", "Q1", "Q2", "Q2", "Q2", "Q3", "Q3",
     ↪  "Q3"],
    "sales": [120, 150, 100, 180, 160, 130, 200, 170, 140]
```

```
})

print("data: ")
data
```

```
data:
```

	product	quarter	sales
0	A	Q1	120
1	B	Q1	150
2	C	Q1	100
3	A	Q2	180
4	B	Q2	160
5	C	Q2	130
6	A	Q3	200
7	B	Q3	170
8	C	Q3	140

4.3 Build and Test the Tools (Before the Agent)

Now that the dataset is available, the next step is to create the *deterministic tools* that the agent will use. This is an important discipline in agent engineering: We do not start by writing the agent loop. We first build tools as independent, testable functions. Only then do we allow an agent to call them.

In this project, we need two tools:

1. A **data retrieval tool** that fetches sales data for a given quarter.
2. An **analysis tool** that computes the top products from the retrieved data.

Tool 1: Query Sales Data

This tool retrieves all sales records for a specified quarter from the dataset. It performs a simple filter operation and returns a clean copy of the matching rows. Its role is strictly data retrieval — it does not perform any analysis or reasoning.

Execution of Tool 1 code:

```
def query_sales_data(quarter: str) -> pd.DataFrame:
    """
    Tool: Retrieve sales data for a given quarter from the dataset.
    """
    return data[data["quarter"] == quarter].copy()

query_sales_data("Q3")
```

	product	quarter	sales
6	A	Q3	200
7	B	Q3	170
8	C	Q3	140

Explanation: we can see that when we give "Q3" as the quarter to this tool, it retrieves all the rows with quarter 3 sales data.

Tool 2: Compute Top Products

This tool analyzes the provided dataframe and computes the total sales for each product. It then ranks the products in descending order of sales and returns the top N entries. Its responsibility is purely analytical — it transforms structured data into a summarized ranking.

Execution of Tool 2 code:

```
def top_products(df: pd.DataFrame, top_n: int = 3) -> pd.Series:
    """
    Tool: Return the top-N products by total sales.
    """
    return (
        df.groupby("product")["sales"]
        .sum()
        .sort_values(ascending=False)
```

```
        .head(top_n)
    )

df_q3 = query_sales_data("Q3")
top_products(df_q3, top_n=2)
```

```
product
A     200
B     170
Name: sales, dtype: int64
```

Explanation: we can see that with help of tool 2 we can not retrieve the top 2 products sold.

This output becomes one of the most important “results” , because it demonstrates that:

- Tool outputs are deterministic.
- They can be verified independently.
- They support the agent’s reasoning loop.

4.4 Define the Agent State (Minimal but Explicit)

Before building the reasoning loop, we must decide what the agent needs to remember. An agent is not a single function call. It operates across multiple steps — reasoning, acting, observing, and updating. To do this coherently, it needs structured memory of what has already happened.

We therefore define an explicit **AgentState** object that will track:

- The original goal (the user’s question)
- The action history (what the agent has attempted so far)
- Observations returned by tools (the results of those actions)
- The iteration count (to enforce loop control and prevent runaway execution)

From a learner’s perspective, think of this state as the agent’s working notebook. At each step, the agent writes down what it tried, what it observed and how many steps it has taken. Without this notebook, the agent would be forced to rely entirely on prompt text to "remember" previous steps. That approach quickly becomes fragile, expensive in terms of tokens, and extremely difficult to debug.

Now we define this structured state explicitly in below code:

```
from dataclasses import dataclass, field
from typing import Any, List

@dataclass
class AgentState:
    goal: str
    iterations: int = 0
    history: List[str] = field(default_factory=list)
    observations: List[Any] = field(default_factory=list)
```

By defining state explicitly in code, we move from an experimental prompt pattern to an engineered system. The agent's reasoning history, observations, and execution progress become inspectable, testable, and controllable.

4.5 Implement the ReAct Loop (First Version: Deterministic Reasoning)

Before connecting a real language model, we deliberately implement the ReAct loop using deterministic and transparent reasoning.

This decision is intentional.

When learners jump directly into LLM-driven agents, the mechanics of the loop often become obscured by model output. By first simulating reasoning deterministically, we clearly expose the architecture itself.

At each iteration of the loop:

- The agent selects an action.
- The system executes the corresponding tool.
- The agent observes the returned result.
- The internal state updates.
- The loop checks termination conditions.

This structured cycle — **Reason → Act → Observe → Update → Check Termination** — is the core of the ReAct architecture.

By implementing it deterministically first, we ensure that:

- The control flow is fully understood,
- Tool integration is verified independently,
- State transitions are visible,
- And termination behavior is predictable.

Only after this structure is clear do we replace deterministic reasoning with model-generated action proposals.

Loop Control

Agent loop runs with some bounds. Even in this simplified example, we enforce a strict maximum number of iterations. This prevents runaway execution and reinforces a core principle of agent engineering that is, autonomy must always operate within defined limits.

Loop control is not an optional safeguard. It is a foundational architectural requirement.

Implementing the First Version of the ReAct Agent

We are now ready to implement our first complete ReAct agent.

This function represents the core reasoning loop of the system. It brings together everything we have built so far:

- The dataset,
- The deterministic tools,
- The structured agent state,
- And bounded loop control.

The function you are about to see performs the following:

1. Initializes the agent state.
2. Iteratively selects an action.
3. Executes the corresponding tool.
4. Stores the observation.

5. Updates the state.
6. Terminates under controlled conditions.

This implementation makes the ReAct structure explicit and transparent before we introduce model-driven reasoning.

```
MAX_ITERATIONS = 5
def react_agent_v1(goal: str) -> str:
    state = AgentState(goal=goal)

    while state.iterations < MAX_ITERATIONS:
        state.iterations += 1

        # Simulated reasoning: decide next action
        if state.iterations == 1:
            action = "QUERY:Q3"
        elif state.iterations == 2:
            action = "ANALYZE:TOP_PRODUCTS"
        elif state.iterations == 3:
            action = "RESPOND"
        else:
            action = "STOP"

        state.history.append(action)

        # Act + Observe
        if action == "QUERY:Q3":
            df = query_sales_data("Q3")
            state.observations.append(("Q3_DATA", df))

        elif action == "ANALYZE:TOP_PRODUCTS":
            label, df = state.observations[-1]
            summary = top_products(df, top_n=3)
            state.observations.append(("TOP3_Q3", summary))

        elif action == "RESPOND":
            label, summary = state.observations[-1]
            top3_list = ", ".join([f"{idx} ({val})" for idx, val
↪  in summary.items()])
```

```
        return f"Top 3 products in Q3 are: {top3_list}."

    elif action == "STOP":
        break

return "Terminated due to iteration limit."
```

```
### Execution:

print("OUTPUT:")
react_agent_v1("What were the top three selling products last
↪  quarter?")
```

```
OUTPUT:
'Top 3 products in Q3 are: A (200), B (170), C (140).'
```

4.6 Walking Through the ReAct Execution step by step

Now that we have seen the code, let us examine how this function embodies the ReAct architecture.

```
def react_agent_v1(goal: str) -> str:
    state = AgentState(goal=goal)
```

We begin by initializing the agent's state. At this moment, the agent knows only its goal. No actions have been taken. No observations exist.

```
    while state.iterations < MAX_ITERATIONS:
        state.iterations += 1
```

This is the control boundary. The loop ensures that the agent cannot run indefinitely. At the start of each cycle, we increment the iteration counter. This makes the progression of the agent explicit and measurable. Without this boundary, a reasoning loop could become unstable or infinite.

```
# Simulated reasoning: decide next action
        if state.iterations == 1:
            action = "QUERY:Q3"
        elif state.iterations == 2:
            action = "ANALYZE:TOP_PRODUCTS"
        elif state.iterations == 3:
            action = "RESPOND"
        else:
            action = "STOP"
```

This block represents the Reasoning step. In a production agent, this decision would be generated by a language model. Here, we simulate reasoning deterministically to make the mechanics transparent. Each iteration determines what action should occur next. This is the "Reason" in ReAct.

```
    state.history.append(action)
```

Every action is recorded in the state. This provides:

- Traceability
- Debuggability
- Transparency of execution.

If something goes wrong, we can inspect the history to see what the agent attempted.

```
if action == "QUERY:Q3":
            df = query_sales_data("Q3")
            state.observations.append(("Q3_DATA", df))
```

This is the Act + Observe phase. The agent calls a tool (query_sales_data), receives structured data, and stores the result inside the state. Notice that we do not mix reasoning and tool logic. The tool remains deterministic.

```
elif action == "ANALYZE:TOP_PRODUCTS":
            label, df = state.observations[-1]
            summary = top_products(df, top_n=3)
            state.observations.append(("TOP3_Q3", summary))
```

The agent now uses the most recent observation as input to another tool. This shows a key property of agent systems like actions depend on prior observations, the system is not executing a fixed pipeline and it is reacting to intermediate results.

```
elif action == "RESPOND":
            label, summary = state.observations[-1]
            top3_list = ", ".join([f"{idx} ({val})" for idx, val
↪  in summary.items()])
            return f"Top 3 products in Q3 are: {top3_list}."
```

Here, the agent decides it has enough information to produce a final response. Notice that the loop terminates by returning immediately. Termination is deliberate and controlled.

```
elif action == "STOP":
    return "Terminated due to iteration limit."
            break
```

This provides an additional safety exit. Even if reasoning logic misbehaves, we retain control. If the loop exits due to reaching MAX_ITERATIONS, we return a clear termination message. This reinforces the principle that autonomy must always operate within bounded execution.

What This Function Demonstrates

This implementation shows a complete ReAct cycle:

- **Reason** (choose action)
- **Act** (call tool)
- **Observe** (store result)
- **Update state**
- **Check termination**

Even though the reasoning step is deterministic here, the architectural structure mirrors that of a real agent.

4.7 Adding an Execution Trace (Making the Loop Visible)

So far, our agent works — but it still behaves like a black box unless we explicitly inspect state. In real agent systems, one of the most important engineering practices is **observability**. We must be able to answer questions like:

- What action did the agent take at each step?
- What tool was called, and with what input?
- What did the tool return?
- Why did the agent stop?

To make the ReAct loop easier to understand (especially for beginners), we now add a **trace-enabled version** of the same agent. This version prints a readable trace during execution so that the agent's reasoning loop becomes visible step by step. This does not change the architecture. It only makes the execution transparent.

```
### A Trace-Enabled Version of the ReAct Agent

MAX_ITERATIONS = 5

def react_agent_v1_with_trace(goal: str) -> str:
    state = AgentState(goal=goal)

    print("=== ReAct Agent Trace ===")
    print(f"Goal: {state.goal}\n")

    while state.iterations < MAX_ITERATIONS:
        state.iterations += 1

        # Simulated reasoning: decide next action
        if state.iterations == 1:
            action = "QUERY:Q3"
        elif state.iterations == 2:
            action = "ANALYZE:TOP_PRODUCTS"
```

```
    elif state.iterations == 3:
        action = "RESPOND"
    else:
        action = "STOP"

    state.history.append(action)

    print(f"[Iteration {state.iterations}]")
    print(f"Action Chosen: {action}")

    # Act + Observe
    if action == "QUERY:Q3":
        df = query_sales_data("Q3")
        state.observations.append(("Q3_DATA", df))
        print("Tool Called: query_sales_data('Q3')")
        print(f"Observation: Retrieved {len(df)} rows\n")

    elif action == "ANALYZE:TOP_PRODUCTS":
        label, df = state.observations[-1]
        summary = top_products(df, top_n=3)
        state.observations.append(("TOP3_Q3", summary))
        print("Tool Called: top_products(df_q3, top_n=3)")
        print("Observation: Top products computed")
        print(summary, "\n")

    elif action == "RESPOND":
        label, summary = state.observations[-1]
        top3_list = ", ".join([f"{idx} ({val})" for idx, val
↪   in summary.items()])
        final_answer = f"Top 3 products in Q3 are:
↪   {top3_list}."
        print("Final Response Generated.")
        print("=== ReAct Agent Trace ===\n")
        return final_answer

    elif action == "STOP":
        print("Stopping early due to STOP signal.")
```

```
            print("=== ReAct Agent Trace ===\n")
            break

    print("Terminated due to iteration limit.")
    print("=== ReAct Agent Trace ===\n")
    return "Terminated due to iteration limit."
```

Run the Trace-Enabled Agent

```
react_agent_v1_with_trace("What were the top three selling products
↪  last quarter?")
```

```
=== ReAct Agent Trace ===
Goal: What were the top three selling products last quarter?

[Iteration 1]
Action Chosen: QUERY:Q3
Tool Called: query_sales_data('Q3')
Observation: Retrieved 3 rows

[Iteration 2]
Action Chosen: ANALYZE:TOP_PRODUCTS
Tool Called: top_products(df_q3, top_n=3)
Observation: Top products computed
product
A    200
B    170
C    140
Name: sales, dtype: int64

[Iteration 3]
Action Chosen: RESPOND
Final Response Generated.
=== ReAct Agent Trace ===
```

```
'Top 3 products in Q3 are: A (200), B (170), C (140).'
```

When you run this, you will see a step-by-step log showing:

- which action was selected
- which tool was called
- what observation was produced
- and when the loop terminated

This trace output is not just for learning. It reflects real production concerns like debugging agent behavior, monitoring tool calls, controlling cost through loop steps, and ensuring the system terminates safely. Before introducing a real language model into the loop, this trace-enabled version helps us confirm that our architecture is correct and observable.

4.8 From Scripted Actions to Model-Driven Reasoning

Until now, the agent's reasoning step has been deterministic.

We explicitly wrote:

```
if state.iterations == 1:
    action = "QUERY:Q3"
```

This allowed us to understand the mechanics of the ReAct loop clearly. However, a real agent must decide dynamically what to do next based on the user's goal and the current state.

In this section, we replace scripted action selection with model-driven reasoning. Importantly, we do not change the architecture. The loop remains bounded. Tools remain deterministic. State remains explicit. Termination remains controlled. Only the reasoning step becomes dynamic.

Designing a Structured Action Format

When a language model proposes an action, it must do so in a structured format. Free-form text is not safe for execution.

We define a simple action schema:

```
{
  "action": "QUERY",
  "arguments": {
    "quarter": "Q3"
  }
}
```

or

```
{
  "action": "ANALYZE",
  "arguments": {
    "top_n": 3
  }
}
```

The model proposes intent. The system parses and validates. The tools execute deterministically. This separation preserves safety.

Simulating a Model Call (Before Using a Real API)

For clarity and reproducibility, we first simulate a model output function. This function mimics what an LLM would produce — structured action proposals.

```
def simulated_model_reasoning(state: AgentState):
    if state.iterations == 1:
        return {"action": "QUERY", "arguments": {"quarter": "Q3"}}
    elif state.iterations == 2:
        return {"action": "ANALYZE", "arguments": {"top_n": 3}}
    else:
        return {"action": "RESPOND", "arguments": {}}
```

Updating the ReAct Loop to Use Structured Actions

Now we modify the reasoning portion of the loop:

```
def react_agent_v2(goal: str) -> str:
    state = AgentState(goal=goal)
```

```
    print("=== ReAct Agent (Model-Driven) ===")

    while state.iterations < MAX_ITERATIONS:
        state.iterations += 1

        action_payload = simulated_model_reasoning(state)
        action = action_payload["action"]
        args = action_payload["arguments"]

        state.history.append(action)

        print(f"[Iteration {state.iterations}] Action: {action}")

        if action == "QUERY":
            df = query_sales_data(args["quarter"])
            state.observations.append(("DATA", df))

        elif action == "ANALYZE":
            label, df = state.observations[-1]
            summary = top_products(df, top_n=args["top_n"])
            state.observations.append(("SUMMARY", summary))

        elif action == "RESPOND":
            label, summary = state.observations[-1]
            top3_list = ", ".join([f"{idx} ({val})" for idx, val
 ↪  in summary.items()])
            return f"Top 3 products are: {top3_list}."

    return "Terminated due to iteration limit."

### Running the Model-Driven Version
react_agent_v2("What were the top three selling products last
 ↪  quarter?")
```

```
=== ReAct Agent (Model-Driven) ===
[Iteration 1] Action: QUERY
```

```
[Iteration 2] Action: ANALYZE
[Iteration 3] Action: RESPOND

'Top 3 products are: A (200), B (170), C (140).'
```

What Changed?

At first glance, the updated implementation may appear significantly different. In reality, only a single component has changed. Previously, the agent selected actions using hardcoded conditional logic. The sequence of steps was explicitly scripted inside the loop. Now, instead of relying on fixed control statements, the system consumes structured action proposals generated by a reasoning function. Everything else remains identical.

We have not altered the architecture of the agent.
We have only evolved the reasoning engine that drives it.

The surrounding system — the guardrails, control boundaries, tool interfaces, and state tracking — remains stable. This demonstrates an important engineering principle:

An agent's intelligence can evolve without destabilizing its architecture.

Why This Step Matters

We have now built a proper separation:

- **Model** → proposes action
- **System** → validates and routes
- **Tool** → executes deterministically
- **State** → updates
- **Loop** → controls execution

This is the foundation of safe agent design.

4.9 Introducing LLMs: Enabling Natural Language Reasoning

Up to this point, we have built a fully structured ReAct agent:

- It maintains explicit state.
- It operates within a bounded control loop.
- It invokes deterministic tools.
- It logs its execution trace.
- It enforces termination conditions.
- It consumes structured action proposals.

Architecturally, the system is sound. However, one critical capability is still missing. Our agent cannot yet understand natural language. Although we refer to the input as a "goal," the current implementation does not truly interpret the user's query. The reasoning step is simulated, meaning the sequence of actions is predetermined. If we change the question slightly:

- "Which product improved the most compared to last quarter?"
- "Is there an upward trend in Q3?"
- "Compare Q2 and Q3 performance."
- "Which items are declining?"

The current system would fail because the agent is not actually *reasoning* about the question. It is executing a scripted sequence. This exposes a fundamental limitation: The architecture exists. The reasoning engine does not.

Why LLMs Are Necessary

To handle open-ended natural language queries, the agent must:

- Interpret user intent.
- Decide which tool to call.
- Choose arguments dynamically.
- Adapt action sequences based on intermediate results.
- Generate coherent explanations.

These are not deterministic rule-based tasks. They require probabilistic reasoning over language. This is precisely where Large Language Models (LLMs) become essential.

LLMs provide:

- Natural language understanding.

- Context-sensitive reasoning.
- Flexible action selection.
- Text generation capabilities.

When integrated properly, the LLM becomes the *reasoning component* inside the agent — not the entire system. The loop, tools, state, and guardrails remain unchanged. Only the reasoning engine is upgraded.

Step 1: Integrating the LLM as the Reasoning Engine

In this step, we connect the agent to a Large Language Model and delegate the decision-making process to it.

The `model_reasoning` function performs three key operations:

1. It constructs a structured prompt from the current agent state.
2. It sends that prompt to the LLM.
3. It enforces that the model returns valid JSON representing the next action.

The LLM does not execute tools directly. It only proposes the next step in structured form. The orchestration layer remains responsible for validation, execution, and control.

By forcing the model to return JSON and parsing it explicitly, we prevent free-form text from entering the execution pipeline. This preserves safety and architectural discipline while enabling natural language reasoning. Below is a provider-neutral function. You can adapt it to OpenAI, Azure, or any LLM provider.

Example using OpenAI-style API:

```
import json , os
from openai import OpenAI

os.environ["OPENAI_API_KEY"] = OPENAI_API_KEY
client = OpenAI()

def model_reasoning(state: AgentState):
    prompt = build_prompt(state)

    response = client.chat.completions.create(
```

```
        model="gpt-4o-mini",
        messages=[{"role": "user", "content": prompt}],
        temperature=0
    )

    content = response.choices[0].message.content

    try:
        return json.loads(content)
    except json.JSONDecodeError:
        raise ValueError("Model returned invalid JSON.")
```

Notice:

- Temperature is set to 0 for determinism.
- Output is parsed strictly as JSON.
- Invalid output raises an exception.

Step 2: Assembling the Complete Agent

This final implementation integrates all the components introduced throughout the lesson into a single working system.

The key elements now operating together are:

- **Explicit State Management**
  The `AgentState` object preserves the user query, tool results, and execution metadata.
  This enables iterative reasoning across multiple steps.
- **Tool Abstraction Layer**
  Each tool enforces structured inputs, validation, and deterministic execution.
  This ensures correctness and prevents arbitrary model execution.
- **Structured Prompt Construction**
  The prompt explicitly defines allowed actions and JSON schema con-

straints.

This limits the model's output space to safe, interpretable actions.

- **LLM-Based Reasoning Step**

  The language model dynamically selects the next action (`CALL_TOOL` or `RESPOND`)

  based on the current state and observations.

- **Guardrails and Loop Control**

  Iteration limits, tool-call caps, and timeout checks enforce bounded execution.

  This prevents runaway behavior and ensures predictable termination.

Together, these components transform a scripted pipeline into a structured, LLM-driven agent.

The model provides adaptive reasoning. The architecture enforces control. We now replace the simulated reasoning function with the real model call. Below is the complete end to end production ready AGENT.

```
# =========================
# 0) Setup: imports + data
# =========================
import os
import json
import time
import pandas as pd
from dataclasses import dataclass, field
from typing import Any, Dict, List, Optional

from openai import OpenAI

# IMPORTANT: Set OPENAI_API_KEY in your environment (recommended)
# os.environ["OPENAI_API_KEY"] = "YOUR_KEY"  # Avoid hardcoding
↪ keys in notebooks

client = OpenAI()

# Sample sales data (your demo dataset)
```

```
data = pd.DataFrame({
    "product": ["A", "B", "C", "A", "B", "C", "A", "B", "C"],
    "quarter": ["Q1", "Q1", "Q1", "Q2", "Q2", "Q2", "Q3", "Q3",
     ↪  "Q3"],
    "sales": [120, 150, 100, 180, 160, 130, 200, 170, 140]
})

print("data:")
display(data)


# =========================================
# 1) Tool Abstraction: validation helpers
# =========================================
def validate(parameters: Dict[str, Any], schema: Dict[str, Any]) ->
 ↪  None:
    """Minimal schema validation (enough for demo + book)."""
    if not isinstance(parameters, dict):
        raise ValueError("Tool parameters must be a dict.")

    required = schema.get("required", [])
    props = schema.get("properties", {})

    for key in required:
        if key not in parameters:
            raise ValueError(f"Missing required parameter: {key}")

    # Simple type checks
    for key, spec in props.items():
        if key in parameters and "type" in spec:
            expected = spec["type"]
            val = parameters[key]
            if expected == "string" and not isinstance(val, str):
                raise ValueError(f"Parameter '{key}' must be a
                 ↪  string.")
            if expected == "integer" and not isinstance(val, int):
                raise ValueError(f"Parameter '{key}' must be an
                 ↪  integer.")
```

```
# ========================
# 2) Tool Abstraction class
# ========================
class Tool:
    def __init__(self, name: str, description: str, input_schema:
     ↪  Dict[str, Any], fn):
        self.name = name
        self.description = description
        self.input_schema = input_schema
        self.fn = fn

    def execute(self, parameters: Dict[str, Any], state:
     ↪  "AgentState") -> Any:
        validate(parameters, self.input_schema)
        return self.fn(parameters, state)


# ========================
# 3) Agent state definition
# ========================
@dataclass
class AgentState:
    user_query: str
    observations: List[Dict[str, Any]] =
↪   field(default_factory=list)
    last_tool_result: Optional[Any] = None
    final_answer: Optional[str] = None
    iterations: int = 0
    start_time: float = field(default_factory=time.time)
    total_tool_calls: int = 0


# ==========================================
# 4) Tools for THIS agent (query + top-N)
# ==========================================
```

```
def tool_query_sales(parameters: Dict[str, Any], state: AgentState)
↪  -> Dict[str, Any]:
    """Query sales rows for a quarter. Supports 'last_quarter'."""
    quarter = parameters["quarter"].strip().upper()

    # Normalize inputs like "Q3 2023" -> "Q3"
    for token in ("Q1", "Q2", "Q3", "Q4"):
        if token in quarter:
            quarter = token
            break

    if quarter in {"LAST_QUARTER", "LAST"}:
        # Determine last quarter present in data
        q_order = {"Q1": 1, "Q2": 2, "Q3": 3, "Q4": 4}
        available = [q for q in data["quarter"].unique() if q in
↪  q_order]
        if not available:
            return {"error": "No valid quarters found in dataset."}
        quarter = max(available, key=lambda q: q_order[q])

    df = data[data["quarter"] == quarter].copy()
    if df.empty:
        return {"error": f"No sales rows found for quarter
         ↪  '{quarter}'.", "quarter": quarter}

    return {
        "quarter": quarter,
        "rows": df.to_dict(orient="records")
    }


def tool_top_selling_products(parameters: Dict[str, Any], state:
↪  AgentState) -> Dict[str, Any]:
    """Compute top-N products from the latest QUERY_SALES
     ↪  result."""
    top_n = parameters["top_n"]
```

```
    last = state.last_tool_result or {}
    rows = last.get("rows", [])
    quarter = last.get("quarter")

    if not rows:
        return {"error": "No queried rows available. Call
        ↪  QUERY_SALES first."}

    df = pd.DataFrame(rows)
    agg = (df.groupby("product", as_index=False)["sales"].sum()
             .sort_values("sales", ascending=False)
             .head(top_n))

    return {
        "quarter": quarter,
        "top_n": top_n,
        "top_products": agg.to_dict(orient="records")
    }


QUERY_SALES = Tool(
    name="QUERY_SALES",
    description="Fetch sales rows for a given quarter. Quarter can
↪   be Q1/Q2/Q3/Q4 or last_quarter.",
    input_schema={
        "type": "object",
        "properties": {"quarter": {"type": "string"}},
        "required": ["quarter"]
    },
    fn=tool_query_sales
)

TOP_PRODUCTS = Tool(
    name="TOP_PRODUCTS",
    description="Compute top-N products by total sales from the
↪   last QUERY_SALES result.",
    input_schema={
```

```
        "type": "object",
        "properties": {"top_n": {"type": "integer"}},
        "required": ["top_n"]
    },
    fn=tool_top_selling_products
)

TOOL_REGISTRY = {
    "QUERY_SALES": QUERY_SALES,
    "TOP_PRODUCTS": TOP_PRODUCTS
}


# ========================
# 5) Prompt construction
# ========================
def build_prompt(state: AgentState) -> List[Dict[str, str]]:
    """
    Return messages list (system+user) so the model sticks to
↪   strict JSON.
    Include last observation so the model can converge quickly.
    """
    last_obs = state.observations[-1] if state.observations else
↪   None

    tool_list = "\n".join(
        [f"- {t.name}: {t.description}" for t in
↪   TOOL_REGISTRY.values()]
    )

    system = f"""
You are an agent that must decide the next step to answer the user.
You can use tools. You must return ONLY valid JSON.

Tools available:
{tool_list}
```

```
Rules:
- Output MUST be a JSON object with keys: action, arguments.
- action must be one of: CALL_TOOL, RESPOND.
- If you need data or computation, CALL_TOOL.
- Use tool names exactly as defined.
- Quarter values MUST be one of Q1, Q2, Q3, Q4, last_quarter (no
↪  year).
- After you have the top products, RESPOND with a clear final
↪  answer.

JSON format:
{{
  "action": "CALL_TOOL" | "RESPOND",
  "arguments": {{
    ...
  }}
}}

If action == CALL_TOOL, arguments must be:
{{
  "tool_name": "<TOOL_NAME>",
  "parameters": {{ ... }}
}}

If action == RESPOND, arguments must be:
{{
  "answer": "<final answer>"
}}
""".strip()

    user = f"""
User question:
{state.user_query}

Latest observation (if any):
{json.dumps(last_obs, ensure_ascii=False)}
""".strip()
```

```
    return [{"role": "system", "content": system},
            {"role": "user", "content": user}]


# ========================
# 6) Model step (JSON only)
# ========================
def model_reasoning(state: AgentState) -> Dict[str, Any]:
    messages = build_prompt(state)
    resp = client.chat.completions.create(
        model="gpt-4o-mini",
        messages=messages,
        temperature=0
    )

    content = resp.choices[0].message.content.strip()

    try:
        obj = json.loads(content)
    except json.JSONDecodeError:
        raise ValueError(f"Model returned invalid
         ↪ JSON:\n{content}")

    if not isinstance(obj, dict):
        raise ValueError("Model output must be a JSON object.")
    return obj


# ========================
# 7) Agent loop (ReAct-ish)
# ========================
def run_agent(user_query: str,
              max_iterations: int = 10,
              max_tool_calls: int = 5,
              timeout_seconds: int = 20,
              debug: bool = True) -> str:
```

```
    state = AgentState(user_query=user_query)

    for i in range(1, max_iterations + 1):
        state.iterations = i

        # Guardrail: timeout
        if time.time() - state.start_time > timeout_seconds:
            return "Terminated: timeout exceeded."

        if debug:
            print(f"\n--- Iteration {i}/{max_iterations} ---")

        step = model_reasoning(state)

        if debug:
            print("Model step:", step)

        action = step.get("action")
        args = step.get("arguments", {}) or {}

        if action == "RESPOND":
            answer = args.get("answer") if isinstance(args, dict)
↪ else None
            state.final_answer = answer or "No answer produced."
            if debug:
                print(" RESPOND. Done.")
            return state.final_answer

        if action != "CALL_TOOL":
            # Hard stop for invalid action
            return f"Terminated: invalid action '{action}'."

        # Guardrail: tool calls cap
        state.total_tool_calls += 1
        if state.total_tool_calls > max_tool_calls:
            return "Terminated: tool call limit exceeded."
```

```
        tool_name = args.get("tool_name")
        params = args.get("parameters", {}) or {}

        if tool_name not in TOOL_REGISTRY:
            obs = {"error": "unknown_tool", "tool_name": tool_name,
↪   "allowed": list(TOOL_REGISTRY.keys())}
            state.observations.append(obs)
            state.last_tool_result = obs
            if debug:
                print("Observation:", obs)
            continue

        tool = TOOL_REGISTRY[tool_name]

        try:
            result = tool.execute(params, state)
        except Exception as e:
            result = {"error": str(e), "tool_name": tool_name,
↪   "parameters": params}

        # Update state (short-term memory)
        obs = {"tool_name": tool_name, "parameters": params,
↪   "result": result}
        state.observations.append(obs)
        state.last_tool_result = result

        if debug:
            print("Observation:", obs)

    return "Terminated: iteration limit reached."


# =========================
# 8) Test
# =========================
answer = run_agent("What were the top three selling products last
↪   quarter?", debug=True)
```

```
print("\nFINAL ANSWER:\n", answer)
```

data:

	product	quarter	sales
0	A	Q1	120
1	B	Q1	150
2	C	Q1	100
3	A	Q2	180
4	B	Q2	160
5	C	Q2	130
6	A	Q3	200
7	B	Q3	170
8	C	Q3	140

```
--- Iteration 1/10 ---
Model step: {'action': 'CALL_TOOL', 'arguments':
↪ {'tool_name': 'QUERY_SALES', 'parameters': {'quarter':
↪ 'last_quarter'}}}
Observation: {'tool_name': 'QUERY_SALES', 'parameters':
↪ {'quarter': 'last_quarter'}, 'result': {'quarter': 'Q3',
↪ 'rows': [{'product': 'A', 'quarter': 'Q3', 'sales':
↪ 200}, {'product': 'B', 'quarter': 'Q3', 'sales': 170},
↪ {'product': 'C', 'quarter': 'Q3', 'sales': 140}]}}

--- Iteration 2/10 ---
Model step: {'action': 'RESPOND', 'arguments': {'answer':
↪ 'The top three selling products last quarter (Q3) were:
↪ 1. Product A with 200 sales, 2. Product B with 170
↪ sales, and 3. Product C with 140 sales.'}}
 RESPOND. Done.
```

```
FINAL ANSWER:
 The top three selling products last quarter (Q3) were: 1.
  ↪ Product A with 200 sales, 2. Product B with 170 sales,
  ↪ and 3. Product C with 140 sales.
```

ReAct Reasoning Agent Architecture

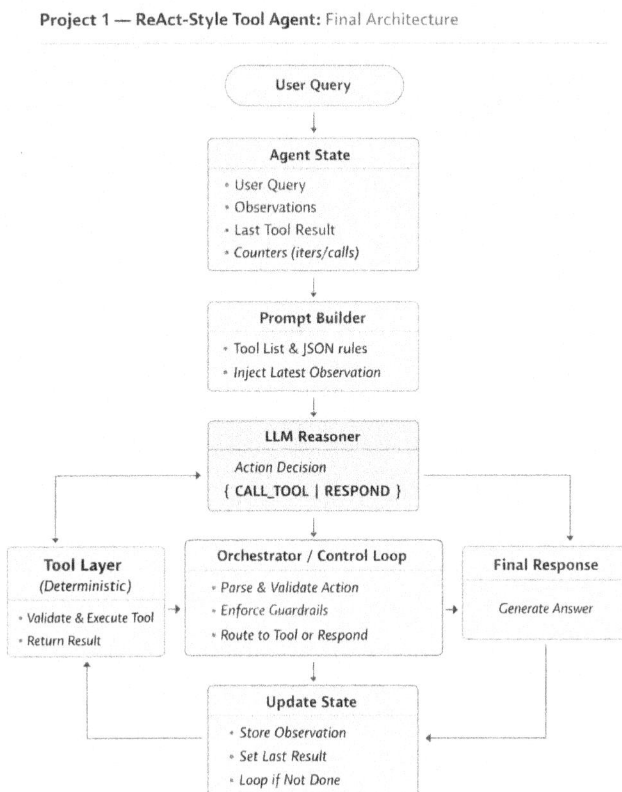

4.10 Conclusion: Building a Controlled, LLM-Driven Agent

In this project, we moved beyond simple language model prompts and constructed a complete agent architecture. We did not merely "call an LLM." We designed a system.

We introduced:

- Explicit state management
- Deterministic tool abstraction
- Structured input validation
- Controlled orchestration
- Guardrails and bounded execution
- A ReAct-style reasoning loop
- An LLM-powered decision policy

The result is not a script. It is an adaptive agent. The model no longer generates a single response. It decides what action to take next.

Yet despite introducing probabilistic reasoning, we preserved architectural discipline:

- Tools remain deterministic
- Execution remains validated
- State remains explicit
- Termination remains bounded

This balance is essential. An agent system is not intelligent because it can generate text. It becomes powerful when it can reason, decide, act, and stop safely.

You have now built a minimal production-structured agent. It can interpret natural language intent, select tools, execute deterministic operations, update its internal state, and produce a controlled final response.

Most importantly, you have done so without surrendering control to the model. This is the foundation of real-world agent design.

Project 2: The Tool-Using Data Analyst Agent

Key Objectives

- Problem Statement: From Fixed Tools to Open-Ended Analysis
- Architectural Evolution of the Agent
- Designing the Safe SQL Execution Layer
- Step I: Creating the Analytical Dataset
- Step II: Implementing the Safe SQL Execution Tool
- Step III: SQL-Aware Reasoning: Prompting the Model to Generate Safe Queries
- Step IV: Integrating SQL Execution into the Agent Loop
- Step V: End-to-End Execution: Running the SQL-Aware Agent
- Practical understanding: From Question to SQL to Answer
- Failure and Recovery: When the Model Is Wrong
- Conclusion: Controlled Generative Execution

5.1 Problem Statement: From Fixed Tools to Open-Ended Analysis

In Project 1, our agent operated within a well-defined environment.
It selected from a small set of deterministic tools:

- Query a dataset.

- Compute top-performing items.
- Return a structured response.

The space of possible actions was limited. The execution logic was predetermined. The architecture was flexible, but the operations were fixed.

Now consider a more realistic analytical scenario.

A user asks:

- "What is total revenue by region?"
- "Which product category performed best in Q1?"
- "Who are the top five customers by purchase volume?"
- "Compare electronics and furniture sales."

These questions are fundamentally different from those in Project 1. They are not variations of a single predefined function. They require dynamic filtering, grouping, aggregation, joins across tables, and derived calculations.

The analytical space has expanded.

A fixed set of Python functions can no longer scale. If we attempt to handle each new question by writing another function, the system becomes rigid and unmaintainable. Every additional query type increases complexity linearly.

This approach does not generalize. To build an agent capable of flexible analysis, we need a different abstraction. We need a system that can generate the analytical logic itself. This is precisely the role of SQL.

Instead of hard-coding logic paths, we allow the model to synthesize a query that expresses the user's intent in a structured, executable form. The database engine then performs the computation deterministically.

However, this introduces a new challenge. In Project 1, the model selected from known tools. In Project 2, the model generates executable code. That shift is significant. Generating SQL dynamically is powerful — but also potentially dangerous. Without constraints, a model could produce destructive statements, malformed queries, or unsafe operations.

Therefore, this project introduces a critical architectural boundary. The model may propose SQL. The system must **validate** it before execution. We are building a controlled generative execution pipeline.

5.2 Architectural Evolution of the Agent

Project 2 does extend the architecture built in Project 1. In the previous project, the agent operated within a structured reasoning loop:

1. The model proposed an action.
2. The system validated the action.
3. A deterministic tool executed.
4. The result was stored in state.
5. The loop continued until termination.

That structure remains intact. What changes is the nature of the tool itself. The tool becomes a database execution engine. The model must generate a SQL query that expresses the user's analytical intent.

This introduces three architectural upgrades.

- First, the tool interface must now accept arbitrary queries rather than structured parameters. The input surface has expanded.
- Second, execution safety becomes essential. SQL is powerful. It can modify, delete, or corrupt data if not controlled. We must therefore introduce validation rules before execution. Only read-only, schema-compliant queries will be permitted.
- Third, the output is no longer predictable. A database query may return any number of rows and columns. The agent must parse and structure results dynamically before generating a response.

Despite these upgrades, one principle remains unchanged. The model does not execute code directly. The model proposes. The system enforces. The reasoning engine remains probabilistic. The execution engine remains deterministic.

Project 2 therefore represents an architectural deepening, not a redesign. The core loop survives. The execution boundary becomes more sophisticated. The agent is no longer choosing among tools. It is generating the analytical logic itself — under strict control.

5.3 Designing the Safe SQL Execution Layer

The moment we allow a language model to generate SQL, we introduce risk. SQL is not a simple function call. It is a declarative language capable of modifying, deleting, and restructuring data. In production systems, an uncontrolled SQL execution pathway can result in catastrophic consequences.

Therefore, the most important architectural component in Project 2 is the validation layer between the model and the database.

1. The Execution Boundary

In this architecture, the boundary is explicit:

1. The model generates a SQL query.
2. The system validates the query.
3. Only if the query satisfies safety constraints, it is executed.
4. The result is returned in structured form.

This boundary preserves determinism.

2. Enforcing Read-Only Constraints

The first and most critical rule is simple: Only `SELECT` queries are allowed.

Any query containing destructive keywords must be rejected. This includes: - `DROP` - `DELETE` - `UPDATE` - `INSERT` - `ALTER` - `CREATE`

The database in this project is local and controlled. However, the architectural discipline we apply here mirrors production practice. Even in a demonstration environment, we enforce the same safety principles we would apply to live systems.

3. Schema Awareness

A model generating SQL must be constrained by the database schema.

The agent must know:

- Which tables exist.
- Which columns belong to each table.

If a query references non-existent tables or columns, execution should fail gracefully rather than propagate errors silently. This introduces an important pattern that the model reasons within a declared schema context. By exposing the schema explicitly in the prompt, we reduce hallucination and guide generation.

4. Limiting Result Size

Another safety consideration is result volume. Unbounded queries can return extremely large result sets. In production systems, this leads to increased latency, memory strain, excess token usage and poor response formatting.

To prevent this, the execution layer may enforce: - A maximum row limit - Automatic `LIMIT` injection - Row-count validation before returning results

This ensures the agent remains responsive and bounded.

5. Structured Output Handling

Unlike Project 1, where tool outputs were predictable, SQL queries can return arbitrary column sets.

The execution layer must:

- Retrieve column names.
- Map rows into structured dictionaries.
- Return consistent JSON-like objects.

This transforms raw database output into a format that the reasoning layer can interpret and summarize.

6. Error Handling and Recovery

Even with constraints, SQL generation may fail. The model may:

- Misspell a column name.
- Use incorrect aggregation syntax.
- Reference an unavailable table.
- Construct malformed joins.

Instead of crashing the system, the execution layer should:

- Catch database errors.

- Return structured error feedback.
- Allow the agent loop to attempt correction.

This introduces a controlled feedback mechanism between execution and reasoning.

The Core Principle

This project introduces a powerful but delicate pattern: **Generative logic + deterministic enforcement.** The model is free to propose analytical queries. The system decides whether they are valid. It is the foundation of safe agent design.

5.4 Step I: Creating the Analytical Dataset

Before the agent can generate SQL, it must have something to query. For that we introduce a relational database layer.

This is a deliberate architectural shift. The agent will generate SQL statements that are executed against a structured database schema. To keep this project self-contained and reproducible, we use **SQLite**, an embedded database engine that ships with Python. It requires no installation, no server, and no configuration.

The goal is not to teach SQL infrastructure.
The goal is to simulate a realistic analytical environment.

Schema Design

We define three simple tables:

- `products` — information about available products
- `customers` — customer details
- `orders` — transactional purchase records

This schema introduces relationships and aggregation opportunities, enabling questions such as:

- "What is total revenue by product?"
- "Which customer placed the most orders?"

- "Which products performed best last month?"

The schema defines the **boundaries of reasoning**.
The model must respect:

- Table names
- Column names
- Relational structure
- SQL syntax

These constraints are essential. They create the environment in which safe generative execution can occur. Once the database is created, we will enforce strict execution rules around it. The agent will be allowed to read from this database. It will not be allowed to modify it.

SQLite Setup (Embedded Database)

```
# ========================================
# SQLite Setup (Embedded Database)
# ========================================

import sqlite3

# Create in-memory SQLite database
connection = sqlite3.connect(":memory:")
cursor = connection.cursor()

# --------------------------
# Create Tables
# --------------------------
cursor.execute("""
CREATE TABLE products (
    id INTEGER PRIMARY KEY,
    name TEXT,
    category TEXT,
    price REAL
);
""")
```

```
cursor.execute("""
CREATE TABLE customers (
    id INTEGER PRIMARY KEY,
    name TEXT,
    region TEXT
);
""")

cursor.execute("""
CREATE TABLE orders (
    id INTEGER PRIMARY KEY,
    customer_id INTEGER,
    product_id INTEGER,
    quantity INTEGER,
    order_date TEXT,
    FOREIGN KEY(customer_id) REFERENCES customers(id),
    FOREIGN KEY(product_id) REFERENCES products(id)
);
""")

# --------------------------
# Insert Sample Data
# --------------------------
products_data = [
    (1, "Laptop", "Electronics", 1200),
    (2, "Phone", "Electronics", 800),
    (3, "Desk", "Furniture", 300)
]

customers_data = [
    (1, "Alice", "North"),
    (2, "Bob", "South"),
    (3, "Charlie", "West")
]

orders_data = [
```

```
    (1, 1, 1, 2, "2024-01-10"),
    (2, 2, 2, 1, "2024-01-12"),
    (3, 3, 3, 4, "2024-02-01"),
    (4, 1, 2, 3, "2024-02-15"),
    (5, 2, 1, 1, "2024-03-05")
]

cursor.executemany("INSERT INTO products VALUES (?, ?, ?, ?);",
↪   products_data)
cursor.executemany("INSERT INTO customers VALUES (?, ?, ?);",
↪   customers_data)
cursor.executemany("INSERT INTO orders VALUES (?, ?, ?, ?, ?);",
↪   orders_data)
connection.commit()
print("SQLite in-memory database created successfully.")
```

```
SQLite in-memory database created successfully.
```

5.5 Step II: Implementing the Safe SQL Execution Tool

With the architectural constraints clearly defined, we now implement the execution layer that enforces them. The objective is to run SQL safely. The tool we build must:

- Accept a model-generated SQL string.
- Validate that it is read-only.
- Ensure it conforms to schema boundaries.
- Prevent destructive operations.
- Limit result size.
- Return structured results.
- Handle errors gracefully.

This tool becomes the controlled gateway between generative reasoning and deterministic database execution.

Implementation

Below is a minimal but disciplined implementation of a safe SQL execution function using SQLite.

```
# ========================================
# Safe SQL Execution Tool
# ========================================
import re

ALLOWED_TABLES = {"products", "customers", "orders"}

FORBIDDEN_KEYWORDS = {
    "DROP", "DELETE", "UPDATE", "INSERT",
    "ALTER", "CREATE", "REPLACE", "TRUNCATE"
}

MAX_ROWS = 50


def is_select_query(query: str) -> bool:
    return query.strip().upper().startswith("SELECT")


def contains_forbidden_keywords(query: str) -> bool:
    upper_query = query.upper()
    return any(keyword in upper_query for keyword in
     ↪  FORBIDDEN_KEYWORDS)


def references_only_allowed_tables(query: str) -> bool:
    tables_in_query = set(re.findall(r"FROM\s+(\w+)|JOIN\s+(\w+)",
 ↪  query, re.IGNORECASE))
    flat_tables = {t for pair in tables_in_query for t in pair if
 ↪  t}
    return flat_tables.issubset(ALLOWED_TABLES)
```

```
def enforce_limit(query: str) -> str:
    if "LIMIT" not in query.upper():
        query = query.rstrip(";") + f" LIMIT {MAX_ROWS};"
    return query


def execute_safe_sql(query: str, connection):
    # 1. Validate SELECT-only
    if not is_select_query(query):
        return {"error": "Only SELECT queries are allowed."}

    # 2. Block destructive keywords
    if contains_forbidden_keywords(query):
        return {"error": "Query contains forbidden SQL keywords."}

    # 3. Restrict tables
    if not references_only_allowed_tables(query):
        return {"error": "Query references unauthorized tables."}

    # 4. Enforce row limit
    safe_query = enforce_limit(query)

    try:
        cursor = connection.cursor()
        cursor.execute(safe_query)
        rows = cursor.fetchall()
        columns = [col[0] for col in cursor.description]

        results = [dict(zip(columns, row)) for row in rows]

        return {
            "query": safe_query,
            "row_count": len(results),
            "results": results
        }

    except Exception as e:
```

```
        return {"error": str(e), "query": query}
```

What This Tool Enforces

This implementation ensures:

- Only read-only `SELECT` queries are allowed.
- Destructive SQL statements are rejected.
- Only predefined tables may be accessed.
- Result size is bounded.
- Errors are captured and returned in structured form.

Notice that this tool does not assume the model is correct. It assumes the model may be wrong. That assumption is what makes the system robust.

Architectural Observation

Now the tool accepts generated code. That is a substantial increase in surface area. The validation layer is therefore not optional — it is the core of safe generative execution. This function now becomes the primary tool the agent will call when handling analytical queries.

The model proposes SQL. This function decides whether it runs.

5.6 Step 3: SQL-Aware Reasoning: Prompting the Model to Generate Safe Queries

Now that we have a safe execution tool, we need the model to produce SQL query in a controlled and schema-aware way. The model must generate a SQL query string. This increases flexibility — but also increases risk.

To reduce failure modes, we constrain the model using three techniques:

1. **Schema exposure** — we explicitly tell the model which tables and columns exist.
2. **Strict output format** — the model must return JSON only.

3. **Safety rules in the prompt** — the model is instructed to generate read-only SQL.

Exposing the Database Schema

- `products(product_id, product_name, category, price)`
- `customers(customer_id, region)`
- `orders(order_id, product_id, customer_id, quantity, order_date)`

This dramatically reduces hallucinated column names.

The SQL-Generation Prompt

The reasoning step returns one of two actions:

- `CALL_TOOL` → execute SQL through the safe execution layer

- `RESPOND` → finalize the answer using the latest query results

Prompt construction code

```
# =========================
# Prompt construction (SQL-aware, strict JSON)
# =========================
import json
from typing import List, Dict

SCHEMA_SUMMARY = """
Tables:
1) products(id, name, category, price)
2) customers(id, name, region)
3) orders(id, customer_id, product_id, quantity, order_date)

Join keys:
- orders.product_id = products.id
- orders.customer_id = customers.id

Derived metric:
- revenue = orders.quantity * products.price
""".strip()
```

```
def build_sql_prompt(state) -> List[Dict[str, str]]:
    """
    Returns chat messages (system + user) that strictly constrain
↪   the model
    to output machine-parseable JSON with tool_name=RUN_SQL when
↪   calling tools.
    """
    last_obs = state.observations[-1] if state.observations else
↪   None

    system = f"""
You are a data analyst agent. Answer the user's question by
↪   generating SAFE SQL.

Schema (use ONLY these tables/columns):
{SCHEMA_SUMMARY}

Hard Rules:
- Only generate SELECT queries (read-only).
- Never use: UPDATE, DELETE, INSERT, DROP, ALTER, CREATE, REPLACE,
↪   TRUNCATE.
- Use ONLY the tables and columns shown in the schema.
- If you need data, call the tool RUN_SQL.
- Return ONLY valid JSON. No markdown. No explanations.

JSON Contract (MUST follow exactly):

Your output MUST be a JSON object with EXACTLY these keys:
{{
  "action": "CALL_TOOL" | "RESPOND",
  "arguments": {{ ... }}
}}

If action == "CALL_TOOL", arguments MUST be:
{{
  "tool_name": "RUN_SQL",
```

```
  "parameters": {{
    "query": "<SQL query string>"
  }}
}}

If action == "RESPOND", arguments MUST be:
{{
  "answer": "<final answer in natural language>"
}}

Important:
- Do NOT omit "arguments".
- Do NOT omit "tool_name".
- Do NOT output anything outside the JSON object.
""".strip()

    user = f"""
User question:
{state.user_query}

Latest observation (if any):
{json.dumps(last_obs, ensure_ascii=False)}
""".strip()

    return [
        {"role": "system", "content": system},
        {"role": "user", "content": user},
    ]
```

Model Reasoning Step (JSON-Only)

This is the same structural pattern as Project 1: the model proposes a structured action object, and we parse it deterministically.

```
from openai import OpenAI
import os
```

```
os.environ["OPENAI_API_KEY"] = OPENAI_API_KEY
client = OpenAI()


def model_reasoning(state):
    messages = build_sql_prompt(state)
    resp = client.chat.completions.create(
        model="gpt-4o-mini",
        messages=messages,
        temperature=0
    )

    content = resp.choices[0].message.content.strip()

    try:
        obj = json.loads(content)
    except json.JSONDecodeError:
        raise ValueError(f"Model returned invalid
         ↪ JSON:\n{content}")

    return obj
```

Why This Works

This prompt does not try to make the model "smart."
It tries to make the model bounded.

- The schema limits hallucination.
- The JSON format makes output machine-interpretable.
- The safety rules reduce dangerous queries.
- The execution layer still validates everything.

The system decides whether it is executed.

5.7 Step 4: Integrating SQL Execution into the Agent Loop

At this point, we have two critical components:

1. A **SQL-aware reasoning step** that outputs structured JSON actions

2. A **safe SQL execution tool** that validates and executes read-only queries

Now we connect them inside a bounded control loop.
The loop remains conceptually identical to Project 1:

- The model proposes the next action.
- The system validates the proposal.
- A deterministic tool executes under constraints.
- The state updates with observations.
- The loop repeats until the model produces a final response.

What changes is the tool: instead of calling fixed analytical functions, the agent now calls a safe database execution gateway.

Wiring the SQL Tool into the Loop

For this project, we expose a single tool:

- `RUN_SQL(query: str)` → validates the SQL and executes it against SQLite

This keeps Project 2 intentionally small while still demonstrating a powerful pattern of controlled generative execution.

Agent Loop Implementation

```
# ==========================
# Agent State (short-term memory)
# ==========================
from dataclasses import dataclass, field
from typing import Any, Dict, List, Optional
```

```
import time

@dataclass
class AgentState:
    user_query: str
    observations: List[Dict[str, Any]] =
 ↪  field(default_factory=list)
    last_tool_result: Optional[Any] = None
    final_answer: Optional[str] = None
    iterations: int = 0
    start_time: float = field(default_factory=time.time)
    total_tool_calls: int = 0


# ==========================
# Tool wrapper for RUN_SQL
# ==========================
def run_sql_tool(parameters: Dict[str, Any], state: AgentState) ->
 ↪  Dict[str, Any]:
    query = parameters.get("query", "")
    return execute_safe_sql(query, connection)  # execute_safe_sql
     ↪  defined earlier


TOOL_REGISTRY = {
    "RUN_SQL": run_sql_tool
}


# ==========================
# Agent loop (ReAct-style)
# ==========================
def run_agent(user_query: str,
              max_iterations: int = 8,
              max_tool_calls: int = 5,
              timeout_seconds: int = 20,
              debug: bool = True) -> str:
```

```
state = AgentState(user_query=user_query)

for i in range(1, max_iterations + 1):
    state.iterations = i

    # Guardrail: timeout
    if time.time() - state.start_time > timeout_seconds:
        return "Terminated: timeout exceeded."

    if debug:
        print(f"\n--- Iteration {i}/{max_iterations} ---")

    # 1) Model proposes next action
    step = model_reasoning(state)  # JSON action object

    if debug:
        print("Model step:", step)

    action = step.get("action")

    if "arguments" not in step:
        return f"Invalid model output: missing 'arguments'
         ↪ field. Output was: {step}"

    args = step["arguments"]
    # 2) If RESPOND, terminate
    if action == "RESPOND":
        answer = args.get("answer") if isinstance(args, dict)
↪ else None
        state.final_answer = answer or "No answer produced."
        if debug:
            print(" RESPOND. Done.")
        return state.final_answer

    # 3) Only one allowed non-terminal action: CALL_TOOL
    if action != "CALL_TOOL":
```

```
            return f"Terminated: invalid action '{action}'."

        # Guardrail: tool calls cap
        state.total_tool_calls += 1
        if state.total_tool_calls > max_tool_calls:
            return "Terminated: tool call limit exceeded."

        tool_name = args.get("tool_name")
        params = args.get("parameters", {}) or {}

        # 4) Validate tool name
        if tool_name not in TOOL_REGISTRY:
            obs = {
                "error": "unknown_tool",
                "tool_name": tool_name,
                "allowed": list(TOOL_REGISTRY.keys())
            }
            state.observations.append(obs)
            state.last_tool_result = obs
            if debug:
                print("Observation:", obs)
            continue

        # 5) Execute tool deterministically
        try:
            result = TOOL_REGISTRY[tool_name](params, state)
        except Exception as e:
            result = {"error": str(e), "tool_name": tool_name,
↪ "parameters": params}

        # 6) Update state (short-term memory)
        obs = {"tool_name": tool_name, "parameters": params,
↪ "result": result}
        state.observations.append(obs)
        state.last_tool_result = result

        if debug:
```

```
        print("Observation:", obs)

    return "Terminated: iteration limit reached."
```

What This Loop Guarantees

Even though the model is generating SQL dynamically, the system remains fully controlled:

- SQL is executed only through `RUN_SQL`.
- Queries are validated before execution.
- Results are structured and stored in state.
- Execution is bounded by guardrails (iterations, tool calls, timeout).

This preserves the core agent design principle:

The model decides what to attempt.
The system decides what is allowed to run.

Tool-Using Data Analyst Agent Architecture

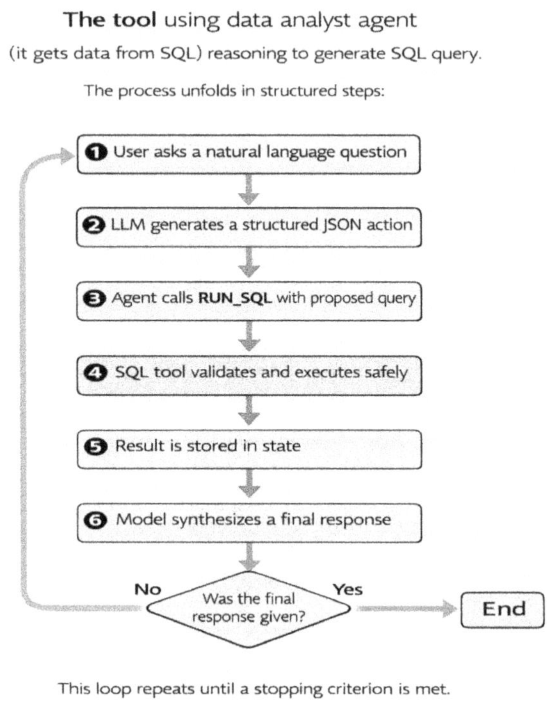

5.8 Step 5: End-to-End Execution: Running the SQL-Aware Agent

Up to this point, we have defined:

- The SQLite analytical dataset
- The safe SQL execution tool

- The structured JSON prompt
- The bounded agent loop

The architecture is complete. Now we execute it. In this section, we run the agent and observe:

- The SQL generated by the model
- The validation layer enforcing safety
- The structured results returned from the database
- The final response synthesized by the model

This confirms that the system works as a controlled generative agent.

Running the Agent

```
print(run_agent("What is the total revenue by product?",
↪ debug=True))
```

```
--- Iteration 1/8 ---
Model step: {'action': 'CALL_TOOL', 'arguments':
↪ {'tool_name': 'RUN_SQL', 'parameters': {'query': 'SELECT
↪ products.name, SUM(orders.quantity * products.price) AS
↪ total_revenue FROM orders JOIN products ON
↪ orders.product_id = products.id GROUP BY
↪ products.name'}}}
```

```
Observation: {'tool_name': 'RUN_SQL', 'parameters':
 ↪  {'query': 'SELECT products.name, SUM(orders.quantity *
 ↪  products.price) AS total_revenue FROM orders JOIN
 ↪  products ON orders.product_id = products.id GROUP BY
 ↪  products.name'}, 'result': {'query': 'SELECT
 ↪  products.name, SUM(orders.quantity * products.price) AS
 ↪  total_revenue FROM orders JOIN products ON
 ↪  orders.product_id = products.id GROUP BY products.name
 ↪  LIMIT 50;', 'row_count': 3, 'results': [{'name': 'Desk',
 ↪  'total_revenue': 1200.0}, {'name': 'Laptop',
 ↪  'total_revenue': 3600.0}, {'name': 'Phone',
 ↪  'total_revenue': 3200.0}]}}

--- Iteration 2/8 ---
Model step: {'action': 'RESPOND', 'arguments': {'answer':
 ↪  'The total revenue by product is as follows: Desk -
 ↪  $1200.00, Laptop - $3600.00, Phone - $3200.00.'}}
  RESPOND. Done.
The total revenue by product is as follows: Desk - $1200.00,
 ↪  Laptop - $3600.00, Phone - $3200.00.
```

What You See in Debug Mode

When debug=True, the system displays:

- The iteration number
- The model's proposed JSON action
- The SQL query generated
- The validated query (with enforced LIMIT)
- The structured database results
- The final RESPOND action

This execution trace demonstrates something critical: The model does not execute SQL directly. It proposes SQL. The system decides whether it is safe to run.

What Happens Internally

The execution cycle follows a controlled sequence:

1. The model receives the user question.
2. It generates a JSON action proposing `RUN_SQL`.
3. The SQL query is validated:
    - Must be `SELECT` only
    - Must not contain destructive keywords
    - Must reference only allowed tables
    - Must enforce a row limit
4. The validated query is executed against SQLite.
5. Results are stored in structured form.
6. The model receives the observation.
7. The model responds with a final answer.
8. The loop terminates safely.

No unvalidated SQL is ever executed.

5.9 Practical understanding: From Question to SQL to Answer

Now that the SQL-aware agent loop is integrated, we test the system with real analytical queries. This is where the architecture becomes tangible. Let us observe this behavior with a few examples.

Example 1 — Aggregation Query

User Question:

> "What is the total revenue by product?"

Typical Model Action:

```
{
  "action": "CALL_TOOL",
  "arguments": {
```

```
    "tool_name": "RUN_SQL",
    "parameters": {
      "query": "SELECT product, SUM(revenue) as total_revenue FROM
       ↪ sales GROUP BY product;"
    }
  }
}
```

The SQL tool:

Validates that this is a SELECT statement. - Confirms only allowed tables are referenced. - Executes the query. - Returns structured rows.

The model then produces:

```
{
  "action": "RESPOND",
  "arguments": {
    "answer": "Product A generated the highest total revenue,
     ↪ followed by Product B and Product C."
  }
}
```

Notice what happened:

The model did not directly compute totals. It generated code that computed totals. The system executed that code safely.

Example 2 — Top-N Query

User Question:

"Show the top 3 products by revenue."

The model generates SQL with ordering and limits:

```
SELECT product, SUM(revenue) as total_revenue
FROM sales
GROUP BY product
ORDER BY total_revenue DESC
LIMIT 3;
```

The loop remains identical. The only difference is the SQL proposed by the model. This demonstrates that the reasoning is dynamic and the execution pipeline is stable.

Example 3 — Comparative Query

User Question:

> "Which product improved the most compared to Q2?"

Now the model must:

- Filter by quarter
- Aggregate values
- Compare across periods

The generated SQL becomes more complex. Yet the execution process remains controlled and identical. This is the key architectural insight: **The complexity grows in the reasoning layer — not in the control layer.**

What These Examples Demonstrate

- Natural language → SQL translation
- Structured output parsing
- Safe execution through validation
- Deterministic tool behavior
- Controlled iterative reasoning
- Clear termination via `RESPOND`

The tool surface area has expanded dramatically. Instead of passing structured parameters, the model is now generating executable code. The architecture, however, remains disciplined. That discipline is what makes generative agents usable in real systems.

5.10 Failure and Recovery: When the Model Is Wrong

So far, we have observed successful runs. But real systems are not judged by their successes. They are judged by how they handle failure. When the model generates SQL, mistakes are inevitable:

- A column name may not exist.
- A table may be referenced incorrectly.
- Aggregations may be malformed.
- Filters may be logically incorrect.

If such failures crash the system, the architecture is fragile. Our design prevents that.

A Deliberate Failure Example

User Question:

> "Show revenue by region."

Suppose the database does not contain a region column.

The model might generate:

```
SELECT region, SUM(revenue)
FROM sales
GROUP BY region;
```

The safe SQL tool attempts execution and returns:

```
{
  "error": "no such column: region"
}
```

Notice what happens next:

- The system does not crash.
- The loop does not terminate abruptly.
- The error is captured in structured form.
- The error is appended to the agent's state.

- The failure becomes an observation.

Iterative Self-Correction

On the next iteration, the model sees:

- The original user query
- The previous SQL attempt
- The structured error message

It can now revise its reasoning. For example, it might instead generate:

```
SELECT product, SUM(revenue)
FROM sales
GROUP BY product;
```

The system validates the new query. The database executes it successfully. The result is returned to the model. The agent continues until it produces:

```
{
  "action": "RESPOND",
  "arguments": {
    "answer": "Revenue is available by product, not by region.
      ↪ Product A generated the highest total revenue."
  }
}
```

This is the first time in the book we demonstrate **closed-loop correction**. The model proposes. The system validates. The environment responds. The model adapts. That cycle is the foundation of **resilient agent** systems.

5.11 Conclusion: Controlled Generative Execution

In this project, we moved beyond structured parameter passing and entered a far more powerful domain: The model now generates executable code. That shift dramatically increases flexibility and risk.

The key architectural lesson: **Generative systems must never execute model output directly.** They must mediate it. The reasoning layer becomes more flexible. The control layer becomes more strict. That balance is what makes generative agents usable in production environments. With Project 2, you have now built:

- A safe code-executing agent
- A SQL-generating analytical assistant
- A bounded reasoning system with recovery

You have expanded from deterministic tools to controlled generative execution.

Project 3: The Memory-Augmented Agent

Key Objectives

- Why Memory Is the Next Architectural Leap
- Session Memory vs Long-Term Memory
- The Hidden Complexity of Memory
- Designing a Memory-Aware Agent Architecture
- Session Memory Summarization (Conceptual Implementation)
- Long-Term Memory: Persistence Across Sessions
- Controlled Retrieval
- Memory-Aware Prompt Construction
- Integrating Memory into the Agent Loop
- From Reactive Assistant to Persistent Intelligence

6.1 Why Memory Is the Next Architectural Leap

Up to this point, our agents have operated within tightly controlled reasoning loops. They could interpret instructions, call tools, validate outputs, and terminate safely. Architecturally, they were sound. Yet something essential was missing.

Continuity

Every interaction began in isolation. The agent had no awareness of what had occurred moments earlier, let alone across sessions. It responded correctly — but only within the boundaries of the current prompt.

Consider a user interacting with an analytical assistant: > "Show me total revenue by product."

The agent responds. Moments later, the user says: > "Now only for Electronics."

Without memory, the second instruction is ambiguous. What does "now" refer to? What context should be preserved? What assumptions are being carried forward?

This limitation becomes obvious the moment interactions extend beyond a single query. A user does not think in isolated instructions. They think in threads. They refine , adjust , reference earlier results and change constraints mid-conversation. Hence an agent with memory is a must to understand that conversations are evolving processes. Agent with memory ensures continuity.

Memory fundamentally alters the agent's operating model. The system must now maintain state beyond a single reasoning loop. It must decide which pieces of context are relevant, which should persist, and which can be discarded. It must manage growth, because memory that expands without control eventually becomes unusable.

In other words, memory introduces **time** into the architecture.

This introduces persistence. The agent is no longer merely reactive; it becomes cumulative. Its behavior is influenced not just by the current query, but by what came before. However, this expansion comes with responsibility. Memory must be structured. It must be bounded. It must be curated. Uncontrolled memory leads to noise, confusion, and degraded reasoning.

The architectural challenge, therefore, is not simply adding storage. It is designing intelligent memory.

Getting started with the project by creating the initial data using SQLite

```
# ========================================
# Project 3 (LLM Upgrade) - Memory-Augmented Agent (E2E)
```

```
# Persistent Analytics Assistant + SQLite + Safe SQL
# ==========================================

import os
import re
import json
import time
import sqlite3
from dataclasses import dataclass, field
from typing import Any, Dict, List, Optional

from openai import OpenAI

# -----------------------------
# 0) OpenAI client (NO HARDCODING)
# -----------------------------

os.environ["OPENAI_API_KEY"] = OPENAI_API_KEY
client = OpenAI()

# ===========================
# 1) SQLite setup + dataset
# ===========================

def create_demo_db() -> sqlite3.Connection:
    conn = sqlite3.connect(":memory:")
    cur = conn.cursor()

    cur.executescript("""
    CREATE TABLE products (
        product_id INTEGER PRIMARY KEY,
        product_name TEXT,
        category TEXT,
        price REAL
    );

    CREATE TABLE customers (
```

```
    customer_id INTEGER PRIMARY KEY,
    region TEXT
);

CREATE TABLE orders (
    order_id INTEGER PRIMARY KEY,
    product_id INTEGER,
    customer_id INTEGER,
    quantity INTEGER,
    order_date TEXT,
    quarter TEXT,
    FOREIGN KEY(product_id) REFERENCES products(product_id),
    FOREIGN KEY(customer_id) REFERENCES customers(customer_id)
);
""")

cur.executemany(
    "INSERT INTO products(product_id, product_name, category,
    ↪ price) VALUES (?, ?, ?, ?)",
    [
        (1, "A", "Core", 100.0),
        (2, "B", "Core", 150.0),
        (3, "C", "Addon", 80.0),
        (4, "D", "Addon", 50.0),
    ],
)

cur.executemany(
    "INSERT INTO customers(customer_id, region) VALUES (?, ?)",
    [
        (1, "North"),
        (2, "South"),
        (3, "West"),
        (4, "East"),
    ],
)
```

```
    cur.executemany(
        "INSERT INTO orders(order_id, product_id, customer_id,
        ↪ quantity, order_date, quarter) VALUES (?, ?, ?, ?, ?,
        ↪ ?)",
        [
            # Q2
            (1, 1, 1, 10, "2023-06-05", "Q2"),
            (2, 2, 2,  6, "2023-06-18", "Q2"),
            (3, 3, 3,  8, "2023-06-22", "Q2"),
            (4, 4, 4, 12, "2023-06-25", "Q2"),
            # Q3
            (5, 1, 1, 14, "2023-08-02", "Q3"),
            (6, 2, 2,  7, "2023-08-11", "Q3"),
            (7, 3, 1, 10, "2023-08-19", "Q3"),
            (8, 2, 3,  4, "2023-09-01", "Q3"),
            (9, 4, 4,  9, "2023-09-10", "Q3"),
        ],
    )

    conn.commit()
    return conn

# ==========================
# 2) Safe SQL tool (SELECT-only)
# ==========================

ALLOWED_TABLES = {"products", "customers", "orders"}
FORBIDDEN_KEYWORDS = {"DROP", "DELETE", "UPDATE", "INSERT",
↪  "ALTER", "CREATE", "REPLACE", "TRUNCATE"}
MAX_ROWS = 50

def is_select_query(query: str) -> bool:
    return query.strip().upper().startswith("SELECT")

def contains_forbidden_keywords(query: str) -> bool:
    uq = query.upper()
    return any(k in uq for k in FORBIDDEN_KEYWORDS)
```

```
def references_only_allowed_tables(query: str) -> bool:
    matches = re.findall(r"(?:FROM|JOIN)\s+([A-Za-z_]\w*)", query,
    ↪ flags=re.IGNORECASE)
    tables = set(m.lower() for m in matches)
    return tables.issubset(ALLOWED_TABLES)

def enforce_limit(query: str) -> str:
    if "LIMIT" not in query.upper():
        query = query.rstrip().rstrip(";") + f" LIMIT {MAX_ROWS};"
    return query

def normalize_quarter_filter(query: str) -> str:
    """
    Optional guardrail:
    Converts quarter = 3 -> quarter = 'Q3'
    Only applies to quarter comparisons with 1..4.
    """
    # examples handled:
    #   quarter = 3
    #   orders.quarter=4
    return re.sub(
        r"(\b(?:orders\.)?quarter\b)\s*=\s*([1-4])\b",
        r"\1 = 'Q\2'",
        query,
        flags=re.IGNORECASE
    )

def run_sql_safe(conn: sqlite3.Connection, query: str) -> Dict[str,
↪ Any]:
    if not is_select_query(query):
        return {"error": "Only SELECT queries are allowed."}
    if contains_forbidden_keywords(query):
        return {"error": "Query contains forbidden SQL keywords."}
    if not references_only_allowed_tables(query):
        return {"error": f"Query references unauthorized tables.
        ↪ Allowed: {sorted(ALLOWED_TABLES)}"}
```

```
query = normalize_quarter_filter(query)  # <-- FIX/guardrail
safe_query = enforce_limit(query)

try:
    cur = conn.cursor()
    cur.execute(safe_query)
    rows = cur.fetchall()
    cols = [c[0] for c in cur.description]
    results = [dict(zip(cols, r)) for r in rows]
    return {"query": safe_query, "row_count": len(results),
     ↪ "results": results}
except Exception as e:
    return {"error": str(e), "query": query}
```

6.2 Session Memory vs Long-Term Memory

Once we decide that an agent must remember, the next architectural question is not *how* to store memory — but *what kind* of memory we are building.

Memory in agent systems is layered. In human cognition, short-term memory allows us to track the current thread of thought, while long-term memory stores durable knowledge accumulated over time. Agent architectures benefit from a similar distinction.

Session Memory (Short-Term Memory)

Session memory exists only within the boundaries of an active interaction. It captures:

- Recent user queries
- Tool calls and results
- Intermediate reasoning steps
- Temporary context required for continuity

This memory is volatile. It does not persist once the session ends. Session memory is what allows an agent to interpret statements like: > "Now filter by region."
> "Use the previous result."
> "Compare this to what we saw earlier."

Without session memory, such instructions would be meaningless.

Architecturally, session memory is not just a chat log. It must be structured and integrated into the agent's state. It grows during the loop and feeds directly into the reasoning step.

Long-Term Memory (Persistent Memory)

Long-term memory extends beyond a single session. It stores durable information that should influence future interactions. This may include:

- User preferences
- Historical summaries
- Learned constraints
- Domain-specific knowledge
- Prior analytical conclusions

Unlike session memory, long-term memory must persist across sessions. It must survive restarts. It must be retrievable later. Long-term memory transforms an agent from a reactive assistant into a personalized system.

If session memory provides continuity within a conversation, long-term memory provides continuity across conversations. The distinction between these two layers is foundational.

Session memory ensures contextual coherence.
Long-term memory enables adaptation over time.

Demonstration: Memory-Driven Continuity in Practice

Let us consider a realistic analytical workflow that necessitate the use of session memory and long term memory.

Scenario 1 — Session Memory in Action

User: "Analyze revenue performance for Product A in Q3."

The agent queries data, summarizes results, and stores the structured outcome in session memory. Later in the same conversation:

User: "Now compare that with the previous quarter."

This instruction contains no explicit reference to Product A. It relies entirely on conversational continuity. With session memory, the agent retrieves the prior product analyzed, the quarter discussed and the relevant metrics.

It constructs the appropriate comparison automatically. The reasoning remains bounded. The conversation remains coherent. Session memory has solved a contextual ambiguity problem.

Scenario 2 — Long-Term Memory in Action

Now consider a cross-session scenario.

Session 1

User: "When presenting revenue analysis, always include a regional breakdown."

The agent stores this as a long-term preference.

Session 2 (Days Later)

User: "Show Q4 revenue performance."

The user does not mention regions. However, the agent retrieves the stored preference and includes a regional breakdown automatically. The system does not ask for repetition. It does not ignore historical context. It adapts. This is not randomness. It is structured continuity.

The following code defines the memory structures used by the agent to maintain session context, store long-term knowledge, and track observations while generating a response.

```
from dataclasses import dataclass, field
from typing import List, Dict, Any
import time


# =========================
```

```
# 3) Memory + state
# =========================

@dataclass
class MemoryItem:
    kind: str  # "preference" | "fact" | "summary"
    content: str
    tags: List[str] = field(default_factory=list)
    timestamp: float = field(default_factory=time.time)


@dataclass
class AgentState:
    user_query: str
    # short-term
    session_buffer: List[str] = field(default_factory=list)
    # long-term
    long_term_store: List[MemoryItem] = field(default_factory=list)
    # traces
    observations: List[Dict[str, Any]] =
↪   field(default_factory=list)
    final_answer: Optional[str] = None
    iterations: int = 0
    start_time: float = field(default_factory=time.time)
    total_tool_calls: int = 0
```

6.3 The Hidden Complexity of Memory

Adding memory to an agent sounds simple: store past messages and append them to the prompt. In practice, this fails. Every interaction adds tokens. Tool outputs add structured data. Clarifications expand context. Over time, the prompt becomes large, noisy, and expensive. Eventually, it exceeds the model's context window.

The real problem is not storage. It is relevance. Not every past interaction should influence the present decision. Some details are temporary. Others are durable. Without filtering, memory becomes clutter. Clutter reduces signal. Reduced signal weakens reasoning.

Memory must therefore be managed — not accumulated. This leads to two essential policies:

- **Summarization** — compress older interactions while preserving meaning.
- **Pruning** — discard information that no longer contributes value.

6.4 Designing a Memory-Aware Agent Architecture

To manage memory properly, we must integrate it into the agent's architecture. A memory-aware agent includes three additional components:

1. **Memory Store** — structured storage for session and long-term entries.
2. **Memory Management Logic** — rules for summarizing, pruning, and persisting.
3. **Memory Retrieval Layer** — selective injection of relevant memory into the prompt.

We do not inject all memory into every prompt. We retrieve selectively. The core loop remains unchanged:

User → Reasoning → Tool Execution → Observation → Update State

But now, "Update State" includes memory management.

The model proposes.

The system enforces.

Memory is governed.

6.5 Session Memory Summarization (Conceptual Implementation)

Session memory is stored inside the agent's state. Session memory is structured, bounded and continuously updated. It enables conversational continuity without context overflow.

```
# ==========================
# 4) Session memory management (LLM summarization)
# ==========================

MAX_SESSION_LINES = 12  # trigger threshold

def add_session(state: AgentState, line: str) -> None:
    state.session_buffer.append(line)

def summarize_session_with_llm(state: AgentState, keep_last_n: int
↪   = 5) -> None:
    """
    Summarize older session lines into a single SUMMARY line using
↪   the LLM.
    Keeps the last keep_last_n lines verbatim.
    """
    if len(state.session_buffer) <= MAX_SESSION_LINES:
        return
    head = state.session_buffer[:-keep_last_n]
    tail = state.session_buffer[-keep_last_n:]
    text = "\n".join(head)
    messages = [
        {"role": "system", "content": (
            "You compress conversation history for an agent.\n"
            "Return a concise summary capturing stable facts,
            ↪  preferences, and conclusions.\n"
            "Do NOT include fluff. Keep it under 80 words."
        )},
        {"role": "user", "content": text}]
```

```
    resp = client.chat.completions.create(
        model="gpt-4o-mini",
        messages=messages,
        temperature=0)

    summary = resp.choices[0].message.content.strip()
    state.session_buffer = [f"SUMMARY: {summary}"] + tail
```

6.6 Long-Term Memory: Persistence Across Sessions

Long-term memory must survive restarts. This implies the memory must persist. Long-term memory must also remain clean and bounded.

We enforce this through:

- Pruning — limit total stored entries
- Deduplication — update existing preferences instead of appending duplicates

Long-term memory is durable, curated and selectively retrieved. Together, session and long-term memory create a memory-aware agent that maintains continuity without sacrificing clarity.

A Minimal Long-Term Memory Structure with persistence

A basic persistence mechanism (for demonstration purposes) could be file-based:

```
# =========================
# 5) Long-term persistence
# =========================

## Defines the JSON file used to persist long-term memory across
↪  sessions.
MEMORY_FILE = "project3_long_term_memory.json"
```

```
## Loads stored memory from disk and converts it into MemoryItem
↪  objects (returns empty list if file does not exist).
def load_long_term_memory(path: str = MEMORY_FILE) ->
↪  List[MemoryItem]:
    try:
        with open(path, "r", encoding="utf-8") as f:
            raw = json.load(f)
        return [MemoryItem(**item) for item in raw]
    except FileNotFoundError:
        return []
    except Exception:
        return []

## Writes the current long-term memory items to disk in JSON
↪  format.
def save_long_term_memory(items: List[MemoryItem], path: str =
↪  MEMORY_FILE) -> None:
    with open(path, "w", encoding="utf-8") as f:
        json.dump([m.__dict__ for m in items], f,
↪  ensure_ascii=False, indent=2)

## Limits long-term memory size by keeping only the most recent
↪  max_items entries.
def prune_long_term(items: List[MemoryItem], max_items: int = 50)
↪  -> List[MemoryItem]:
    if len(items) <= max_items:
        return items
    items = sorted(items, key=lambda x: x.timestamp, reverse=True)
    return items[:max_items]


# ========================
# Preference dedupe helpers
# ========================

## Normalizes text (lowercase, remove punctuation, trim spaces) to
↪  detect semantic duplicates reliably.
```

```
def canonicalize_text(text: str) -> str:
    """Normalize text for duplicate detection."""
    t = text.lower()
    t = re.sub(r"[^\w\s]", "", t)  # remove punctuation
    t = re.sub(r"\s+", " ", t).strip()
    return t

## Adds a new preference if it doesn't exist, or updates the
↪  existing one instead of creating a duplicate.
def upsert_preference(store: List[MemoryItem], content: str, tags:
↪  List[str]) -> str:
    """
    Insert preference if new, otherwise update timestamp.
    Returns: "saved" | "updated"
    """
    canon_new = canonicalize_text(content)
    for m in store:
        if m.kind == "preference" and canonicalize_text(m.content)
         ↪  == canon_new:
            m.timestamp = time.time()
            # optionally merge tags
            m.tags = sorted(set(m.tags) | set(tags))
            return "updated"

    store.append(MemoryItem(kind="preference", content=content,
↪  tags=tags))
    return "saved"

## Cleans up long-term memory by keeping only the most recent
↪  version of each preference.
def dedupe_preferences_keep_latest(items: List[MemoryItem]) ->
↪  List[MemoryItem]:
    """One-time cleanup: keep latest preference per canonical
     ↪  content."""
    best: Dict[str, MemoryItem] = {}
    non_pref: List[MemoryItem] = []
    for m in items:
```

```
        if m.kind != "preference":
            non_pref.append(m)
            continue
        key = canonicalize_text(m.content)
        if key not in best or m.timestamp > best[key].timestamp:
            best[key] = m
    return non_pref + list(best.values())
```

6.7 Controlled Retrieval

Once the memory is stored. The next important aspect is that the entire memory cannot be a part of the prompt. Hence we must also control how it is retrieved.

The agent should **not** inject the entire memory store into every prompt. Instead, it should retrieve only the entries relevant to the current query. This ensures memory remains bounded, irrelevant context does not pollute reasoning and the prompt stays efficient. Long-term memory therefore acts as a controlled augmentation layer. It informs reasoning without overwhelming it.

The system now has three layers of continuity:

- Session memory — maintains conversational flow
- Long-term memory — preserves durable history
- Controlled retrieval — injects only what is relevant

The reasoning loop remains bounded.
The agent gains temporal depth without losing clarity.

```
# =========================
# 6) Preference promotion + retrieval
# =========================

def detect_preference_statement(user_text: str) -> Optional[str]:
    """
    Minimal rule: treat explicit 'always' as a durable preference.
    """
```

```
    t = user_text.lower()
    if "always" in t and ("include" in t or "show" in t):
        return user_text.strip()
    return None

def extract_tags_from_text(text: str) -> List[str]:
    """
    Lightweight tagger for retrieval.
    (Expanded slightly to catch 'breakdown')
    """
    t = text.lower()
    tags = []
    for k in [
        "revenue", "sales",
        "region", "regional", "breakdown",
        "trend", "top", "products",
        "quarter", "q1", "q2", "q3", "q4"
    ]:
        if k in t:
            tags.append("region" if k == "regional" else k)
    return sorted(set(tags))

def retrieve_relevant_long_term(state: AgentState, query: str, k:
 ↪  int = 3) -> List[MemoryItem]:
    q = query.lower()
    scored = []
    for m in state.long_term_store:
        score = sum(1 for tag in m.tags if tag in q)
        if score > 0:
            scored.append((score, m))
    scored.sort(key=lambda x: (-x[0], -x[1].timestamp))
    return [m for _, m in scored[:k]]
```

6.8 Memory-Aware Prompt Construction

Before calling the model, we retrieve relevant memory and provide it to the prompt, so that the prompt has the relevant context for reasoning.

```
# ==========================
# 7) Prompt builder (memory injected)
# ==========================

SCHEMA_SUMMARY = """
Tables:
1) products(product_id, product_name, category, price)
2) customers(customer_id, region)
3) orders(order_id, product_id, customer_id, quantity, order_date,
↪  quarter)

Notes:
- revenue = quantity * price
- joins:
  orders.product_id = products.product_id
  orders.customer_id = customers.customer_id
- IMPORTANT: quarter is TEXT and values look like
↪  'Q1','Q2','Q3','Q4' (e.g., 'Q3')
""".strip()

def build_prompt(state: AgentState) -> List[Dict[str, str]]:
    last_obs = state.observations[-1] if state.observations else
↪   None

    relevant_mem = retrieve_relevant_long_term(state,
↪   state.user_query, k=3)
    mem_text = "\n".join([f"- {m.content}" for m in relevant_mem])
↪   or "(none)"

    session_tail = "\n".join(state.session_buffer[-6:]) if
↪   state.session_buffer else "(none)"

    system = f"""
```

```
You are a memory-aware analytics agent.

You MUST return ONLY valid JSON.
You can call exactly one tool: RUN_SQL.

Database schema:
{SCHEMA_SUMMARY}

Long-term memory (preferences/facts):
{mem_text}

Recent session context:
{session_tail}

Rules:
- If needed, CALL_TOOL with tool_name "RUN_SQL" and a SELECT-only
 ↪ query.
- Use only tables/columns from the schema.
- Prefer simple queries.
- Always respect long-term preferences when relevant (unless user
 ↪ overrides).
- After you have enough evidence, RESPOND with a clear final
 ↪ answer.
- Output MUST be JSON with keys: action, arguments.

JSON format:
{{
  "action": "CALL_TOOL" | "RESPOND",
  "arguments": {{ ... }}
}}

If action == CALL_TOOL:
{{
  "tool_name": "RUN_SQL",
  "parameters": {{
    "query": "<SQL query>"
  }}
```

```
}}

If action == RESPOND:
{{
  "answer": "<final answer>"
}}
""".strip()

    user = f"""
User question:
{state.user_query}

Latest observation (if any):
{json.dumps(last_obs, ensure_ascii=False)}
""".strip()

    return [{"role": "system", "content": system},
            {"role": "user", "content": user}]
```

6.9 Integrating Memory into the Agent Loop

At this point, we have designed:

- Session memory
- Long-term memory
- Summarization strategies
- Pruning policies
- Retrieval approach

But memory components alone do not create intelligence. They must participate in the reasoning loop. This section brings everything together. The agent now carries context across turns — and across sessions.

The Memory-Enhanced Reasoning Flow

The original agent loop followed this pattern: User → Reasoning → Tool Execution → Observation → Update State

The memory-aware loop evolves into: User → Retrieve Relevant Memory → Build Prompt with Memory → Model Reasoning → Tool Execution → Update Session Memory → Summarize / Prune → Promote Important Insights to Long-Term Memory → Termination Check

What Has Changed Architecturally?

The reasoning loop still exists. The guardrails still exist. The tools remain deterministic. But the agent now has temporal depth. It can remember user preferences, maintain analytical continuity, adapt across sessions and evolve its contextual understanding. The architecture remains controlled. The intelligence becomes layered.

With this now the conversations remain coherent over time. Context windows remain bounded. Token growth is controlled. Long-term knowledge becomes structured influence. The agent feels persistent — not transactional. This is the first time in the book where the agent evolves beyond the immediate present.

It now carries history — deliberately, selectively, and safely.

```
# 8) Model reasoning (strict JSON)
# ==========================


def model_reasoning(state: AgentState) -> Dict[str, Any]:
    messages = build_prompt(state)
    resp = client.chat.completions.create(
        model="gpt-4o-mini",
        messages=messages,
        temperature=0
    )
    content = resp.choices[0].message.content.strip()

    try:
```

```
        obj = json.loads(content)
    except json.JSONDecodeError:
        # One repair attempt (bounded)
        fix_msgs = [
            {"role": "system", "content": "Fix the following into
↪   valid JSON only. No explanations."},
            {"role": "user", "content": content}
        ]
        fixed = client.chat.completions.create(
            model="gpt-4o-mini",
            messages=fix_msgs,
            temperature=0
        ).choices[0].message.content.strip()
        obj = json.loads(fixed)

    if not isinstance(obj, dict):
        raise ValueError("Model output must be a JSON object.")
    return obj


# =========================
# 9) Agent loop (bounded + memory lifecycle)
# =========================

def run_memory_agent(
    conn: sqlite3.Connection,
    user_query: str,
    max_iterations: int = 8,
    max_tool_calls: int = 5,
    timeout_seconds: int = 20,
    debug: bool = True
) -> str:
    state = AgentState(user_query=user_query)
    state.long_term_store = load_long_term_memory()

    # One-time safety: ensure stored preferences are deduped (cheap
     ↪  + deterministic)
```

```
    state.long_term_store =
↪   dedupe_preferences_keep_latest(state.long_term_store)
    save_long_term_memory(prune_long_term(state.long_term_store))

    # Session: add user query
    add_session(state, f"USER: {user_query}")

    # Promotion: if user states a durable preference, upsert it
     ↪ (dedupe-aware)
    pref = detect_preference_statement(user_query)
    if pref:
        status = upsert_preference(
            state.long_term_store,
            content=pref,
            tags=extract_tags_from_text(pref),
        )
        state.long_term_store =
↪   prune_long_term(state.long_term_store)
        save_long_term_memory(state.long_term_store)

        if status == "updated":
            add_session(state, f"PREF_UPDATED: {pref}")
        else:
            add_session(state, f"PREF_SAVED: {pref}")

        # Continue loop so the agent can act on it if needed

    for i in range(1, max_iterations + 1):
        state.iterations = i

        # Guardrail: timeout
        if time.time() - state.start_time > timeout_seconds:
            return "Terminated: timeout exceeded."

        if debug:
            print(f"\n--- Iteration {i}/{max_iterations} ---")
            rel = retrieve_relevant_long_term(state, user_query)
```

```
        print("Relevant long-term memory:", [m.content for m
         ↪ in rel])

    step = model_reasoning(state)

    if debug:
        print("Model step:", step)

    action = step.get("action")
    args = step.get("arguments", {}) or {}

    if action == "RESPOND":
        answer = args.get("answer") if isinstance(args, dict)
↪   else None
        state.final_answer = answer or "No answer produced."
        add_session(state, f"ANSWER: {state.final_answer}")

        summarize_session_with_llm(state)
        if debug:
            print("\nSession buffer (bounded):")
            for line in state.session_buffer:
                print("  ", line)

        return state.final_answer

    if action != "CALL_TOOL":
        return f"Terminated: invalid action '{action}'."

    # Tool-call guardrail
    state.total_tool_calls += 1
    if state.total_tool_calls > max_tool_calls:
        return "Terminated: tool call limit exceeded."

    tool_name = args.get("tool_name")
    params = args.get("parameters", {}) or {}
    query = params.get("query") if isinstance(params, dict)
↪   else None
```

```
        if tool_name != "RUN_SQL" or not query:
            obs = {"error": "invalid_tool_call", "tool_name":
↪ tool_name, "allowed": ["RUN_SQL"]}
            state.observations.append(obs)
            add_session(state, f"OBS: {obs}")
            summarize_session_with_llm(state)
            continue

        # Execute tool
        result = run_sql_safe(conn, query)

        obs = {"tool": "RUN_SQL", "parameters": {"query": query},
↪ "result": result}
        state.observations.append(obs)
        add_session(state, f"OBS: {json.dumps(obs,
↪ ensure_ascii=False)[:600]}")

        if debug:
            if "query" in result:
                print("Validated query:", result["query"])
            print("Tool result keys:", list(result.keys()))

        summarize_session_with_llm(state)

    return "Terminated: iteration limit reached."


# ========================
# 10) DEMO: Two sessions (memory benefit)
# ========================

if __name__ == "__main__":
    conn = create_demo_db()

    print("\n============================")
    print("SESSION 1: Set a preference")
```

```python
print("==============================")
ans1 = run_memory_agent(
    conn,
    "Always include regional breakdown when answering revenue
     ↪ questions.",
    debug=True
)
print("\nFINAL ANSWER (Session 1):\n", ans1)

print("\n==============================")
print("SESSION 2: Ask revenue question")
print("==============================")
ans2 = run_memory_agent(
    conn,
    "Show Q3 revenue performance.",
    debug=True
)
print("\nFINAL ANSWER (Session 2):\n", ans2)
```

```
==============================
SESSION 1: Set a preference
==============================

--- Iteration 1/8 ---
Relevant long-term memory: ['Always include regional
 ↪ breakdown when answering revenue questions.', 'When
 ↪ answering revenue questions, include a regional
 ↪ breakdown by default.']
Model step: {'action': 'RESPOND', 'arguments': {'answer':
 ↪ 'This preference is already noted. I will always include
 ↪ a regional breakdown when answering revenue
 ↪ questions.'}}

Session buffer (bounded):
```

```
  USER: Always include regional breakdown when answering
   ↪ revenue questions.
  PREF_UPDATED: Always include regional breakdown when
   ↪ answering revenue questions.
  ANSWER: This preference is already noted. I will always
   ↪ include a regional breakdown when answering revenue
   ↪ questions.

FINAL ANSWER (Session 1):
 This preference is already noted. I will always include a
  ↪ regional breakdown when answering revenue questions.

============================
SESSION 2: Ask revenue question
============================

--- Iteration 1/8 ---
Relevant long-term memory: ['Always include regional
 ↪ breakdown when answering revenue questions.', 'When
 ↪ answering revenue questions, include a regional
 ↪ breakdown by default.']
Model step: {'action': 'CALL_TOOL', 'arguments':
 ↪ {'tool_name': 'RUN_SQL', 'parameters': {'query': "SELECT
 ↪ customers.region, SUM(orders.quantity * products.price)
 ↪ AS revenue FROM orders JOIN products ON
 ↪ orders.product_id = products.product_id JOIN customers
 ↪ ON orders.customer_id = customers.customer_id WHERE
 ↪ orders.quarter = 'Q3' GROUP BY customers.region"}}}
Validated query: SELECT customers.region,
 ↪ SUM(orders.quantity * products.price) AS revenue FROM
 ↪ orders JOIN products ON orders.product_id =
 ↪ products.product_id JOIN customers ON orders.customer_id
 ↪ = customers.customer_id WHERE orders.quarter = 'Q3'
 ↪ GROUP BY customers.region LIMIT 50;
```

```
Tool result keys: ['query', 'row_count', 'results']

--- Iteration 2/8 ---
Relevant long-term memory: ['Always include regional
↪ breakdown when answering revenue questions.', 'When
↪ answering revenue questions, include a regional
↪ breakdown by default.']
Model step: {'action': 'RESPOND', 'arguments': {'answer':
↪ {'Q3_revenue_performance': [{'region': 'East',
↪ 'revenue': 450.0}, {'region': 'North', 'revenue':
↪ 2200.0}, {'region': 'South', 'revenue': 1050.0},
↪ {'region': 'West', 'revenue': 600.0}]}}}

Session buffer (bounded):
  USER: Show Q3 revenue performance.
  OBS: {"tool": "RUN_SQL", "parameters": {"query": "SELECT
   ↪ customers.region, SUM(orders.quantity *
   ↪ products.price) AS revenue FROM orders JOIN products
   ↪ ON orders.product_id = products.product_id JOIN
   ↪ customers ON orders.customer_id =
   ↪ customers.customer_id WHERE orders.quarter = 'Q3'
   ↪ GROUP BY customers.region"}, "result": {"query":
   ↪ "SELECT customers.region, SUM(orders.quantity *
   ↪ products.price) AS revenue FROM orders JOIN products
   ↪ ON orders.product_id = products.product_id JOIN
   ↪ customers ON orders.customer_id =
   ↪ customers.customer_id WHERE orders.quarter = 'Q3'
   ↪ GROUP BY customers.region LIMIT 50;", "ro
  ANSWER: {'Q3_revenue_performance': [{'region': 'East',
   ↪ 'revenue': 450.0}, {'region': 'North', 'revenue':
   ↪ 2200.0}, {'region': 'South', 'revenue': 1050.0},
   ↪ {'region': 'West', 'revenue': 600.0}]}

FINAL ANSWER (Session 2):
```

```
{'Q3_revenue_performance': [{'region': 'East', 'revenue':
↪ 450.0}, {'region': 'North', 'revenue': 2200.0},
↪ {'region': 'South', 'revenue': 1050.0}, {'region':
↪ 'West', 'revenue': 600.0}]}
```

6.10 From Reactive Assistant to Persistent Intelligence

Chapter 6 marks a turning point in the evolution of our agent architecture. What began as a controlled reasoning loop has now become a memory-aware system capable of continuity across turns and across sessions.

The agent does not merely answer a question; it remembers intent, enforces guardrails, retrieves relevant context, and integrates it into structured reasoning. The loop remains bounded, the SQL remains validated, and memory remains curated. Yet the behavior feels persistent and adaptive.

This is the architectural achievement of the lesson. We made the system smarter by introducing structured memory, controlled retrieval, and lifecycle governance. The agent now carries temporal depth — deliberately, selectively, and safely. With this foundation in place, we move beyond reactive assistants and toward systems that accumulate context over time without sacrificing stability.

Chapter 7 — Project 4: Retrieval-Augmented Agent (RAG + Reasoning)

Objectives

By the end of this chapter, you will:

- Why Retrieval Is Needed: The Limits of Parametric Memory
- Embeddings and Vector Search
- Retrieval + Reasoning Integration
- Hallucination Control and Grounded Answer Generation
- Evidence Citation and Verifiable Output
- Failure Analysis and Production Considerations
- RAG as an Agent Pattern (System-Level Reflection)
- From RAG Pipeline to Agent

7.1 Why Retrieval Is Needed: The Limits of Parametric Memory

Large Language Models store knowledge in their parameters. This is called **parametric memory**.

But parametric memory has limitations. It is frozen at training time. It may not contain domain-specific data. It may hallucinate when uncertain. It cannot access private or real-time data.

An agent designed for real-world use must:

1. Access external knowledge.
2. Retrieve only relevant information.
3. Reason over that information.
4. Produce grounded answers.

This is where Retrieval-Augmented Generation (RAG) becomes essential.

The Core Idea of RAG

Instead of asking: "LLM, answer from whatever you remember." We change the flow to:

1. Retrieve relevant documents.
2. Inject them into the prompt.
3. Ask the model to reason over them.
4. Constrain it to answer using only retrieved evidence.

Now the model does not rely purely on memory. It becomes a **grounded reasoning system**.

High-Level Architecture

A minimal RAG agent contains:

- Document loader - that loads all relevant documents.
- Chunking module - Breaks the document text into small readable chunks.
- Embedding model - Converts the text to numbers.
- Vector store - Stores embeddings for future use.
- Retriever - Retrieves query matched embeddings from vector base.
- Reasoning prompt - Sends the query and retrieved chunks to LLM.
- Answer generator - LLM responses from the retrieved chunks only.

We will build this step-by-step.

Step 1 — Define the Knowledge Base

For this project, we assume a domain-specific text corpus.

Example:

```
documents = [
    "Solar panels convert sunlight into electricity using
     ↪ photovoltaic cells.",
    "Wind turbines generate power by converting kinetic energy from
     ↪ wind into mechanical energy.",
    "Battery storage systems help stabilize renewable energy supply
     ↪ during peak demand.",
    "Hydroelectric plants produce electricity by using flowing
     ↪ water to spin turbines.",
    "Inverters convert direct current (DC) from solar panels into
     ↪ alternating current (AC)."
]
```

In a real system, these would come from: PDFs, manuals, technical logs & knowledge base articles. For now, we begin small to understand the mechanics.

Why We Cannot Directly Embed Whole Documents

If we embed the entire corpus as one block retrieval becomes coarse, irrelevant information pollutes context, token limits get exhausted and precision of response drops. So we must break documents into smaller units. This is called **chunking**.

Chunking improves:

- Retrieval granularity
- Context relevance
- Token efficiency
- Hallucination control

Chunk size is a design decision. Too small leads to loss of context. Too large causes retrieval noise. We will begin with simple chunking method.

Step 2 — Basic Chunking Implementation

For demonstration, assume character-based chunking:

```
def chunk_text(text, chunk_size=100, overlap=20):
    chunks = []
    start = 0
    while start < len(text):
        end = start + chunk_size #chunk_size means fixed 100
↪   characters in each chunk.
        chunks.append(text[start:end])
        start += chunk_size - overlap
    return chunks

all_chunks = []

for doc in documents:
    chunks = chunk_text(doc)
    all_chunks.extend(chunks)
print(all_chunks)
```

```
['Solar panels convert sunlight into electricity using
↪  photovoltaic cells.', 'Wind turbines generate power by
↪  converting kinetic energy from wind into mechanical
↪  energy.', 'cal energy.', 'Battery storage systems help
↪  stabilize renewable energy supply during peak demand.',
↪  'd.', 'Hydroelectric plants produce electricity by using
↪  flowing water to spin turbines.', '.', 'Inverters
↪  convert direct current (DC) from solar panels into
↪  alternating current (AC).', ' (AC).']
```

7.2 Embeddings and Vector Search

Once we have chunks, they are still just text. Computers cannot measure semantic similarity between raw strings in a meaningful way. To enable intelligent retrieval, we must convert text into numerical representations. These representations are called **embeddings**.

An embedding is a dense vector representation of text. Instead of storing: "Battery storage systems help stabilize renewable energy supply". We store something like: [0.012, -0.883, 0.442, ..., 0.193]. Each chunk becomes a point in high-dimensional space. Semantically similar chunks are positioned closer together. This allows us to perform **similarity search** instead of keyword search.

Why Embeddings Matter in RAG

Embeddings enable:

- Semantic retrieval (not just keyword match)
- Context-aware search
- Domain-specific knowledge lookup
- Ranking by similarity

Without embeddings, retrieval becomes shallow and brittle. With embeddings, retrieval becomes meaning-driven.

Step 3 — Generating Embeddings

For demonstration, we will use a sentence-transformer model. A sentence-transformer model converts a sentence into a dense numerical vector (embedding) that captures its semantic meaning for similarity comparison.

```
from sentence_transformers import SentenceTransformer
import numpy as np

embedding_model = SentenceTransformer("all-MiniLM-L6-v2")

print("done")
# First chunk the documents
all_chunks = []
for doc in documents:
    chunks = chunk_text(doc)
    all_chunks.extend(chunks)

print(all_chunks)
# Encode in smaller batches
batch_size = 8
all_embeddings = []
```

```
for i in range(0, len(all_chunks), batch_size):
    batch = all_chunks[i:i + batch_size]
    batch_embeddings = embedding_model.encode(
        batch,
        batch_size=batch_size,
        convert_to_numpy=True,
        show_progress_bar=False
    )
    all_embeddings.append(batch_embeddings)

chunk_embeddings = np.vstack(all_embeddings)
print(chunk_embeddings.shape)
```

Now each chunk has a vector representation. All vectors have equal dimensionality. We can compare them numerically.

Understanding Similarity: Cosine Similarity

To retrieve relevant chunks, we measure similarity between:

- User query embedding
- Stored chunk embeddings

Cosine similarity is commonly used. It measures the angular similarity between two vectors. Its value ranges between 1 and -1.

- 1 → Very similar
- 0 → Unrelated
- -1 → Opposite direction

Step 4 — Implementing Similarity Search

```
from sklearn.metrics.pairwise import cosine_similarity

def retrieve_top_k(query, chunk_embeddings, chunks, k=2):
    query_embedding = embedding_model.encode([query])
    similarities = cosine_similarity(query_embedding,
↪   chunk_embeddings)[0]
```

```
    top_indices = similarities.argsort()[-k:][::-1]
    return [(chunks[i], similarities[i]) for i in top_indices]

query = "How is solar energy converted into usable electricity?"
results = retrieve_top_k(query, chunk_embeddings, all_chunks, k=2)

for text, score in results:
    print(f"Score: {score:.4f}")
    print(text)
    print("-" * 50)
```

```
Score: 0.7619
Solar panels convert sunlight into electricity using
↪ photovoltaic cells.
--------------------------------------------------
Score: 0.6439
Inverters convert direct current (DC) from solar panels into
↪ alternating current (AC).
--------------------------------------------------
```

What We Have Achieved

We now have:

- Chunked documents
- Generated embeddings
- Implemented semantic retrieval
- Ranked results by similarity

At this stage, we have built a **retriever**.

7.3 Retrieval & Reasoning Integration

At this point, we have a working **retriever**. But retrieval alone is not enough. Returning the top-k similar chunks does not automatically produce a reliable answer. We now need to integrate retrieval with structured reasoning. This is the step where a retriever becomes a **Retrieval-Augmented Agent**.

From Retrieval to Generation

So far, our pipeline looks like this:

1. User asks a question
2. Convert question into embedding
3. Retrieve top-k similar chunks

Now we extend it:

4. Inject retrieved chunks into the prompt
5. Ask the language model to reason using only that context
6. Generate a grounded answer

This changes the model's behavior from: **"Answer from memory"** to **"Answer using the provided evidence"**

Reasoning enforces structure. It encourages the model to identify relevant facts, connect them logically and produce a supported conclusion.

Step 5 — Constructing a Grounded Prompt

We now build a structured prompt template.

```
def build_prompt(query, retrieved_chunks):
    context = "\n\n".join(retrieved_chunks)

    prompt = f"""
You are a helpful assistant.
Use ONLY the information provided in the context below.
If the answer is not present, say "Insufficient information."

Context:
{context}

Question:
{query}

Answer step-by-step before giving the final answer.
"""
    return prompt
```

This prompt does three important things:

- Constrains the model to the retrieved context
- Allows refusal when information is missing
- Encourages step-by-step reasoning

Step 6 — Integrating Retrieval + Prompt

```
def rag_pipeline(query):
    # Retrieve relevant chunks
    results = retrieve_top_k(query, chunk_embeddings, all_chunks,
    ↪ k=2)
    retrieved_texts = [text for text, _ in results]

    # Build structured prompt
    prompt = build_prompt(query, retrieved_texts)

    return prompt
```

7.4 Hallucination Control and Grounded Answer Generation

Even with retrieved context, the model can still hallucinate. Because retrieval does not guarantee relevance. It only guarantees similarity. We must explicitly enforce **grounding discipline** in our pipeline so that the model does not hallucinate.

Problem 1 — Irrelevant Retrieval

If similarity scores are low, the retrieved chunks may not truly answer the question. So we introduce a **similarity threshold**. If no chunk passes the threshold, we refuse to answer.

Step 7 — Threshold-Based Filtering

```
def retrieve_with_threshold(query, chunk_embeddings, chunks, k=3,
↪ threshold=0.55):
    query_embedding = embedding_model.encode([query])
    similarities = cosine_similarity(query_embedding,
↪ chunk_embeddings)[0]
    # Get top-k
    top_indices = similarities.argsort()[-k:][::-1]
    # Filter by threshold
    filtered = [
        (chunks[i], similarities[i])
        for i in top_indices
        if similarities[i] >= threshold]

    return filtered
```

Now retrieval is not just "top-k". It is "top-k above a minimum confidence".

Step 8 — Full Grounded RAG Pipeline

We now connect everything into one functional pipeline.

```
def answer_query(query):

    # 1. Retrieve relevant chunks
    results = retrieve_with_threshold(
        query, chunk_embeddings, all_chunks, k=3, threshold=0.55)

    if not results:
        return "Insufficient information to answer the question."

    retrieved_texts = [text for text, _ in results]

    # 2. Build grounded prompt
    prompt = build_prompt(query, retrieved_texts)

    # 3. Call LLM (placeholder)
```

```
    # Replace with actual LLM call (OpenAI, local model, etc.)
    response = llm.generate(prompt)   # pseudo-call

    return response
```

This function now:

- Retrieves relevant knowledge
- Rejects weak matches
- Injects grounded context
- Calls the language model
- Returns an answer constrained by evidence

We now have a **functionally connected RAG agent**.

Problem 2 — Fabricated Evidence

Even with threshold filtering, the model may:

- Add external facts
- Infer beyond context
- Present confident but unsupported claims

To reduce this risk, we enforce citation. The model must reference the exact retrieved chunks.

7.5 Evidence Citation and Verifiable Output

Trust is built through transparency. Instead of returning only an answer, we return:

- Final answer
- Supporting evidence
- Similarity scores

This helps us trace the reasoning process of the agent. It also helps us validate if the responses provided by the agent are correct or not.

Step 9 — Structured Answer Format

```
def answer_query_with_citation(query):

    results = retrieve_with_threshold(
        query, chunk_embeddings, all_chunks, k=3, threshold=0.55
    )

    if not results:
        return {
            "answer": "Insufficient information to answer the
             ↪ question.",
            "sources": []
        }

    retrieved_texts = [text for text, _ in results]
    prompt = build_prompt(query, retrieved_texts)

    response = llm.generate(prompt)   # pseudo-call

    return {
        "answer": response,
        "sources": [
            {"text": text, "similarity": float(score)}
            for text, score in results
        ]
    }
```

Now the system produces:

- A grounded answer
- Explicit source attribution
- Measurable retrieval confidence

This completes the functional RAG agent.

What We Have Built

End-to-end system:

- Knowledge base
- Chunking
- Embeddings
- Semantic retrieval
- Threshold filtering
- Grounded prompt construction
- LLM reasoning
- Evidence citation

This is no longer a retriever. This is a **Retrieval-Augmented Generation with reasoning and hallucination control**.

7.6 Failure Analysis and Production Considerations

We have built a fully functional Retrieval-Augmented Agent. But building a working system is only the beginning. Engineering reliable systems requires understanding where they fail. This section focuses on practical limitations and production thinking.

1. Retrieval Misses

Sometimes the correct answer exists in the knowledge base, but the retriever does not surface it. This could be because of poor chunking boundaries, weak embedding model, query phrasing mismatch or similarity threshold being too high. This can be avoided by following steps:

- Tune chunk size and overlap
- Experiment with better embedding models
- Lower threshold carefully
- Use query rewriting techniques

2. Noisy or Overlapping Chunks

If chunks are too large:

- Irrelevant information enters context
- Reasoning becomes confused

If chunks are too small:

- Context gets fragmented
- Logical coherence breaks

Production systems often use:

- Token-aware chunking
- Semantic chunking
- Sliding window overlap

Chunking is not preprocessing. It is a strategic design decision.

3. Over-Reliance on Similarity Scores

High cosine similarity does not guarantee correctness. Similarity measures semantic closeness, not factual sufficiency. You must still constrain reasoning, enforce refusal when evidence is incomplete and return citations. This helps ensure that the responses are backed by strong factual evidences.

4. Latency vs Accuracy Trade-Off

Increasing:

- k (number of retrieved chunks)
- Embedding dimensionality
- Model size
- Re-ranking steps

Improves answer quality.
But increases:

- Latency
- Token cost
- Infrastructure requirements

Production systems balance:

- Precision vs cost
- Depth vs speed

Agent design is always about trade-offs.

5. Evaluating RAG Systems

Commonly used evaluation signals for RAG systems are:

- Retrieval accuracy (was the correct chunk retrieved?)
- Answer grounding (does output rely on retrieved evidence?)
- Hallucination rate
- Refusal correctness

Evaluation often combines automated checks, manual review and test question suites.

7.7 RAG as an Agent Pattern

RAG is not just a retrieval technique — it is a design pattern in agent engineering. At its core, RAG solves one problem: "How can an agent access external knowledge reliably?"

Its structured flow is: - Knowledge Base - Retrieval - Context Injection - Reasoned Generation

RAG is fundamentally about **knowledge grounding**.

RAG vs Memory-Augmented Agents

- Memory stores prior interactions.
- RAG retrieves external domain knowledge.

Memory answers: "What happened before? RAG answers: "What does the knowledge base say? These systems solve different problems and are often combined.

RAG vs Tool-Using Agents

Tool-using agents: - Execute actions (SQL, APIs, calculations) - Interact with structured systems

RAG agents: - Retrieve unstructured knowledge - Generate grounded responses

If the task requires computation → use tools.
If the task requires document knowledge → use RAG.

7.8 From RAG Pipeline to Agent

So far, we have built a disciplined Retrieval-Augmented Generation (RAG) system. It retrieves knowledge, applies similarity thresholds, constructs grounded prompts, generates answers, and returns citations. This system is reliable. But it is still a linear pipeline.

An agent introduces one additional capability: It evaluates intermediate results and decides what to do next.

What Changes When We Introduce Agency?

A RAG pipeline:

- Retrieves top-k chunks
- Generates an answer
- Returns the result

An agent:

- Evaluates retrieval quality
- Decides whether to retry
- Verifies grounding
- Refuses when unsupported
- Exposes its reasoning trace

Agency emerges from control.

Adding a Minimal Agent Loop

We now introduce a lightweight control loop. The agent will:

1. Retrieve evidence.
2. Decide if retrieval is sufficient.
3. Retry once with a rewritten query if needed.
4. Verify that the generated answer is supported.

5. Return answer with trace.

This transforms a pipeline into a decision-driven system.

Agentic Version of the Answer Function

```
from openai import OpenAI
import os

os.environ["OPENAI_API_KEY"] = OPENAI_API_KEY
client = OpenAI()

def generate_llm_response(prompt):
    response = client.chat.completions.create(
        model="gpt-4o-mini",
        messages=[{"role": "user", "content": prompt}],
        temperature=0
    )
    return response.choices[0].message.content

def answer_query_agentic(query, max_retries=1, k=3,
↪   threshold=0.55):

    current_query = query

    for attempt in range(max_retries + 1):

        # Step 1: Retrieve
        results = retrieve_with_threshold(
            current_query, chunk_embeddings, all_chunks, k=k,
↪   threshold=threshold
        )

        # Step 2: Decide - is retrieval sufficient?
        if not results:
            if attempt < max_retries:
                current_query = f"Explain clearly: {current_query}"
                continue
```

```
        return {
            "answer": "Insufficient information to answer the
              ↪ question.",
            "sources": [],
            "trace": ["retrieval_failed"]
        }

    retrieved_texts = [text for text, _ in results]

    # Step 3: Generate grounded answer
    prompt = build_prompt(query, retrieved_texts)
    answer = generate_llm_response(prompt)

    # Step 4: Verify grounding
    verification_prompt = build_verification_prompt(answer,
↪ retrieved_texts)
    verdict = llm.generate(verification_prompt)  # pseudo-call

    if "SUPPORTED" in verdict:
        return {
            "answer": answer,
            "sources": [{"text": t, "similarity": float(s)}
              ↪ for t, s in results],
            "trace": ["retrieval_ok", "verified_supported"]
        }

    return {
        "answer": "Answer could not be verified from retrieved
          ↪ sources.",
        "sources": [{"text": t, "similarity": float(s)} for t,
          ↪ s in results],
        "trace": ["verification_failed"]
    }

prompt = "How do solar panels generate electricity?"
answer = generate_llm_response(prompt)
print(answer)
```

```
Solar panels generate electricity through a process called
↪ the photovoltaic effect. Here's a step-by-step
↪ explanation of how this process works:

1. **Photovoltaic Cells**: Solar panels are made up of many
↪ individual solar cells, typically made from silicon.
↪ These cells are designed to absorb sunlight.

2. **Absorption of Sunlight**: When sunlight (composed of
↪ particles called photons) hits the solar cells, the
↪ energy from the photons is absorbed by the silicon atoms
↪ in the cells.

3. **Excitation of Electrons**: The absorbed energy excites
↪ electrons in the silicon, giving them enough energy to
↪ break free from their atomic bonds. This creates free
↪ electrons and holes (the absence of an electron) in the
↪ silicon.

4. **Electric Field Creation**: Solar cells are constructed
↪ with two layers of silicon: one layer is doped with
↪ phosphorus (n-type), which has extra electrons, and the
↪ other is doped with boron (p-type), which has fewer
↪ electrons. The junction between these two layers creates
↪ an electric field that drives the free electrons toward
↪ the n-type layer and the holes toward the p-type layer.

5. **Flow of Current**: As the electrons move toward the
↪ n-type layer, they create a flow of electric current.
↪ This flow can be harnessed by connecting the solar cells
↪ to an external circuit.
```

```
6. **Inverter Conversion**: The electricity generated by the
↪ solar panels is in the form of direct current (DC). Most
↪ homes and businesses use alternating current (AC), so an
↪ inverter is used to convert the DC electricity into AC
↪ electricity.

7. **Power Usage**: The converted AC electricity can then be
↪ used to power electrical devices, feed into the
↪ electrical grid, or charge batteries for later use.

Overall, solar panels convert sunlight directly into
↪ electricity through the interaction of photons with
↪ semiconductor materials, enabling a clean and renewable
↪ source of energy.
```

This version introduces:

- Decision-making (evaluate retrieval results)
- Action selection (rewrite and retry)
- Verification before response
- Transparent execution trace
- Explicit refusal policy

The system now adapts based on intermediate outcomes. It does not simply execute steps. It evaluates, adjusts, and enforces constraints. That is the essence of an agent.

Project 5: Planner–Executor Agent

Key Objectives

- Planner Executor Concept
- The Tool Layer — Actions the Agent Executes
- Plan Schema — Why an Agent Needs Structure
- The Planner — Turning a Goal into an Executable Blueprint
- Validation and Repair — Engineering for Reliability
- Dependency Ordering — How the Agent Knows What to Execute First
- The Executor - Turning the Plan into Action (Retry + Fallback)
- The Orchestrator — Bringing the Agent to Life
- Running the Agent — Observing Agentic Behavior

8.1 Planner Executor Concept

A Planner–Executor agent separates "thinking" from "doing". **Planner** converts a user goal into a structured plan (tasks + dependencies). **Executor** runs tasks in order, handling failures, retries, and fallbacks. This separation is what makes the system agentic. It can **decide a sequence of actions**, track progress, and adapt when a step fails.

This starts with a goal. For example: "Create a 3-day beginner workout plan and save it to a Markdown file."

The agent will:

1. Ask the LLM to **create a plan** (tasks + dependencies).
2. Execute tasks using small local "tools":
    - generate text (LLM)
    - validate constraints (Python)
    - write a file (Python)
3. If something fails, it will retry or use a fallback.
4. Return a final answer with a brief **execution trace**.

8.2 The Tool Layer — Actions the Agent Executes

In a Planner–Executor architecture, tools are the **action layer** of the agent. The planner decides *what to do*. The executor calls tools to actually do it. Without tools, the system only generates text.
With tools, it can:

- Generate structured content
- Validate outputs
- Perform side tasks (like writing files)
- Recover from failures

This is what makes the system operational. Different tools used in this project are:

1. `tool_generate_workout_plan(days)` : A model-powered tool that creates the workout plan in Markdown. This is the creative step and may fail — which allows retries and fallback.

2. `tool_validate_markdown_has_days(md, days)` : A guardrail tool that checks whether required day headings exist. If validation fails, it raises an error — enabling controlled retries. This introduces verification before progression.

3. `tool_write_file(path, content)` : A side tasks tool that writes the plan to disk. This turns the agent from a text generator into a system actor.

4. `tool_fallback_short_plan(days)` : A deterministic fallback if LLM generation fails. This ensures graceful degradation instead of crashing.

TOOL_REGISTRY : Maps tool names (from the planner) to actual Python functions. This keeps planning abstract and execution concrete.

TOOL_SIGNATURES : Defines allowed inputs per tool. The planner is generative and may invent fields. The executor enforces strict contracts. The planner proposes. The executor enforces.

This tool layer is what converts reasoning into reliable execution.

```
# ============
# Step I: LLM Set Up
# ============


import json
import time
import re
import inspect
import os
from dataclasses import dataclass, field
from typing import Any, Dict, List, Optional

# ---- LLM client (OpenAI Responses API) ----
# Official quickstart shows client.responses.create(...).
↪ :contentReference[oaicite:2]{index=2}
from openai import OpenAI
# client = OpenAI()

def llm_text(prompt: str, model: str = "gpt-5.2", temperature:
↪ float = 0.2) -> str:
    """Call the LLM and return aggregated text output."""
    resp = client.responses.create(
        model=model,
        input=prompt,
        temperature=temperature,
    )
    return resp.output_text

os.environ["OPENAI_API_KEY"] = OPENAI_API_KEY
```

```python
client = OpenAI()

# ============
# Step II: Building tools
# ============

def tool_generate_workout_plan(days: int) -> str:
    """LLM tool: generate a beginner workout plan in Markdown."""
    prompt = f"""
Create a {days}-day beginner workout plan in Markdown.

Constraints:
- Each day has: warm-up, main workout, cooldown
- Beginner-friendly and safe tone
- No medical claims
Return ONLY Markdown.
"""
    return llm_text(prompt, temperature=0.3)

def tool_validate_markdown_has_days(md: str, days: int) -> str:
    """Guardrail tool: ensure Day headings exist."""
    missing = [d for d in range(1, days + 1) if f"Day {d}" not in
↪ md]
    if missing:
        raise ValueError(f"Missing headings for: {missing}")
    return "Validation passed."

def tool_write_file(path: str, content: str) -> str:
    """Side-effect tool: write content to disk."""
    with open(path, "w", encoding="utf-8") as f:
        f.write(content)
    return f"Wrote file: {path}"

def tool_fallback_short_plan(days: int) -> str:
    """Fallback tool: deterministic plan if LLM generation
     ↪ fails."""
    out = [f"# {days}-Day Beginner Workout Plan\n"]
```

```
    for d in range(1, days + 1):
        out.append(
            f"## Day {d}\n"
            f"- Warm-up: 5 min walk\n"
            f"- Main: 3× (10 squats, 10 wall push-ups)\n"
            f"- Cooldown: 5 min stretch\n"
        )
    return "\n".join(out)


TOOL_REGISTRY = {
    "generate_workout_plan": tool_generate_workout_plan,
    "validate_markdown_has_days": tool_validate_markdown_has_days,
    "write_file": tool_write_file,
    "fallback_short_plan": tool_fallback_short_plan,
}

# Tool signatures (used to validate/repair planner outputs)
TOOL_SIGNATURES = {
    "generate_workout_plan": ["days"],
    "validate_markdown_has_days": ["md", "days"],
    "write_file": ["path", "content"],
}
```

8.3 Plan Schema - Why an Agent Needs Structure

A Planner–Executor agent cannot operate on free-form text alone. If the planner simply returns a paragraph describing what to do, the executor has nothing reliable to execute. An agent needs structure. It needs to know what exact steps must be performed, the order of these steps, which tools should be used and with what inputs and finally what to do when something fails.

That is why we define a **Plan Schema**. Instead of letting the planner output loose instructions, we require it to return a structured object: A plan that represents the overall goal and a list of tasks that represent executable steps to achieve the goal.

Each task encodes the operational requirements of an agent:

- **Tool selection** (what action to take)
- **Dependency tracking** (what must happen first)
- **Retry policy** (how resilient the step is)
- **Fallback behavior** (how to recover from failure)

This transforms planning from "reasoning in text" into "reasoning as a program." In other words the planner does not describe the solution. It produces a blueprint. And that blueprint must be structured enough for the executor to run it safely and deterministically. That is the purpose of the Plan and Task definitions.

```
# ============
# Step III: PLAN SCHEMA
# ============
@dataclass
class Task:
    id: str
    description: str
    tool: str
    inputs: Dict[str, Any] = field(default_factory=dict)
    depends_on: List[str] = field(default_factory=list)
    retries: int = 1
    fallback_tool: Optional[str] = None

@dataclass
class Plan:
    goal: str
    tasks: List[Task]
```

8.4 The Planner - Turning a Goal into an Executable Blueprint

A Planner–Executor agent begins with a goal. The system must first transform that goal into a structured sequence of actions. That transformation is the role of the **Planner**.

In this implementation, the planner itself is powered by the LLM. However, we do not allow it to respond freely. We constrain it. Instead of asking: "How would you solve this?" we ask: "Convert this goal into STRICT JSON following this exact schema."

This is a crucial shift. The LLM is no longer producing prose. It is producing a structured execution blueprint.

Why Strict JSON?

Large language models are generative by nature. If left unconstrained, they may add extra fields, invent different tool names, reorder certain steps and omit required inputs. That unpredictability is unacceptable in an agent system. By forcing strict JSON:

- We define a contract between Planner and Executor.
- We limit tool choices.
- We enforce valid inputs.
- We control dependency order.

This turns the LLM from a storyteller into a structured planner.

Why Fix the Tool List in the Prompt?

Notice that the planner is told:

- Exactly which tools are allowed.
- Exactly what inputs each tool accepts.
- Exactly how tasks must depend on one another.

This prevents "tool hallucination." The planner can reason creatively about *how* to solve the goal, but it cannot invent new capabilities. This separation of freedom (reasoning) and constraint (execution schema) is essential in reliable agent systems.

```
# ============
# Step IV: PLANNER (LLM)
# ============
def plan_tasks(goal: str, model: str = "gpt-5.2") -> Plan:
```

```
    """
    LLM planner returns a small task plan.
    We keep the schema tight, and we will validate/repair before
↪   execution.
    """
    planner_prompt = f"""
You are a planner. Create a compact executable plan for this goal.

Goal:
{goal}

Return STRICT JSON with this schema:
{{
  "goal": "<string>",
  "days": <int>,
  "tasks": [
    {{
      "id": "t1",
      "description": "<string>",
      "tool": "<generate_workout_plan | validate_markdown_has_days
↪   | write_file>",
      "inputs": {{ }},
      "depends_on": ["t0", "..."],
      "retries": 1,
      "fallback_tool": "<fallback_short_plan or null>"}}]}}

Rules:
- Use exactly these tools and only these tools.
- Use ONLY valid inputs for each tool:
  - generate_workout_plan inputs: {{ "days": <int> }}
  - validate_markdown_has_days inputs: {{ "md": "{{t1}}", "days":
↪   <int> }}
  - write_file inputs: {{ "path": "workout_plan.md", "content":
↪   "{{t2}}" }}
- Use 3 tasks in this order (with dependencies):
  t1 generate -> t2 validate -> t3 write_file
- Set fallback_tool on t1 as "fallback_short_plan".
```

```
- Ensure depends_on links reflect the order.
"""
    raw = llm_text(planner_prompt, model=model,
↪   temperature=0.0).strip()

    # Strip accidental code fences
    if raw.startswith("```"):
        raw = raw.strip("`")
        raw = raw.replace("json\n", "", 1)

    data = json.loads(raw)
    tasks = [Task(id=t["id"],
                  description=t["description"],
                  tool=t["tool"],
                  inputs=t.get("inputs", {}) or {},
                  depends_on=t.get("depends_on", []) or [],
                  retries=int(t.get("retries", 1)),
                  fallback_tool=t.get("fallback_tool", None),)
             for t in data["tasks"]]
    return Plan(goal=data["goal"], tasks=tasks)
```

8.5 Validation and Repair — Engineering for Reliability

The planner uses an LLM, and LLMs can make small mistakes. They might forget required inputs, add extra fields, or arrange steps incorrectly. If we run that plan as-is, the agent can crash. Real systems cannot rely on "maybe it will work." They must check and fix plans before execution. That is why we add a validation and repair layer to ensure that the plan is safe and executable.

The repair layer acts as a bridge between the planner and the executor.

It ensures:

- Required parameters always exist
- Tool inputs match function signatures
- Dependencies are correctly wired

- Fallback policies are present
- Minimal executable structure is guaranteed

This transforms “likely to work” into “guaranteed to run.”

Below functions are added to achieve implement validation and repair layers:

- **extract_days_from_goal** : The function that extracts the number of days from the goal demonstrates an important idea: The agent should not depend entirely on the planner for simple facts. Some information can be deterministically inferred from the user request. This reduces unnecessary planner complexity and increases robustness.
- **filter_inputs_for_tool** : This mechanism ensures that only valid parameters reach each tool and any planner-invented keys are ignored. This is critical because planners can hallucinate.
- **resolve_refs** : Planner-generated inputs may reference previous task outputs using placeholders like: `{t1}` The resolution step converts those symbolic references into actual runtime values. This is what allows tasks to depend on each other. Without this, dependency tracking would remain theoretical.
- **repair_plan** : The repair function reconstructs a minimal, canonical plan if needed to generate content, validate or write the same. This ensures that even if the planner deviates slightly, the executor still receives a consistent, executable structure.

The Validation + Repair step ensures that the agent always runs in one go. Failures are handled deliberately. Structure is enforced before action. It is not a workaround. It is a design necessity in real-world agent systems.

```
# ============
# Step V: VALIDATION + REPAIR (MAKES IT RUN IN ONE GO)
# ============

def extract_days_from_goal(goal: str, default: int = 3) -> int:
    m = re.search(r"(\d+)\s*-\s*day|(\d+)\s*day", goal.lower())
    if not m:
        return default
    return int(next(x for x in m.groups() if x))
```

```
def filter_inputs_for_tool(tool_fn, inputs: Dict[str, Any]) ->
↪ Dict[str, Any]:
    """Ignore any planner-invented keys (e.g., 'level')."""
    sig = inspect.signature(tool_fn)
    allowed = set(sig.parameters.keys())
    return {k: v for k, v in inputs.items() if k in allowed}

def resolve_refs(inputs: Dict[str, Any], outputs: Dict[str, Any])
↪ -> Dict[str, Any]:
    """Resolve placeholders like {{t1}} into actual previous
    ↪ outputs."""
    out = {}
    for k, v in inputs.items():
        if isinstance(v, str) and v.startswith("{{") and
        ↪ v.endswith("}}"):
            ref = v[2:-2].strip()
            out[k] = outputs.get(ref)
        else:
            out[k] = v
    return out

def repair_plan(plan: Plan) -> Plan:
    """
    Deterministic repair so the executor never fails due to missing
↪   required inputs.
    This is the difference between a demo and an engineered agent.
    """
    days = extract_days_from_goal(plan.goal, default=3)

    # Ensure the canonical 3-task structure exists; if planner
    ↪ deviates, normalize.
    # We'll rebuild minimal tasks if needed.
    by_tool = {t.tool: t for t in plan.tasks}

    # Create or fix t1: generate
    t1 = by_tool.get("generate_workout_plan") or Task(
        id="t1", description="Generate workout plan",
        ↪ tool="generate_workout_plan"
```

```
)
t1.id = "t1"
t1.inputs = {"days": days}
t1.depends_on = []
t1.retries = max(1, t1.retries)
t1.fallback_tool = "fallback_short_plan"

# Create or fix t2: validate
t2 = by_tool.get("validate_markdown_has_days") or Task(
    id="t2", description="Validate plan headings", tool="validate_markdown_has_days"
)
t2.id = "t2"
t2.inputs = {"md": "{{t1}}", "days": days}
t2.depends_on = ["t1"]
t2.retries = max(1, t2.retries)

# Create or fix t3: write
t3 = by_tool.get("write_file") or Task(
    id="t3", description="Write plan to file", tool="write_file"
)
t3.id = "t3"
t3.inputs = {"path": "workout_plan.md", "content": "{{t1}}"}
# Note: write can depend on validate (better), but content comes from t1.
t3.depends_on = ["t2"]
t3.retries = max(0, t3.retries)

plan.tasks = [t1, t2, t3]
return plan
```

8.6 Dependency Ordering — How the Agent Knows What to Execute First

A Planner–Executor agent runs tasks in the order they are **allowed** to run. The order is determined by dependencies. This is essential because later tasks often require outputs produced earlier (for example: validate the content after it is generated, write the file after it is validated).

The planner produces tasks as a small dependency graph (a DAG). Without dependency ordering, the executor might run tasks in a broken sequence and fail due to missing inputs. In order to avoid all such issues, the execution rule is: **Always execute tasks whose dependencies are already satisfied**.

The `topo_order` function:

1. Builds a dependency graph from the plan
2. Finds tasks with **zero prerequisites**
3. Executes them first
4. Unlocks dependent tasks as prerequisites complete
5. Continues until all tasks are ordered

Dependency ordering is a core agent capability. It enables multi-step execution. It ensures correct sequencing. It allows plans to scale beyond linear workflows. It makes the executor reliable even when plans become complex. In short the planner defines what must happen. Dependency ordering defines what can happen next. The executor uses that to run safely.

```
# ============
# Step VI: DEPENDENCY ORDERING
# ============

def topo_order(tasks: List[Task]) -> List[Task]:
    by_id = {t.id: t for t in tasks}
    indeg = {t.id: 0 for t in tasks}
    graph = {t.id: [] for t in tasks}

    for t in tasks:
        for dep in t.depends_on:
```

```
            if dep not in by_id:
                raise ValueError(f"Task {t.id} depends on unknown
                    ↪ task {dep}")
            graph[dep].append(t.id)
            indeg[t.id] += 1

    q = [tid for tid, d in indeg.items() if d == 0]
    ordered = []

    while q:
        cur = q.pop(0)
        ordered.append(by_id[cur])
        for nxt in graph[cur]:
            indeg[nxt] -= 1
            if indeg[nxt] == 0:
                q.append(nxt)

    if len(ordered) != len(tasks):
        raise ValueError("Cycle detected in task dependencies.")
    return ordered
```

8.7 The Executor - Turning the Plan into Action (Retry + Fallback)

Planning is only half the job. An agent becomes real when it can **execute**. The executor is the runtime engine of the Planner–Executor architecture. It takes the structured plan and performs the tasks, one by one, in the correct dependency order. This is where agent behavior becomes visible: it runs actions, it tracks state, it handles errors and it adapts when a step fails.

A reliable executor needs five capabilities:

1. **Execute tasks in dependency order**
   It starts with `topo_order(plan.tasks)` so tasks run only when prerequisites are satisfied.

2. **Maintain state across steps**
   It stores task outputs in outputs so later tasks can use earlier results.

3. **Resolve dependencies at the data level**
   Plans often include references like `{t1}`.
   The executor must replace these placeholders with the actual output values at runtime.

4. **Enforce tool contracts**
   The planner may accidentally include extra inputs.
   The executor filters inputs to match the tool signature so execution does not crash.

5. **Recover from failure**
   When a tool fails, the executor retries.
   If retries are exhausted and a fallback exists, it runs the fallback tool instead.

Retry: Why It Matters

Failures are normal in agent systems: transient API issues, flaky network, occasional model formatting issues and validation failures. A retry policy prevents the agent from failing immediately. It gives the system resilience at low cost.

Fallback: Why It Matters Even More

Sometimes retries are not enough. Fallbacks allow graceful degradation. The agent still produces usable output. The workflow completes. The user gets a result instead of an error. This is the practical meaning of robustness in agents.

Trace: Making the Agent Observable

The executor logs each attempt into `trace`: which task ran, which tool was used, success or failure, attempt number and error message (if any). This trace helps developers to debug. It also ensures transparency for users and monitoring systems. It allows the agent to explain what happened, not just return a result.

```
# ============
# step VII: EXECUTOR (RETRY + FALLBACK)
# ============

def execute_plan(plan: Plan) -> Dict[str, Any]:
    ordered = topo_order(plan.tasks)
    outputs: Dict[str, Any] = {}
    trace: List[Dict[str, Any]] = []

    for task in ordered:
        tool_fn = TOOL_REGISTRY[task.tool]

        attempt = 0
        last_err = None

        while attempt <= task.retries:
            try:
                attempt += 1

                # Resolve references (e.g., md="{{t1}}")
                resolved = resolve_refs(task.inputs, outputs)

                # Filter inputs to match tool signature (ignore
                 ↪  hallucinated keys)
                safe_inputs = filter_inputs_for_tool(tool_fn,
 ↪  resolved)

                result = tool_fn(**safe_inputs)
                outputs[task.id] = result

                trace.append({
                    "task": task.id, "tool": task.tool,
                    "status": "success", "attempt": attempt
                })
                break

            except Exception as e:
```

```
                last_err = str(e)
                trace.append({
                    "task": task.id, "tool": task.tool,
                    "status": "failed", "attempt": attempt,
                     ↪ "error": last_err
                })
                time.sleep(0.2)

                # fallback only after retries exhausted
                if attempt > task.retries and task.fallback_tool:
                    fb_fn = TOOL_REGISTRY[task.fallback_tool]
                    resolved = resolve_refs(task.inputs, outputs)
                    safe_fb_inputs = filter_inputs_for_tool(fb_fn,
↪  resolved)

                    fb_result = fb_fn(**safe_fb_inputs)
                    outputs[task.id] = fb_result
                    trace.append({
                        "task": task.id, "tool":
                         ↪  task.fallback_tool,
                        "status": "fallback_success", "attempt":
                         ↪  attempt
                    })
                    break

        if task.id not in outputs:
            raise RuntimeError(f"Task {task.id} failed:
             ↪  {last_err}")

    return {"goal": plan.goal, "outputs": outputs, "trace": trace}
```

8.8 The Orchestrator — Bringing the Agent to Life

All previous components — planner, repair layer, executor — are building blocks. The orchestrator is what turns them into a complete agent. It defines the full lifecycle of a request:

1. **Plan**
2. **Validate and repair**
3. **Execute**
4. **Respond**

This function represents the agent's outer control loop.

- **Step 1 — Planning** : The user provides a goal. The LLM converts that goal into a structured plan. At this stage, the system has reasoning — but not action.
- **Step 2 — Repair** : Before execution begins, the plan is validated and normalized. This ensures required inputs exist, dependencies are correct and fallbacks are present. This step guarantees that execution will succeed in one go.
- **Step 3 — Execution** : The executor runs the plan: resolves dependencies, calls tools, retries on failure, uses fallback if necessary and records a trace. Now the system has acted. It has produced real output.
- **Step 4 — Agentic Response** : The orchestrator now asks the LLM to: review what happened (using the execution trace), confirm what was produced, mention whether fallback was used and communicate clearly to the user.

The final response is not speculative. It is grounded in actual execution results. The LLM is now summarizing actions that truly occurred. This function demonstrates a complete agent lifecycle: Reason → Constrain → Execute → Reflect → Respond. That is what makes it an end-to-end Planner–Executor agent.

```
# ============
# Step VIII: ORCHESTRATOR (END-TO-END AGENT)
# ============

def run_planner_executor_agent(goal: str) -> Dict[str, Any]:
    # 1) Plan (LLM)
    plan = plan_tasks(goal)

    # 2) Repair (deterministic guardrail that ensures one-go
     ↪  execution)
```

```
    plan = repair_plan(plan)

    # 3) Execute (dependencies + retry + fallback)
    run = execute_plan(plan)

    # 4) Produce final agentic response based on what actually
     ↪  happened
    summary_prompt = f"""
You executed a plan.

Goal:
{run["goal"]}

Trace (JSON):
{json.dumps(run["trace"], indent=2)}

Write a short response that:
- confirms the file was created
- mentions if fallback was used
- points to workout_plan.md
"""
    final_answer = llm_text(summary_prompt, temperature=0.2)

    return {"plan": plan, "run": run, "final_answer": final_answer}
```

8.9 Running the Agent — Observing Agentic Behavior

With all components in place, we now give the agent a goal: "Create a 3-day beginner workout plan and save it to a Markdown file." This single line triggers the entire lifecycle:

1. The planner decomposes the goal into structured tasks.
2. The repair layer validates and normalizes the plan.

3. The executor runs each task with dependency control, retries, and fallback.
4. The orchestrator generates a final grounded response.

When we print `result["final_answer"]`, we see the agent's user-facing explanation of what it accomplished. When we print the `TRACE`, we see something more important:

- Which tools were executed
- In what order
- Whether any retries occurred
- Whether fallback was used

By inspecting both the final answer and the trace, we verify that the system did not merely respond — it executed.

```
# ============
# Step IX: Execution
# ============

goal = "Create a 3-day beginner workout plan and save it to a
↪ Markdown file."
result = run_planner_executor_agent(goal)

print(result["final_answer"])
print("\nTRACE:")
for row in result["run"]["trace"]:
    print(row)
```

```
Created the workout plan file at **workout_plan.md**. No
↪ fallback was used; all steps completed successfully.

TRACE:
{'task': 't1', 'tool': 'generate_workout_plan', 'status':
↪ 'success', 'attempt': 1}
{'task': 't2', 'tool': 'validate_markdown_has_days',
↪ 'status': 'success', 'attempt': 1}
```

```
{'task': 't3', 'tool': 'write_file', 'status': 'success',
↪  'attempt': 1}
```

8.10 Lesson Summary — Planner–Executor Agent

In this chapter, we built a complete Planner–Executor agent from first principles. We did not rely on a single prompt to "do everything." Instead, we separated responsibilities: The **Planner** converts a goal into structured tasks. The **Repair layer** enforces execution contracts. The **Executor** runs tasks with dependency control. **Retries and fallback** provide resilience. The **Orchestrator** delivers a grounded, user-facing response.

This architecture demonstrates a fundamental shift: From generating answers to designing systems that reason, act, adapt, and report. By combining structured planning, dependency management, validation, and controlled execution, we created an agent that does not merely respond — it completes work reliably. It is a foundational building block for complex, multi-step, real-world AI systems.

Project 6: Multi-Agent Collaboration System

Key Objectives

- Why Multi-Agent Systems?
- Role Specialization — Designing Agents with Clear Boundaries
- Shared State and Agent Communication
- The Agent Abstraction
- Specialized Agents
- The Coordinator — Conflict Resolution and Final Composition
- Orchestration - Coordinating the Rounds
- Running the System and Interpreting Output

9.1 Why Multi-Agent Systems?

Many real-world problems are not single-perspective problems. For example: launching a startup, drafting a policy, evaluating risk, designing a product — these require multiple viewpoints.They are based on different rules and different knowledge base. In real life too, such goals are achieved by a team of people with varied specialization.

The same happens in agentic AI domain. A single agent can reason broadly. A multi-agent system can reason *from distinct roles*. Hence a team of AI agents is what helps in such scenarios.

When one model handles everything like market assumptions, strategy, financial planning and risk analysis, it tends to blend perspectives. There is no real disagreement. No structured tension. No governance layer. It becomes just one single long prompt — not a team.

A multi-agent system introduces:

- **Specialization** — each agent has a specialized responsibility
- **Structured interaction** — agents communicate intentionally
- **Shared memory** — all agents operate on the same evolving context
- **Conflict resolution** — disagreements are surfaced and resolved

This mirrors how real organizations operate.

We will construct a Multi-Agent Startup Launch Planning System. The agents will simulate a small startup team:

- **Research Agent** — market & positioning
- **Strategy Agent** — go-to-market plan
- **Finance Agent** — pricing & budget
- **Risk/Critic Agent** — conflict & risk detection
- **Coordinator Agent** — decision-making & final synthesis

The system will:

1. Accept a product goal
2. Generate independent proposals
3. Detect conflicts
4. Apply resolution logic
5. Produce one consolidated launch plan

Architectural Shift

- Multiple agents propose.
- A critic challenges.
- A coordinator governs.

This is no longer linear execution. This is structured collaboration.

9.2 Role Specialization — Designing Agents with Clear Boundaries

A multi-agent system only works if each agent has a clearly defined role. Without boundaries, multiple agents simply repeat similar reasoning. They become redundant instead of collaborative. True collaboration requires specialization.

In real organizations researchers analyze markets, strategists design execution plans, finance teams evaluate feasibility, risk teams challenge assumptions and leaders make final decisions. Each role sees the same goal — but through a different lens.

Multi-agent systems mirror this structure. Instead of one model attempting to think from every perspective, we assign distinct cognitive responsibilities.

What Happens Without Specialization?

If multiple agents share identical instructions outputs overlap, conflicts are superficial, no real negotiation emerges and the system becomes parallel prompting.To create structured collaboration, we must:

- Define scope
- Restrict responsibility
- Clarify authority

That is what role specialization enforces.

Roles in This Project

In this system, we define five roles:

1. **Research Agent** focuses on:

- Target users
- Market positioning
- Differentiation
- Market risks

Strategy Agent focuses on:

- Go-to-market phases

- Channel selection
- KPIs

Finance Agent focuses on:

- Pricing model
- Budget assumptions
- Unit economics

4. **Risk/Critic Agent** focuses on:

- Conflict detection
- Unrealistic assumptions
- Risk surfacing

5. **Coordinator Agent** focuses on:

- Merging proposals
- Resolving conflicts
- Producing final output

Each agent has a narrow cognitive scope, a defined output format and no authority outside its domain.

Architectural Principle

In multi-agent systems diversity of reasoning comes from diversity of constraints. Each agent is constrained differently. That is what creates meaningful collaboration.

Step 1 — System Initialization

We begin by setting up the runtime environment for the multi-agent system. At this stage, we define the model configuration, the API client and a reusable helper function for LLM calls.

The `llm_text()` function provides a consistent interface for all agents to interact with the language model.
By centralizing the model call, we ensure that configuration changes—such as model selection or temperature adjustments—can be managed in one place. This

setup establishes the foundation upon which the agents, shared state, and communication mechanisms will operate.

The following code initializes this base layer.

```
# ------------------------------
# Step I : Config and LLM helper
# ------------------------------
import json
import time
import os
from dataclasses import dataclass, field
from typing import Any, Dict, List, Optional
from openai import OpenAI

# ------------------------------
# Config
# ------------------------------
MODEL = "gpt-4o-mini"  # change to your preferred model
TEMPERATURE = 0.2

os.environ["OPENAI_API_KEY"] = OPENAI_API_KEY
client = OpenAI()
# ------------------------------
# LLM helper
# ------------------------------
def llm_text(prompt: str, *, system: str = "", model: str = MODEL,
↪  temperature: float = TEMPERATURE) -> str:
    """Simple text call using the Responses API."""
    resp = client.responses.create(
        model=model,
        input=[
            {"role": "system", "content": system} if system else
↪  {"role": "system", "content": "You are helpful."},
            {"role": "user", "content": prompt},
        ],
        temperature=temperature,
    )
    return resp.output_text.strip()
```

9.3 Shared State and Agent Communication

A multi-agent system requires a shared working memory. If each agent operates independently, their outputs remain isolated and cannot influence one another. To enable collaboration, all agents must work over a common state.

In this project, coordination is built around two core components: **Message** and **SharedState**.

The `Message` structure defines how agents communicate. Every message clearly specifies the sender, the intended recipient (either a specific agent or `"ALL"`), the type of message (proposal, critique, question, answer, or final), and the content itself. This ensures that communication remains structured and traceable rather than conversational and ambiguous.

The `SharedState` acts as the central memory of the system. It stores the original goal, product information, intermediate artifacts such as proposals, recorded decisions, and the full message history. Every agent reads from this shared state and writes back to it.

Before generating output, each agent receives a compact snapshot of the current state. This keeps context focused and prevents uncontrolled memory growth while still enabling collaboration.

Together, the messaging structure and shared state transform independent LLM calls into a coordinated multi-agent system.

The following code defines this communication and memory layer.

```
# ----------------------------
# Step II: Shared State + Messaging
# ----------------------------
@dataclass
class Message:
    sender: str
    recipient: str  # "ALL" or agent name
    kind: str       # "proposal" | "critique" | "question" |
↪   "answer" | "final"
    content: str
    meta: Dict[str, Any] = field(default_factory=dict)

@dataclass
```

```
class SharedState:
    """A minimal shared state store used by all agents."""
    goal: str
    product: Dict[str, Any]
    artifacts: Dict[str, Any] = field(default_factory=dict)  #
↪   proposals, drafts, etc.
    decisions: List[Dict[str, Any]] = field(default_factory=list)
    messages: List[Message] = field(default_factory=list)

    def post(self, msg: Message) -> None:
        self.messages.append(msg)

    def inbox(self, recipient: str) -> List[Message]:
        return [m for m in self.messages if m.recipient in
         ↪  (recipient, "ALL")]

    def snapshot(self) -> Dict[str, Any]:
        """A compact snapshot passed to agents."""
        return {
            "goal": self.goal,
            "product": self.product,
            "artifacts": self.artifacts,
            "decisions": self.decisions[-10:],  # keep it short
            "recent_messages": [
                {"sender": m.sender, "recipient": m.recipient,
↪   "kind": m.kind, "content": m.content, "meta": m.meta}
                for m in self.messages[-12:]]}
```

9.4 The Agent Abstraction

With shared memory and messaging in place, the next step is to define what an agent is within this system. Rather than writing completely separate logic for each role, we introduce a common base class. This establishes a consistent structure that all specialized agents will follow.

Every agent in this project has:

- A `name` , that identifies it in the system
- A `role_system_prompt` that defines its perspective
- A `run()` method that executes its task
- Access to the shared state

The `run()` method is intentionally left undefined in the base class. Each specialized agent must implement its own behavior. This enforces role clarity and prevents generic reasoning from leaking across responsibilities.

The `_context_prompt()` method prepares the information that each agent receives before generating output. It packages a snapshot of the shared state into a structured prompt. This ensures that all agents reason from the same source of truth while maintaining their distinct roles.

This abstraction provides three important benefits:

- Consistency across agents
- Clear separation of responsibilities
- Centralized context construction

```
# ------------------------------
# Step III: Agent base
# ------------------------------
class Agent:
    name: str = "Agent"
    role_system_prompt: str = "You are a helpful assistant."

    def run(self, state: SharedState) -> None:
        raise NotImplementedError

    def _context_prompt(self, state: SharedState) -> str:
        snap = state.snapshot()
        return (
            "You are part of a multi-agent startup launch planning
             ↪ system.\n\n"
            "Shared State (JSON):\n"
            f"{json.dumps(snap, indent=2)}\n\n"
            "Instructions:\n"
            "- Be concise and specific.\n"
            "- Use bullet points where helpful.\n"
```

```
        "- Do not invent external sources; reason from general
        ↪ knowledge.\n")
```

9.5 Specialized Agents

With the base agent structure in place, we now define the specialized roles. Each agent inherits from the common `Agent` class but defines a distinct `name`, a role-specific system prompt and a focused `run()` implementation. This is where role specialization becomes operational.

Research Agent

The Research Agent focuses on market understanding. It generates structured output covering:

- Target users and pain points
- Positioning and differentiation
- Market-level risks

Its responsibility is analytical. It does not propose execution tactics or financial assumptions. The output is returned in JSON format and sent to the Coordinator as a proposal.

Strategy Agent

The Strategy Agent defines how the product will be launched. Its scope is execution planning. The structured proposal is again sent to the Coordinator. It proposes:

- Launch phases
- Channel selection
- Key performance indicators

Finance Agent

The Finance Agent evaluates feasibility. It introduces cost realism into the plan. It proposes:

- Pricing structure
- Three-month budget allocation
- Unit economics assumptions

Critic Agent

The Critic Agent does not create a new proposal. Instead, it evaluates the outputs of other agents. This step introduces structured tension into the system. It identifies:

- Conflicts between proposals
- Missing assumptions
- High-risk areas
- Suggested mitigations

Why This Structure Matters

Each agent:

- Has a clearly bounded responsibility
- Produces structured output
- Communicates through the shared state

```
# ----------------------------
# Step IV: Specialized agents
# ----------------------------
class ResearchAgent(Agent):
    name = "Research"
    role_system_prompt = (
        "You are the Research Agent. Provide market/user insights
         ↪ and competitor landscape at a high level. "
        "Focus on assumptions, target users, and differentiation
         ↪ angles."
```

```
    )

    def run(self, state: SharedState) -> None:
        prompt = self._context_prompt(state) + (
            "\nTask:\n"
            "Write a proposal for a startup launch plan section
             ↪ covering:\n"
            "1) Target users + key pain points\n"
            "2) Positioning + differentiators\n"
            "3) Top 3 risks from market perspective\n"
            "Return JSON with keys: target_users, positioning,
             ↪ differentiators, market_risks.\n"
        )
        out = llm_text(prompt, system=self.role_system_prompt,
 ↪  temperature=0.3)
        state.post(Message(sender=self.name,
 ↪  recipient="Coordinator", kind="proposal", content=out))


class StrategyAgent(Agent):
    name = "Strategy"
    role_system_prompt = (
        "You are the Strategy Agent. Create a practical
         ↪ go-to-market (GTM) plan: channels, messaging, timeline,
         ↪ and KPIs."
    )

    def run(self, state: SharedState) -> None:
        prompt = self._context_prompt(state) + (
            "\nTask:\n"
            "Propose a GTM plan for the product:\n"
            "1) Launch phases (pre-launch, launch week,
             ↪ post-launch)\n"
            "2) Channel mix and why\n"
            "3) Key KPIs and how to measure\n"
            "Return JSON with keys: phases, channels, kpis.\n"
        )
```

```
        out = llm_text(prompt, system=self.role_system_prompt,
↪   temperature=0.3)
        state.post(Message(sender=self.name,
↪   recipient="Coordinator", kind="proposal", content=out))


class FinanceAgent(Agent):
    name = "Finance"
    role_system_prompt = (
        "You are the Finance Agent. Provide a simple but realistic
         ↪   budget, pricing, and unit economics assumptions."
    )

    def run(self, state: SharedState) -> None:
        prompt = self._context_prompt(state) + (
            "\nTask:\n"
            "Propose financial assumptions for launch:\n"
            "1) Pricing model (tiers)\n"
            "2) 3-month budget (rough buckets)\n"
            "3) Simple unit economics assumptions (CAC, payback,
             ↪   conversion assumptions)\n"
            "Return JSON with keys: pricing, budget_3mo,
             ↪   unit_econ.\n"
        )
        out = llm_text(prompt, system=self.role_system_prompt,
↪   temperature=0.2)
        state.post(Message(sender=self.name,
↪   recipient="Coordinator", kind="proposal", content=out))


class CriticAgent(Agent):
    name = "Critic"
    role_system_prompt = (
        "You are the Risk/Critic Agent. Your job is to find flaws,
         ↪   conflicts, missing pieces, and unrealistic assumptions.
         ↪   "
        "Be strict but constructive."
```

```
    )

    def run(self, state: SharedState) -> None:
        prompt = self._context_prompt(state) + (
            "\nTask:\n"
            "Review the latest proposals from other agents (in
             ↪ recent_messages). Identify:\n"
            "1) Conflicts between proposals\n"
            "2) Unclear assumptions\n"
            "3) High-risk items\n"
            "4) Concrete fixes/mitigations\n"
            "Return JSON with keys: conflicts, missing_assumptions,
             ↪ high_risks, mitigations.\n"
        )
        out = llm_text(prompt, system=self.role_system_prompt,
↪   temperature=0.0)
        state.post(Message(sender=self.name,
↪   recipient="Coordinator", kind="critique", content=out))
```

9.6 The Coordinator — Conflict Resolution and Final Composition

With multiple specialized proposals generated, the system now requires a governing role. The Coordinator Agent performs this function. It does not introduce new domain knowledge. Instead, it consolidates, evaluates, and finalizes. This role acts as the decision authority in the system.

The Coordinator:

- Collects all proposals from the shared inbox
- Retrieves the latest critique
- Parses structured outputs
- Logs conflict resolution decisions
- Produces a single consolidated launch plan

Conflict Handling

If the Critic Agent identifies conflicts or risks, the Coordinator must acknowledge them.
Rather than ignoring disagreements, the system records them in the `decisions` log along with a resolution rule. This introduces transparency. Every conflict becomes part of the system's reasoning history.

Structured Consolidation

The Coordinator then generates the final plan using only:

- The structured proposals
- The critique analysis
- The shared state

It does not invent new information outside these inputs. The final output includes:

- Product summary
- Target users and positioning
- Launch phases
- Channel strategy
- Pricing and budget
- KPIs
- Risks and mitigations
- Explicit trade-offs decided

This ensures that the final plan is grounded in collaborative inputs rather than a single-agent rewrite. The Coordinator integrates, resolves and formalizes. It transforms distributed reasoning into a coherent, unified outcome.

```
# ------------------------------
# Step V: Coordinator (conflict resolver + final composer)
# ------------------------------
class CoordinatorAgent(Agent):
    name = "Coordinator"
    role_system_prompt = (
        "You are the Coordinator Agent. Combine proposals into one
        ↪  coherent launch plan. "
```

```
        "Resolve conflicts using explicit trade-offs. Prefer
         ↪ clarity and feasibility."
    )

    def _safe_json_load(self, s: str) -> Dict[str, Any]:
        s = s.strip()
        if s.startswith("```"):
            s = s.strip("`").replace("json\n", "", 1)
        try:
            return json.loads(s)
        except Exception:
            # fallback: wrap as text
            return {"_raw": s}

    def run(self, state: SharedState) -> None:
        # Collect latest proposals/critique
        inbox = state.inbox("Coordinator")
        proposals = {m.sender: m for m in inbox if m.kind ==
↪   "proposal"}
        critique = next((m for m in reversed(inbox) if m.kind ==
↪   "critique"), None)

        # Parse
        parsed = {k: self._safe_json_load(v.content) for k, v in
↪   proposals.items()}
        parsed_critique = self._safe_json_load(critique.content)
↪   if critique else {}

        # Store in shared artifacts for transparency
        state.artifacts["proposals"] = parsed
        state.artifacts["critique"] = parsed_critique

        # Conflict resolution policy (lightweight but explicit):
        # - If critic reports conflicts, coordinator must choose
         ↪ and justify in decisions.
        conflicts = parsed_critique.get("conflicts", [])
        mitigations = parsed_critique.get("mitigations", [])
```

```
        # Make a decision log entry (human-readable + structured)
        state.decisions.append({
            "type": "conflict_resolution",
            "conflicts": conflicts,
            "resolution_rule": "Prefer feasibility; keep plan
             ↪ small; add mitigations; align KPIs with budget.",
            "timestamp": time.time(),
        })

        # Build final plan with LLM (grounded in the collected
         ↪ JSON)
        prompt = self._context_prompt(state) + (
            "\nTask:\n"
            "Create ONE consolidated startup launch plan in
             ↪ Markdown.\n"
            "It must include:\n"
            "- Product summary (1 paragraph)\n"
            "- Target users + positioning\n"
            "- Differentiators\n"
            "- Launch phases with timeline (3 phases)\n"
            "- Channel plan\n"
            "- Pricing + budget (3 months)\n"
            "- KPIs (top 6)\n"
            "- Risks + mitigations\n"
            "- Final 'Trade-offs decided' section (explicitly
             ↪ mention how conflicts were resolved)\n\n"
            "Use only the information in the shared proposals and
             ↪ critique (JSON in shared state).\n"
        )
        final_md = llm_text(prompt, system=self.role_system_prompt,
↪ temperature=0.2)

        state.post(Message(sender=self.name, recipient="ALL",
↪ kind="final", content=final_md))
        state.artifacts["final_plan_markdown"] = final_md
```

9.7 Orchestration - Coordinating the Rounds

With all agents defined, we now need a control layer that determines **when** each agent runs and in what sequence. This function serves as the orchestrator of the system. It initializes the shared state and then executes the collaboration in structured rounds.

The process unfolds in three stages:

- **1. Proposal Generation**
  The Research, Strategy, and Finance agents independently generate their proposals and post them to the shared state.
- **2. Critique**
  The Critic Agent reviews the proposals already stored in shared memory and posts structured feedback.
- **3. Coordination**
  The Coordinator reads all proposals and critiques, resolves conflicts, and produces the final consolidated launch plan.

The round-based approach ensures that specialists contribute first, critique happens after proposals and finally consolidation happens after evaluation. This mirrors real collaborative workflows.

The function returns the complete `SharedState`, which contains:

- All messages
- Logged decisions
- Structured proposals
- The final consolidated plan

This state provides full traceability of how the final outcome was produced. The following code defines the orchestration logic that drives the multi-agent collaboration.

```
# ------------------------------
# Step VI: Orchestrator: communication rounds
# ------------------------------
def run_multi_agent_launch_planner(
    goal: str,
```

```
    product: Dict[str, Any],
    *,
    max_rounds: int = 2
) -> SharedState:
    """
    Round 1: specialists propose
    Round 1b: critic reviews
    Round 2: coordinator composes final plan
    (Optional) more rounds if you expand the system later.
    """
    state = SharedState(goal=goal, product=product)

    # Agents
    research = ResearchAgent()
    strategy = StrategyAgent()
    finance = FinanceAgent()
    critic = CriticAgent()
    coordinator = CoordinatorAgent()

    # ROUND 1: proposals
    for agent in (research, strategy, finance):
        agent.run(state)

    # ROUND 1b: critique (reads proposals via shared messages)
    critic.run(state)

    # ROUND 2: coordination + conflict resolution + final plan
    coordinator.run(state)

    return state
```

9.8 Running the System and Interpreting Output

To run the project end to end, we provide a simple demo entry point.

We define:

- A launch goal

- A product description
- Practical constraints (timeline, team size, budget cap)

These inputs become the shared context for all agents. When the orchestrator is called, the system runs through the collaboration rounds and returns a completed shared state object.

The demo prints two things:

- **Final Launch Plan** : This is the consolidated Markdown plan produced by the Coordinator after reading all proposals and critiques.
- **Message Trace** : This is a compact log of the collaboration.

This trace helps confirm that collaboration actually occurred and makes the system easier to debug and extend.

```
# -----------------------------
# Step VII: Demo run
# -----------------------------
if __name__ == "__main__":
    goal = "Create a launch plan for a new AI productivity app
↪   targeted at busy professionals."
    product = {
        "name": "FlowPilot",
        "one_liner": "An AI assistant that turns messy notes and
        ↪   tasks into an executable daily plan.",
        "target_market": "Busy professionals (consultants,
        ↪   managers, founders)",
        "constraints": {
            "timeline": "3 weeks to first public launch",
            "team": "2 engineers + 1 designer",
            "budget_cap_3mo_usd": 15000,
        }
    }

    state = run_multi_agent_launch_planner(goal, product)

    # Print final output + trace-like view of messages
    final_msg = next((m for m in reversed(state.messages) if m.kind
↪   == "final"), None)
```

```python
    print("\n================ FINAL LAUNCH PLAN (Markdown)
     ↪ ================\n")
    print(final_msg.content if final_msg else "No final plan
     ↪ produced.")

    print("\n================ MESSAGE TRACE ================\n")
    for m in state.messages:
        preview = m.content[:120].replace("\n", " ")
        print(f"[{m.kind.upper():8}] {m.sender:11} ->
         ↪ {m.recipient:11} | {preview}...")
```

```
================ FINAL LAUNCH PLAN (Markdown)
 ↪ ================

# FlowPilot Launch Plan

## Product Summary
FlowPilot is an AI productivity app designed for busy
 ↪ professionals, transforming messy notes and tasks into
 ↪ an executable daily plan. By leveraging AI, it
 ↪ simplifies chaotic workflows, enabling users to
 ↪ prioritize and execute their daily tasks efficiently.

## Target Users + Positioning
- **Target Users**: Busy professionals, including
 ↪ consultants, managers, and founders.
- **Positioning**: FlowPilot positions itself as a smart AI
 ↪ assistant that simplifies the chaotic workflow of busy
 ↪ professionals by transforming unstructured notes and
 ↪ tasks into a clear, actionable daily plan.

## Differentiators
- AI-driven organization of notes and tasks, providing
 ↪ personalized daily plans.
```

```
- User-friendly interface designed for quick input and retrieval of information.
- Integration with existing productivity tools (e.g., calendars, task managers) for seamless workflow.

## Launch Phases with Timeline
1. **Pre-launch (Weeks 1-2)**:
   - Finalize product features and user interface.
   - Create a landing page for email sign-ups.
   - Develop promotional materials (videos, graphics).
   - Engage with potential users on social media and forums.

2. **Launch Week (Week 3)**:
   - Officially launch FlowPilot with a press release.
   - Host a live demo/webinar to showcase features.
   - Leverage social media ads targeting busy professionals.
   - Offer a limited-time free trial or discount.

3. **Post-launch (Weeks 4-6)**:
   - Collect user feedback and reviews.
   - Monitor user engagement and retention metrics.
   - Iterate on product features based on feedback.
   - Continue marketing efforts through content and partnerships.

## Channel Plan
- **Social Media (LinkedIn, Twitter)**: Target professionals where they network and share insights.
- **Email Marketing**: Directly reach potential users who signed up on the landing page.
- **Webinars**: Engage users interactively and demonstrate product value.
- **Content Marketing (Blogs, Articles)**: Establish authority in productivity and AI, driving organic traffic.
```

```
- **Paid Ads (Google, Facebook)**: Quickly reach a broad audience of busy professionals.

## Pricing + Budget (3 Months)
- **Pricing Model**: Subscription-based
  - **Basic**: $9.99/month
  - **Pro**: $19.99/month
  - **Enterprise**: $49.99/month

- **Budget Allocation**:
  - Development: $6,000
  - Marketing: $5,000
  - Operations: $3,000
  - Miscellaneous: $1,000
  - **Total**: $15,000

## KPIs (Top 6)
1. User Sign-Ups: Track the number of email sign-ups on the landing page.
2. Trial Conversions: Measure the percentage of users who convert from trial to paid.
3. User Engagement: Monitor daily active users (DAU) and session duration.
4. Customer Feedback Score: Collect and analyze user feedback through surveys.
5. Social Media Engagement: Track likes, shares, and comments on promotional posts.
6. Retention Rate: Measure the percentage of users who continue using the app after the trial period.

## Risks + Mitigations
- **Market Competition**: High competition from established productivity apps.
```

```
  - **Mitigation**: Perform a thorough competitive analysis to identify unique selling points and refine product positioning.

- **User Resistance**: Potential resistance from users accustomed to existing productivity systems.
  - **Mitigation**: Conduct user research to validate assumptions and adjust projections based on findings.

- **Development Timeline**: Rapid changes in AI technology may outpace development.
  - **Mitigation**: Adopt an agile development approach to allow for flexibility in feature finalization.

## Trade-offs Decided
- **Marketing Strategy vs. Budget Allocation**: The marketing strategy was adjusted to prioritize lower-cost channels initially, ensuring alignment with the $5,000 budget. This includes focusing on organic engagement through social media and content marketing rather than extensive paid advertising.

================ MESSAGE TRACE ================

[PROPOSAL] Research    -> Coordinator | ```json {   "target_users": {     "description": "Busy professionals including consultants, managers, and founders.",   ...
[PROPOSAL] Strategy    -> Coordinator | ```json {   "phases": {     "pre-launch": {       "activities": [         "Finalize product features and user interface....
[PROPOSAL] Finance     -> Coordinator | ```json {   "pricing": {     "model": "Subscription-based",     "tiers": [       {         "name": "Basic",         "pri...
```

```
[CRITIQUE] Critic      -> Coordinator | ```json {
↪  "conflicts": [     {       "issue": "Marketing Strategy
↪  vs. Budget Allocation",       "details": "The market...
[FINAL   ] Coordinator -> ALL         | # FlowPilot Launch
↪  Plan  ## Product Summary FlowPilot is an AI productivity
↪  app designed for busy professionals, transfo...
```

Chapter Summary

In this chapter, we built a multi-agent collaboration system from first principles. We introduced:

- Role specialization
- Structured agent communication
- Shared state management
- Conflict detection and resolution
- Coordinated final synthesis

Each agent operated within a clearly defined boundary. All communication flowed through a shared state. Disagreements were surfaced explicitly and resolved through a governing role.

The result is not parallel prompting, but structured collaboration. This pattern reflects how real teams operate: Specialists contribute. Critics evaluate. Leaders consolidate.

With this foundation, multi-agent systems can scale beyond simple tasks into coordinated decision-making environments.

Project 7: Self-Reflective (Critic) Agent

Key Objectives

- Self-Reflective Agents
- System Overview and Architecture
- System Initialization (LLM Setup)
- Writer Agent — Generating the Initial Report
- Critic Agent — Evaluating and Scoring the Report
- Iterative Refinement Loop
- Running the System and Interpreting Output

10.1 Self-Reflective Agents

In most AI applications, a model generates a response and returns it immediately. However, in real-world environments—especially in corporate settings—outputs are rarely accepted without review. Business reports, strategy documents, proposals, and technical summaries typically go through a **review cycle** before being finalized.

This review process improves clarity, logical consistency, completeness and decision usefulness. Self-reflective agents replicate this process in software. Instead of relying on a single generation step, the system introduces a **critic role** that evaluates the output and suggests improvements. The system then refines the output based on that feedback.

This creates a structured loop: Draft → Critique → Improve.

In this project, we will construct a **Self-Reflective Business Report Generator**. The system will simulate a corporate reporting workflow using two agents:

- **Writer Agent** — generates the initial report
- **Critic Agent** — evaluates the report and provides feedback

The critic assigns a **confidence score** and identifies weaknesses such as unclear statements, missing metrics, unsupported claims and weak action items. If the confidence score is below a threshold, the report is revised using the critic's feedback. The process repeats until the quality reaches an acceptable level.

This system introduces three important capabilities:

- **Feedback Loops** : The system evaluates its own outputs.
- **Confidence Scoring** : The critic estimates the reliability of the generated report.
- **Iterative Refinement** : The report improves across multiple passes instead of relying on a single generation.

This pattern is widely used in advanced reasoning systems, evaluation frameworks, and enterprise AI applications where **quality and reliability are critical**.

10.2 System Overview and Architecture

The system we build follows a simple reflective workflow. Instead of producing a single output, the agent evaluates its own result and improves it through structured feedback.

The architecture uses **two specialized agents**:

- **Writer Agent** — generates the initial business report
- **Critic Agent** — evaluates the report, identifies weaknesses, and assigns a confidence score

The process unfolds in a loop.

1. The Writer Agent produces an initial draft.
2. The Critic Agent reviews the draft and provides structured feedback.

3. The Critic also assigns a **confidence score (0–100)** representing report quality.
4. If the confidence score is below a defined threshold, the Writer revises the report using the feedback.
5. The loop continues until the confidence threshold is reached or the iteration limit is met.

The final result is a report that has been reviewed and improved before being returned to the user.

10.3 System Initialization (LLM Setup)

We begin by setting up the runtime environment required for the reflective agent system.

At this stage, we define:

- The language model configuration
- The API client used to interact with the model
- A reusable helper function for generating responses

The helper function provides a consistent interface for making LLM calls. Both the **Writer Agent** and the **Critic Agent** will use this function to generate outputs.

The following code initializes the model configuration and defines the helper function used throughout the system.

```
# ------------------------------
# Step I: Config & LLM Helper
# ------------------------------
import json
import os
import re
import time
from dataclasses import dataclass, field
from typing import Any, Dict, List, Optional

from openai import OpenAI
```

```
MODEL = os.getenv("OPENAI_MODEL", "gpt-4o-mini")  # safe default;
↪  change if you want
TEMP_WRITER = 0.4
TEMP_CRITIC = 0.0
MAX_ITERS = 3
CONF_THRESHOLD = 80

os.environ["OPENAI_API_KEY"] = OPENAI_API_KEY
client = OpenAI()

# -----------------------------
# LLM helper
# -----------------------------
def llm_text(prompt: str, *, system: str = "", model: str = MODEL,
↪  temperature: float = 0.2) -> str:
    resp = client.responses.create(
        model=model,
        input=[
            {"role": "system", "content": system or "You are
↪  helpful."},
            {"role": "user", "content": prompt},
        ],
        temperature=temperature,
    )
    return (resp.output_text or "").strip()

# -----------------------------
# Step II: Data structures
# -----------------------------
@dataclass
class Critique:
    confidence: int
    issues: List[str] = field(default_factory=list)
    improvements: List[str] = field(default_factory=list)
    missing: List[str] = field(default_factory=list)
    risks: List[str] = field(default_factory=list)
```

```
    summary: str = ""
@dataclass
class IterationLog:
    iteration: int
    confidence: int
    critic_summary: str
    top_issues: List[str] = field(default_factory=list)
```

10.4 Writer Agent - Generating the Initial Report

The first component of the system is the **Writer Agent**. Its role is to generate the initial draft of the business report.

The writer receives:

- the **topic**
- the **context**
- the **intended audience**

Using this information, it produces a structured report in Markdown format. The report follows a simple corporate structure so that it can be easily reviewed and refined in later steps.

Typical sections include:

- Executive Summary
- Background
- Key Updates
- Metrics
- Risks
- Next Steps

At this stage, the goal is not perfection. The writer generates a **reasonable first draft** that will later be evaluated by the critic.

The following code defines the Writer Agent and the function responsible for generating the initial report.

```
# ------------------------------
# Step III: Writer Agent
```

```python
# ----------------------------
WRITER_SYSTEM = (
    "You are a business report writer. Write clearly, concisely,
     ↪ and professionally. "
    "Use headings, bullets, and measurable statements where
     ↪ possible. "
    "Avoid making up precise numbers; if unknown, label as 'TBD' or
     ↪ 'Assumption'.")

def writer_draft(topic: str, context: str, audience: str =
↪ "Leadership team") -> str:
    prompt = f"""
Write a business report in Markdown.
Topic:
{topic}
Audience:
{audience}
Context:
{context}

Requirements:
- Start with an Executive Summary (4-6 bullets)
- Include: Background, Key Updates, Metrics (with TBD where
↪ needed), Risks, Next Steps
- Use crisp, corporate tone
- Keep it 1-2 pages worth of text
Return ONLY Markdown.
"""
    return llm_text(prompt, system=WRITER_SYSTEM,
     ↪ temperature=TEMP_WRITER)

def writer_refine(topic: str, context: str, prior_report_md: str,
↪ critique: Critique, audience: str = "Leadership team") -> str:
    prompt = f"""
You will revise a business report using critic feedback.
Topic:
{topic}
```

```
Audience:
{audience}
Context:
{context}
Current report (Markdown):
{prior_report_md}

Critic feedback (JSON):
{json.dumps({
  "confidence": critique.confidence,
  "issues": critique.issues,
  "missing": critique.missing,
  "risks": critique.risks,
  "improvements": critique.improvements,
  "summary": critique.summary
}, indent=2)}

Revision rules:
- Address the critic's top issues first.
- Add missing sections/items explicitly.
- Do NOT invent precise metrics; use TBD/Assumption labels.
- Keep the structure consistent and polished.
Return ONLY the revised Markdown.
"""
    return llm_text(prompt, system=WRITER_SYSTEM,
     ↪ temperature=TEMP_WRITER)
```

10.5 Critic Agent — Evaluating and Scoring the Report

Once the initial report is generated, the next step is evaluation. This responsibility belongs to the **Critic Agent**. Its role is not to produce new content, but to review the existing report and assess its quality.

The critic examines the report for common issues found in business writing, such as:

- unclear or vague statements
- unsupported claims
- missing metrics or assumptions
- weak action items
- structural gaps in the report

After reviewing the report, the critic returns structured feedback and assigns a **confidence score between 0 and 100**.

The response typically includes:

- a short evaluation summary
- a list of issues detected in the report
- suggested improvements
- missing elements that should be added

This feedback becomes the guidance used to refine the report in the next step. The following code implements the Critic Agent and defines how the report evaluation and confidence scoring are performed.

```
# -----------------------------
# Step IV: Critic Agent
# -----------------------------
CRITIC_SYSTEM = (
    "You are a strict business quality reviewer. "
    "You judge clarity, structure, evidence, assumptions, and
     ↪ actionability. "
    "Be specific and practical. Score confidence 0-100.")

CRITIC_SCHEMA_INSTRUCTIONS = """
Return STRICT JSON with this schema:
{
  "confidence": 0-100 integer,
  "summary": "<1-2 sentences>",
  "issues": ["<top problems>"],
  "missing": ["<missing sections or info>"],
  "risks": ["<risks like ambiguity, unsupported claims, weak
↪  metrics>"],
  "improvements": ["<concrete edits the writer should make next>"]}
```

```
Rules:
- confidence must be an integer 0..100
- issues/improvements should be actionable
- do not include any Markdown or commentary outside JSON
"""

def _safe_json_load(s: str) -> Optional[Dict[str, Any]]:
    s = (s or "").strip()
    if not s:
        return None
    # strip code fences if present
    if s.startswith("```"):
        s = s.strip("`")
        s = s.replace("json\n", "", 1)
        s = s.strip()
    # best effort: extract first {...} block
    if not s.startswith("{"):
        m = re.search(r"\{.*\}", s, flags=re.DOTALL)
        if m:
            s = m.group(0)
    try:
        return json.loads(s)
    except Exception:
        return None

def critic_review(topic: str, context: str, report_md: str,
↪ audience: str = "Leadership team") -> Critique:
    prompt = f"""
Review this business report for leadership consumption.
Topic:
{topic}
Audience:
{audience}
Context:
{context}
Report (Markdown):
{report_md}
```

```
Evaluation criteria:
- Clarity and structure
- Specificity and actionability
- Metrics discipline (no made-up numbers)
- Risks and assumptions called out
- Strong next steps with ownership-like language

{CRITIC_SCHEMA_INSTRUCTIONS}
"""
    raw = llm_text(prompt, system=CRITIC_SYSTEM,
↪   temperature=TEMP_CRITIC)
    data = _safe_json_load(raw)

    # If parsing fails, create a minimal fallback critique
    if not data:
        return Critique(
            confidence=40,
            summary="Critique parsing failed; treat as low
↪   confidence.",
            issues=["Critic output was not valid JSON."],
            improvements=["Re-run critic or tighten prompt
↪   constraints."],)

    # sanitize confidence
    conf = data.get("confidence", 0)
    try:
        conf = int(conf)
    except Exception:
        conf = 0
    conf = max(0, min(100, conf))

    return Critique(
        confidence=conf,
        summary=str(data.get("summary", "")).strip(),
        issues=[str(x) for x in (data.get("issues") or [])][:8],
        missing=[str(x) for x in (data.get("missing") or [])][:8],
```

```
        risks=[str(x) for x in (data.get("risks") or [])][:8],
        improvements=[str(x) for x in (data.get("improvements") or
 ↪  [])][:10],)
```

10.6 Iterative Refinement Loop

With both the Writer and Critic agents defined, the system can now improve its output through an iterative refinement process. The refinement cycle follows these steps:

1. The Writer generates the first draft.
2. The Critic reviews the draft and assigns a confidence score.
3. If the confidence score is below the threshold, the Writer revises the report using the feedback.
4. The Critic evaluates the revised report again.
5. The process continues until the confidence threshold is reached or a maximum number of iterations is completed.

This loop introduces a structured improvement mechanism. Instead of relying on a single generation step, the system progressively improves the report by incorporating feedback from each evaluation round.

The following code implements the self-reflective orchestration loop.

```
# ----------------------------
# Step V: Orchestrator (self-reflective loop)
# ----------------------------
def run_self_reflective_report_agent(
    topic: str,
    context: str,
    *,
    audience: str = "Leadership team",
    max_iters: int = MAX_ITERS,
    confidence_threshold: int = CONF_THRESHOLD,
) -> Dict[str, Any]:
    trace: List[IterationLog] = []
```

```
    report = writer_draft(topic, context, audience=audience)
    critique = critic_review(topic, context, report,
↪   audience=audience)

    trace.append(IterationLog(
        iteration=1,
        confidence=critique.confidence,
        critic_summary=critique.summary,
        top_issues=critique.issues[:3],
    ))

    it = 1
    while critique.confidence < confidence_threshold and it <
     ↪  max_iters:
        it += 1
        report = writer_refine(topic, context, report, critique,
↪   audience=audience)
        critique = critic_review(topic, context, report,
↪   audience=audience)

        trace.append(IterationLog(
            iteration=it,
            confidence=critique.confidence,
            critic_summary=critique.summary,
            top_issues=critique.issues[:3],
        ))

        time.sleep(0.1)

    return {
        "topic": topic,
        "audience": audience,
        "final_confidence": critique.confidence,
        "final_critic_summary": critique.summary,
        "final_report_markdown": report,
        "trace": [t.__dict__ for t in trace]}
```

10.7 Running the System and Interpreting Output

To demonstrate the reflective agent in action, we include a simple execution block.

In this example, we define:

- a report topic
- background context describing the project
- the intended audience for the report

These inputs simulate a realistic corporate reporting scenario. The program prints three outputs:

- **Final Report**
- **Final Confidence Score**
- **Iteration Trace** (A summary of each refinement round)

The following code runs the reflective agent and displays the results.

```
# ------------------------------
# Step VI: Demo
# ------------------------------
if __name__ == "__main__":
    topic = "Q1 Project Update: Customer Analytics Dashboard"
    context = """
We are building an internal-facing customer analytics dashboard for
↪  sales and customer success.
Current status:
- MVP is feature-complete but needs performance improvements and UX
↪  polish.
- Data sources are stable; data freshness is daily, moving to
↪  hourly is planned.
Constraints:
- Team: 2 engineers, 1 analyst, shared designer.
- Next leadership review is in 10 days.
Risks:
- Stakeholders want more metrics than we can safely validate right
↪  now.
- Performance issues on large accounts.
```

```
Goals:
- Ship a pilot to 3 teams, gather feedback, and define v1 scope.
"""
    result = run_self_reflective_report_agent(
        topic,
        context,
        audience="VP + Directors",
        max_iters=3,
        confidence_threshold=80,
    )

    print("\n================ FINAL REPORT (Markdown)
    ↪  ================\n")
    print(result["final_report_markdown"])

    print("\n================ FINAL CONFIDENCE ================\n")
    print(result["final_confidence"], "-",
    ↪  result["final_critic_summary"])

    print("\n================ ITERATION TRACE ================\n")
    for row in result["trace"]:
        print(f"Iter {row['iteration']}:
        ↪  confidence={row['confidence']} |
        ↪  {row['critic_summary']}")
        if row["top_issues"]:
            print("  Top issues:", "; ".join(row["top_issues"]))
```

```
================ FINAL REPORT (Markdown) ================

```markdown
# Q1 Project Update: Customer Analytics Dashboard

## Executive Summary
- **Project Status:** MVP is feature-complete; performance
↪  improvements and UX polish are in progress.
```
```

```
- **Data Freshness:** Currently daily; transitioning to
↪ hourly updates planned for Q2 2024.
- **Team Composition:** 2 engineers, 1 analyst, and a shared
↪ designer.
- **Next Review:** Leadership review scheduled in 10 days.
- **Goals:** Pilot launch to 3 teams to gather feedback and
↪ define version 1 scope.

## Background
The Customer Analytics Dashboard is an internal tool
↪ designed to enhance the capabilities of our sales and
↪ customer success teams. The dashboard aims to provide
↪ actionable insights into customer behavior, enabling
↪ teams to make data-driven decisions.

## Key Updates
- **MVP Status:** The Minimum Viable Product (MVP) is now
↪ feature-complete. Key functionalities have been
↪ implemented, but ongoing efforts are focused on:
  - Performance optimization for large accounts.
  - User Experience (UX) enhancements based on initial
   ↪ feedback.

- **Data Sources:** All data sources are stable. Current
↪ data refresh frequency is daily, with plans to upgrade
↪ to hourly updates by Q2 2024.

## Metrics
- **MVP Completion:** 100% feature-complete
- **Data Freshness:** Daily (transitioning to hourly,
↪ planned for Q2 2024)
- **Pilot Teams:** 3 teams selected for pilot testing
- **Feedback Collection Timeline:** 2 weeks post-pilot
↪ launch
```

```
- **Success Metrics for Pilot:**
  - User satisfaction score (TBD)
  - Engagement levels (TBD)
  - Adoption rate (TBD)

## Risks
- **Stakeholder Expectations:** There is a risk that stakeholders are requesting more metrics than can be validated within the current timeline, which may affect project scope and timeline.
- **Performance Issues:** Current performance issues on large accounts could hinder user experience and adoption. Specific performance thresholds are targeted at a response time of under 2 seconds for 95% of queries.

## Next Steps
1. **Performance Improvements:**
   - **Owner:** Engineer 1
   - **Timeline:** Complete by March 15, 2024, before pilot launch.

2. **UX Polish:**
   - **Owner:** Shared Designer
   - **Timeline:** Finalize enhancements by March 15, 2024, before pilot launch.

3. **Pilot Launch:**
   - **Owner:** Analyst
   - **Timeline:** Schedule pilot launch to 3 selected teams by March 20, 2024, and define feedback mechanisms.

4. **Prepare for Leadership Review:**
   - **Owner:** Project Manager
```

```
  - **Timeline:** Compile findings and updates for the
    ↪ upcoming leadership review on March 10, 2024.

---

This report outlines the current status and future direction
↪ of the Customer Analytics Dashboard project. Continued
↪ focus on performance, stakeholder alignment, and clear
↪ accountability will be critical for successful
↪ implementation.
```

================ FINAL CONFIDENCE ================

```
75 - The report provides a clear overview of the project
↪ status but lacks specificity in metrics and some action
↪ items. It effectively outlines risks but could benefit
↪ from more detailed next steps.
```

================ ITERATION TRACE ================

```
Iter 1: confidence=75 | The report provides a clear overview
↪ of the project status but lacks specificity in metrics
↪ and next steps. It needs stronger actionability and
↪ clarity around risks and assumptions.
  Top issues: Metrics are vague and lack specific timelines
  ↪ for the transition to hourly updates.; Next steps are
  ↪ not assigned to specific team members or roles.
Iter 2: confidence=75 | The report provides a solid overview
↪ of the project status but lacks specificity in timelines
↪ and metrics, which could hinder decision-making for
↪ leadership.
```

```
  Top issues: Unclear timelines marked as TBD create
  ↪  ambiguity.; Lack of defined success metrics for the
  ↪  pilot may lead to misalignment on goals.
Iter 3: confidence=75 | The report provides a clear overview
↪  of the project status but lacks specificity in metrics
↪  and some action items. It effectively outlines risks but
↪  could benefit from more detailed next steps.
  Top issues: Metrics are vague and labeled as TBD without
  ↪  clear definitions or baselines.; Next steps lack
  ↪  specific deadlines for feedback collection and
  ↪  analysis.
```

Chapter Summary

In this chapter, we built a **Self-Reflective (Critic) Agent** that improves its own outputs through structured feedback.

The system introduced three important capabilities:

- **Feedback loops** where the output is evaluated before being finalized
- **Confidence scoring** to estimate the quality of the generated report
- **Iterative refinement** where the system improves the report across multiple passes

Using a **Writer Agent** and a **Critic Agent**, we implemented a simple but powerful workflow:

- Generate
- Evaluate
- Refine.

This pattern mirrors how real organizations review important documents before sharing them with stakeholders. Self-reflective architectures are widely used in advanced AI systems where **quality, reliability, and reasoning accuracy** are critical.

Observability and Evaluation Framework

Key Objectives

- Why Observability Matters for AI Agents
- System Architecture of the Incident Diagnosis Agent
- Implementing the Observability Layer
- Configuration and LLM Setup
- Building the Observability Component
- Implementing the Incident Knowledge Retrieval Tool
- Generating Troubleshooting Recommendations
- Building the Incident Diagnosis Agent
- Running the Agent
- Key Takeaways

11.1 Why Observability Matters for AI Agents

As AI agents become more capable, they are increasingly integrated into real-world systems such as customer support platforms, research assistants, monitoring tools, and enterprise automation workflows.

However, these agents differ significantly from traditional software applications. Their outputs are generated through probabilistic models, multi-step reasoning processes, and interactions with external tools. Because of this, their internal behavior is often opaque.

Consider a scenario where an AI agent is responsible for diagnosing system incidents. If the agent provides an incorrect recommendation, developers need to understand several key questions:

- What reasoning steps did the agent follow?
- Which tools or data sources were used?
- How long did the process take?
- How many tokens were consumed?
- Where did the failure occur?

Without proper observability, answering these questions becomes extremely difficult. Observability provides visibility into the **internal operations of AI agents**. By capturing execution traces, performance metrics, and response outputs, developers can monitor how agents behave and identify potential issues.

In traditional software engineering, observability is achieved through logging, metrics, and monitoring systems. In AI systems, the same principles apply, but they must be extended to capture additional information such as reasoning chains, tool usage, and token consumption.

By implementing observability, we gain the ability to:

- Debug agent failures more effectively
- Monitor operational costs
- Measure system performance
- Improve reliability over time

In this chapter, we extend our incident diagnosis agent with a lightweight **observability framework** that records key execution events and performance metrics. This approach mirrors how production AI systems are monitored in modern engineering environments.

The result is an agent that is not only capable of diagnosing problems but is also **transparent, measurable, and maintainable**.

11.2 System Architecture of the Incident Diagnosis Agent

The goal of this system is to diagnose incidents and **record and monitor how the agent arrives at its conclusions**. To achieve this, the architecture separates the system into multiple components, each responsible for a specific function.

At a high level, the system processes an incident report, analyzes it using available knowledge, generates troubleshooting recommendations, and records all intermediate steps and performance metrics.

The workflow can be summarized as follows:

Issue Description → Agent Analysis → Knowledge Retrieval → Solution Generation → Observability Logging → Monitoring Output

The architecture contains the following components.

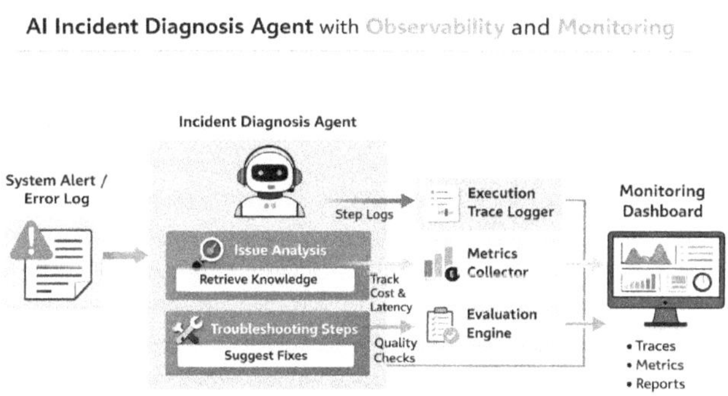

System Alert or Issue Description

The process begins when a user or monitoring system provides an **incident description**. This could include error messages, system alerts, or logs that describe a problem occurring in a software system.

Example: Database connection timeout errors are occurring in the production environment. This input becomes the **starting point for the agent's reasoning process**.

Incident Diagnosis Agent

The **Incident Diagnosis Agent** acts as the central component of the system. Its role is to analyze the incoming issue and determine possible causes and solutions.

The agent performs several tasks:

- Interpreting the issue description
- Retrieving relevant diagnostic knowledge
- Generating troubleshooting steps
- Coordinating interactions with tools

This agent behaves similarly to a **technical support engineer**, analyzing system symptoms and recommending possible fixes.

Knowledge Retrieval Component

To assist with diagnosis, the system uses a **knowledge retrieval mechanism** that searches a small incident knowledge base. This component maps known issues to potential explanations or causes.

For example:

Incident Pattern	Possible Explanation
Database connection timeout	Overloaded database server or network latency
API latency spike	High traffic or slow downstream services
Memory leak	Continuous memory growth due to unreleased resources

This knowledge helps the agent **ground its reasoning in known technical patterns**.

Solution Generation

Once the issue is analyzed, the system generates **troubleshooting recommendations** using the language model.

The model evaluates the analysis and produces actionable steps such as checking system resource utilization, inspecting network connectivity, reviewing configuration settings or investigating traffic spikes. These suggestions simulate the recommendations a **DevOps engineer or system administrator** might provide.

Execution Trace Logger

One of the most important components in this architecture is the **execution trace logger**. Every action taken by the agent is recorded, including:

- Input queries
- Intermediate reasoning steps
- Tool outputs
- Generated responses
- Execution timestamps

These traces provide **full visibility into the agent's behavior**. Without this layer, debugging AI systems becomes extremely difficult.

Metrics Collector

The metrics collector tracks important **operational measurements** during execution. Examples include:

- Response latency
- Token usage
- Total execution time

Monitoring these metrics allows developers to evaluate **performance and operational cost**.

Observability Output

Finally, all traces and metrics are stored as structured logs that can later be analyzed or visualized. This observability output allows developers to answer important questions such as:

- Why did the agent produce a particular recommendation?

- How expensive was the query?
- Which step consumed the most time?

This level of transparency is essential when deploying AI agents in **production environments**. By combining the incident diagnosis logic with an observability layer, this architecture ensures that the agent is not only **useful** but also **transparent, measurable, and maintainable**.

11.3 Implementing the Observability Layer

In the previous sections, we discussed why observability is important and how it fits into the architecture of our incident diagnosis system. The next step is to **implement the observability layer that records how the agent operates during execution**.

Rather than embedding logging logic directly inside the agent code, a better engineering practice is to **separate observability from the agent logic**. This keeps the system modular and allows the same monitoring system to be reused across different agents.

In this project, we implement a lightweight observability component called **ExecutionTracer**. This component is responsible for recording the actions performed by the agent while it analyzes incidents and generates solutions.

The tracer performs three key tasks:

- **Recording agent steps** — logs each major action taken by the agent

- **Tracking operational metrics** — captures execution time and token usage

- **Saving execution traces** — stores logs in a structured JSON file for later inspection

With this design, every time the agent performs an operation—such as analyzing an incident or generating a solution—the tracer records the corresponding input and output. This approach gives developers clear visibility into how the agent behaves during runtime.

11.4 Configuration and LLM Setup

Before implementing the agent components, we begin by configuring the environment and initializing the language model client that will generate troubleshooting recommendations.

```
import os
import json
import time
from datetime import datetime
from dotenv import load_dotenv
from openai import OpenAI

os.environ["OPENAI_API_KEY"] = OPENAI_API_KEY
client = OpenAI()
```

11.5 Building the Observability Component

In this section, we implement the **observability component** of the system. The goal of this component is to record how the agent behaves during execution so that developers can inspect its actions, monitor performance, and analyze system behavior after a run.

To achieve this, we introduce a utility class called **ExecutionTracer**.

The responsibility of this component is to maintain a structured record of the agent's execution. It tracks the sequence of operations performed by the agent and stores performance statistics generated during the process.

The observability component performs three primary functions.

1. Maintaining the Trace Structure

The tracer begins by defining a structured container that stores all execution data. This structure contains steps and metrics. It allows the system to maintain both **behavioral logs** and **performance measurements** in a single place.

2. Recording Agent Execution Steps

The tracer provides a method that records each step performed by the agent. Whenever the agent completes an operation—such as analyzing an incident or generating troubleshooting recommendations—the tracer logs the name of the step, input received, output generated and the timestamp. This helps create a **chronological trace of the agent's workflow**.

3. Tracking Performance Metrics

In addition to logging execution steps, the tracer also records important performance metrics like execution latency and token usage. These measurements help evaluate both **system performance** and **operational cost**.

4. Saving the Execution Trace

After the agent completes its task, the tracer stores all collected information in a structured trace file. The trace is saved in **JSON format**, which provides several advantages:

- easy to read and inspect
- simple to integrate with monitoring tools
- suitable for further analysis or visualization

This saved trace acts as a complete **execution log of the agent run**, enabling developers to review how the system behaved during the task.

With the observability component implemented, the system now has the ability to record and monitor agent behavior.

```
###############################
# OBSERVABILITY COMPONENT
###############################
class ExecutionTracer:

    def __init__(self):
        self.trace = {
            "steps": [],
            "metrics": {}}
```

```
    def log_step(self, name, input_data, output_data):
        self.trace["steps"].append({
            "step": name,
            "input": input_data,
            "output": output_data,
            "timestamp": str(datetime.utcnow())})

    def log_metrics(self, latency, tokens):
        self.trace["metrics"] = {
            "latency_seconds": latency,
            "token_usage": tokens}

    def save_trace(self, filename="agent_trace.json"):
        with open(filename, "w") as f:
            json.dump(self.trace, f, indent=2)
```

11.6 Implementing the Incident Knowledge Retrieval Tool

Before generating troubleshooting recommendations, the agent first needs to **interpret the incoming issue description**. To support this, we introduce a simple knowledge retrieval mechanism that maps common incident patterns to possible explanations.

The system maintains a small **incident knowledge base** that contains known system issues and their likely causes. Each entry links an incident pattern (for example, database timeouts or memory leaks) to a short diagnostic explanation.

When the agent receives an issue description, the retrieval function scans the knowledge base to check whether the description contains any known patterns. If a match is found, the corresponding explanation is returned and used as the initial analysis of the problem.

If no match is detected, the system returns a default message indicating that the issue is not present in the knowledge base. This ensures the agent can still proceed with generating recommendations even when the incident is unfamiliar.

```
##################################
# TOOL: Retrieve Knowledge
##################################
incident_database = {
    "database connection timeout":
        "Possible causes include overloaded DB server or network
        ↪ issues.",
    "api latency spike":
        "May be caused by high traffic or slow downstream
        ↪ services.",
    "memory leak":
        "Application memory usage growing continuously without
        ↪ release."}

def retrieve_incident_knowledge(issue):
    for key in incident_database:
        if key in issue.lower():
            return incident_database[key]
    return "No direct match found in incident database."
```

11.7 Generating Troubleshooting Recommendations

After retrieving the initial analysis, the next step is to generate **troubleshooting recommendations**.

The system constructs a prompt using the retrieved analysis and sends it to the language model. The model then produces a set of actionable steps that could help diagnose or resolve the issue.

Along with the generated response, the function also returns the **token usage** associated with the request. This information is later used by the observability component to track system cost and performance.

This step allows the agent to transform a simple incident description into **practical troubleshooting guidance**.

```
##################################
# TOOL: Suggest Fix
```

```
##################################
def suggest_fix(analysis):

    prompt = f"""
    Based on the following system issue analysis, suggest
↪   troubleshooting steps:

    {analysis}
    """

    response = client.chat.completions.create(
        model="gpt-4o-mini",
        messages=[{"role":"user","content":prompt}])

    return response.choices[0].message.content,
     ↪  response.usage.total_tokens
```

11.8 Building the Incident Diagnosis Agent

After implementing the observability component and the supporting tools, we now build the **main agent that orchestrates the entire workflow**. The Incident-DiagnosisAgent acts as the central controller that coordinates incident analysis, solution generation, and observability tracking.

The agent integrates three key components:

- Knowledge retrieval
- Language model reasoning
- Execution tracing

Agent Initialization

When the agent is created, it initializes an instance of the **ExecutionTracer**. This tracer will record the steps performed by the agent and capture performance metrics during execution.

By attaching the tracer to the agent, we ensure that every important action taken by the system can be monitored and logged.

Running the Agent Workflow

The core logic of the agent is implemented in the `run()` method. This method receives an **issue description** and executes the full diagnostic workflow.

The workflow follows three main stages:

1. **Incident Analysis**: The agent first analyzes the incoming issue using the knowledge retrieval tool.
   This step attempts to match the issue description with known incident patterns stored in the knowledge base. The result of this analysis is then recorded by the observability system so that the reasoning step can be inspected later.

2. **Solution Generation**: Once the incident has been analyzed, the agent invokes the language model to generate troubleshooting recommendations. The model receives the diagnostic explanation and produces actionable steps that could help resolve the issue. This step is also recorded by the tracer, capturing both the analysis used as input and the generated response.

3. **Performance Tracking**: After the solution is generated, the agent calculates the **total execution time** and records the number of **tokens consumed** during the language model interaction. These metrics are stored by the tracer and later written to the execution trace file.

Saving the Execution Trace

Once the workflow is complete, the tracer saves the entire execution record. This trace contains:

- the sequence of agent actions
- the inputs and outputs of each step
- the overall performance metrics

The trace file provides a clear view of how the agent processed the request, making it easier to debug issues or evaluate system behavior.

Final Output

Finally, the agent returns the generated troubleshooting recommendations to the user. The user receives the solution, while the system retains a detailed record of the agent's internal operations for monitoring and analysis.

```
################################
# AGENT
################################
class IncidentDiagnosisAgent:
    def __init__(self):
        self.tracer = ExecutionTracer()

    def run(self, issue_description):

        start_time = time.time()
        total_tokens = 0

        # Step 1: Analyze issue
        analysis = retrieve_incident_knowledge(issue_description)

        self.tracer.log_step(
            "incident_analysis",
            issue_description,
            analysis)

        # Step 2: Generate troubleshooting steps
        solution, tokens = suggest_fix(analysis)
        total_tokens += tokens
        self.tracer.log_step(
            "generate_solution",
            analysis,
            solution)

        latency = time.time() - start_time
        self.tracer.log_metrics(
            latency,
            total_tokens)
```

```
        self.tracer.save_trace()
        return solution
```

11.9 Running the Agent

The final step of the project is to execute the agent and observe how the system processes an incident request end-to-end. This section acts as the **entry point of the program**, where the agent is initialized and provided with an issue description to diagnose.

This final step demonstrates how all the components like knowledge retrieval, language model reasoning, and observability tracking, work together to form a complete incident diagnosis system.

```
################################
# RUN AGENT
################################

if __name__ == "__main__":
    agent = IncidentDiagnosisAgent()
    issue = "Our system is facing database connection timeout
↪   errors."
    result = agent.run(issue)

    print("\n===== AGENT RESPONSE =====\n")
    print(result)
```

```
===== AGENT RESPONSE =====

To troubleshoot the issue based on the analysis of a
 ↪  potentially overloaded database (DB) server or network
 ↪  issues, you can follow these systematic steps:

### Step 1: Assess Current Server Load
```

```
1. **Check Server Metrics:**
   - Monitor CPU usage, memory consumption, and disk I/O on the database server. Use tools like `top`, `htop`, or system monitoring software (e.g., Nagios, Grafana).

2. **Analyze Database Performance:**
   - Check database-specific metrics such as query response time, number of active connections, and transaction throughput.
   - Use the database's performance monitoring tools or logs (e.g., `EXPLAIN` commands for SQL databases).

### Step 2: Review Database Configuration
1. **Configuration Tuning:**
   - Ensure that the database’s configuration parameters are optimized for your workload (e.g., buffer sizes, connection pool size).
   - Adjust settings based on the observed load and database performance.

### Step 3: Identify Slow Queries
1. **Query Analysis:**
   - Identify and optimize slow-running queries. Use SQL execution plans to pinpoint inefficiencies.
   - Implement indexes if they are missing on frequently accessed tables.

### Step 4: Check for Blocking or Deadlocks
1. **Monitor Locks:**
   - Investigate for locking issues by checking for blocked processes or deadlocks in the database.
   - Resolve any contention issues by optimizing queries or adjusting transaction isolation levels.
```

```
### Step 5: Network Diagnostics
1. **Test Network Performance:**
   - Use tools like `ping`, `tracert`, or `traceroute` to
    ↪ check network latency and packet loss between the
    ↪ client and the server.
   - Check for saturation on network interfaces or abnormal
    ↪ behaviors in the network.

2. **Review Firewall and Security Settings:**
   - Ensure that firewalls are not inadvertently dropping
    ↪ packets or causing latency. Check for any new
    ↪ security rules that may affect connectivity.

### Step 6: Log Analysis
1. **Review Logs:**
   - Check the database server logs for any errors,
    ↪ warnings, or unexpected behaviors during peak usage
    ↪ times.
   - Look for network-related logs on both the server and
    ↪ client-side.

### Step 7: Load Testing
1. **Simulate Load:**
   - Conduct load testing to reproduce the issue. This can
    ↪ help narrow down if the problem truly lies with the
    ↪ database capacity or the network.
   - Use tools like JMeter or LoadRunner to simulate user
    ↪ traffic and monitor system performance.

### Step 8: Scaling Considerations
1. **Consider Scaling Solutions:**
   - If the database server is consistently overloaded,
    ↪ consider vertical scaling (upgrading hardware) or
    ↪ horizontal scaling (sharding or clustering).
```

```
   - Review database performance characteristics in a scaled
    ↪  environment if possible.

### Step 9: Seek Expert Help
1. **Database Admin Consultation:**
   - If you're unable to identify the issue, consult with a
    ↪  database administrator or network specialist for
    ↪  deeper analysis and recommendations.

By following these troubleshooting steps, you should be able
 ↪  to pinpoint whether the problem lies with the database
 ↪  server's performance or if it's related to network
 ↪  connectivity issues.
```

11.10 Key Takeaways

In this project, we built an **AI-powered Incident Diagnosis Agent** capable of analyzing system issues and generating troubleshooting recommendations.

More importantly, we introduced an **observability layer** that records how the agent operates during execution. This allows developers to monitor system behavior, inspect reasoning steps, and track performance metrics such as latency and token usage. Through this project, we combined three essential components of production-grade AI systems:

- **Knowledge retrieval** to interpret incident patterns
- **Language model reasoning** to generate troubleshooting guidance
- **Observability mechanisms** to monitor and evaluate system behavior

This design ensures that the agent is not only capable of solving problems but is also **transparent, traceable, and easier to maintain**. In real-world AI systems, observability plays a crucial role in debugging failures, monitoring operational costs, and improving system reliability over time.

Cost-Aware Multi-Model Routing Agent

Key Objectives

- Understanding Cost-Aware Model Routing
- System Architecture of the Cost-Aware Routing Agent
- Defining Model Profiles
- Estimating Task Complexity
- Managing Budget Constraints
- Estimating Request Cost
- Designing the Routing Engine
- Executing the Selected Model
- Monitoring Routing Decisions
- Building the Cost-Aware Routing Agent
- Running the Cost-Aware Routing Agent
- Key Takeaways

12.1 Understanding Cost-Aware Model Routing

As AI applications scale, the cost of running language models becomes a major operational factor. Each model interaction consumes computational resources and contributes to the overall system cost. In many enterprise environments, thousands or even millions of requests may be processed daily. If every request is sent to the most powerful model, operational costs can increase dramatically.

At the same time, many requests are relatively simple and do not require advanced reasoning capabilities. For example, a request asking for a brief definition or summary does not require the same computational power as a request asking for a system architecture design.

This creates an important engineering challenge:

How can we allocate AI resources efficiently while maintaining response quality?

Cost-aware routing addresses this problem by introducing a **decision layer** between the user request and the model execution stage. Instead of sending every request directly to a model, the system first evaluates the request and determines which model is best suited for the task.

The routing decision typically considers several factors:

- **Task Complexity** Some tasks require advanced reasoning, while others are relatively simple.
- **Latency Requirements** Certain applications require faster responses and may prioritize low-latency models.
- **Operational Budget** Organizations often operate under cost constraints that limit how expensive each request can be.

By considering these factors, the system can dynamically select the most appropriate model for each request.

The routing agent evaluates the incoming query, estimates its complexity, checks available budget, and selects a model that provides the best balance between **performance, latency, and cost**.

This approach mirrors how many real-world AI systems operate today, allowing organizations to build **scalable and economically sustainable AI applications**.

12.2 System Architecture of the Cost-Aware Routing Agent

Before implementing the routing logic, it is important to understand how the different components of the system interact with each other. The Cost-Aware Routing Agent is designed as a modular system where each component handles a specific responsibility within the routing workflow.

At a high level, the system receives a user query, evaluates its complexity, determines the most appropriate model based on budget and latency considerations, and then executes the selected model to generate a response.

The architecture consists of the following key components.

- **User Query** : The process begins when a user submits a request. This request may vary in complexity—from simple informational queries to complex analytical or architectural questions. The query acts as the **input signal** that triggers the routing pipeline.
- **Complexity Analyzer** : The first component that processes the query is the **Complexity Analyzer**. Its role is to estimate how difficult the task is before invoking a language model. The analyzer evaluates the query using simple rule-based heuristics, such as detecting specific keywords or evaluating query length. Based on this analysis, the task is classified into one of three categories: **Low Complexity, Medium Complexity or High Complexity**
- **Routing Engine** : Once the complexity level is identified, the request is passed to the **Routing Engine**. The routing engine is responsible for selecting the most suitable model by considering task complexity, latency preference and budget available for inference. Instead of blindly selecting a model, the routing engine evaluates multiple candidates and selects the one that best satisfies these constraints.
- **Budget Manager** : It tracks the amount of money available for AI inference. Each request consumes a certain amount of budget depending on the model used and the number of tokens processed. Before executing a request, the routing system checks whether enough budget remains to

safely process the request. If the estimated cost exceeds the available budget, the system automatically selects a low cost model. This mechanism prevents the system from exceeding its operational cost limits.

- **Model Execution Layer** : Once a model has been selected, the request is forwarded to the **Model Execution Layer**. This component sends the query to the chosen language model and retrieves the generated response. The system also records token usage and response latency during execution.
- **Routing Observability** : To make the routing decisions transparent, the system records routing events such as detected query complexity, selected model, estimated cost, actual token usage and remaining budget. These logs allow developers to inspect how the routing system behaved and evaluate whether the routing decisions were optimal.

By organizing the system into these components, the routing agent achieves three important goals:

- Efficient resource utilization
- Controlled operational cost
- Transparent routing decisions

12.3 Defining Model Profiles

For the routing agent to make intelligent decisions, it must first understand the **characteristics of the available models**. Different models vary in terms of capability, response latency, and operational cost. Instead of treating all models the same, the routing system defines **model profiles** that describe these attributes.

A model profile acts as a configuration record that stores key information about each model. These profiles allow the routing engine to compare models and determine which one is most suitable for a given request.

Each model profile in the system includes several important attributes.

- **Model Name** : The identifier used when calling the model through the API.
- **Latency Category** : An indicator of how quickly the model typically responds. In this project, models are categorized as *fast*, *medium*, or *slow*.

- **Quality Level** : A relative measure of the model's capability. More powerful models provide better reasoning and higher-quality responses but are typically more expensive.
- **Token Cost** : The operational cost associated with processing input and output tokens. Tracking this information allows the system to estimate how expensive a request will be before executing it.
- **Supported Complexity Levels** : Each model is assigned the types of tasks it is capable of handling. For example, lightweight models may support low and medium complexity tasks, while more advanced models are reserved for high-complexity problems.

By defining these attributes, the routing agent gains a structured understanding of the available models. Instead of making arbitrary decisions, the system can evaluate models using **objective criteria such as cost, latency, and capability**.

Implementing the Model Profiles

With the conceptual structure defined, we now implement the model profiles in the system.

```
import os
import time
from dotenv import load_dotenv
from openai import OpenAI

load_dotenv()

os.environ["OPENAI_API_KEY"] = OPENAI_API_KEY
client = OpenAI()

######################################################
# MODEL CONFIGURATION
######################################################

MODEL_PROFILES = {
    "cheap_model": {
```

```
        "name": "gpt-4o-mini",
        "latency": "fast",
        "quality": "good",
        "input_cost_per_1k": 0.00015,
        "output_cost_per_1k": 0.00060,
        "complexity_support": ["low", "medium"]
    },
    "balanced_model": {
        "name": "gpt-4.1-mini",
        "latency": "medium",
        "quality": "better",
        "input_cost_per_1k": 0.00040,
        "output_cost_per_1k": 0.00160,
        "complexity_support": ["medium", "high"]
    },
    "powerful_model": {
        "name": "gpt-4.1",
        "latency": "slow",
        "quality": "best",
        "input_cost_per_1k": 0.00200,
        "output_cost_per_1k": 0.00800,
        "complexity_support": ["high"]
    }
}
```

12.4 Estimating Task Complexity

Before the routing system can select an appropriate model, it must first determine **how difficult the incoming request is**. To enable this decision-making process, the system includes a **Complexity Analyzer**. The purpose of this component is to evaluate the incoming query and classify it into one of three categories:

- **Low Complexity** – simple informational requests such as definitions, short explanations, or basic summaries
- **Medium Complexity** – moderately detailed questions requiring explanation or structured responses

- **High Complexity** – analytical or design-oriented tasks that require deeper reasoning and more sophisticated responses

The complexity analyzer uses a **rule-based approach** to estimate task difficulty. It scans the incoming query for specific keywords that typically indicate simple or complex tasks. For example, queries containing words such as *define*, *list*, or *briefly explain* are often simple informational requests. In contrast, queries containing words like *design*, *analyze*, *optimize*, or *architecture* usually represent more complex tasks.

The analyzer also considers the **length of the query**. Longer queries often indicate that the user is requesting deeper analysis or more detailed responses.

By combining keyword detection with query length evaluation, the system can quickly estimate the complexity of the task before selecting a model. This step is important because it prevents the system from unnecessarily using powerful and expensive models for tasks that can be solved by smaller models.

In the next code segment, we implement the **ComplexityAnalyzer**, which performs this classification and provides the routing engine with the complexity label required for model selection.

```
#####################################################
# COMPLEXITY ANALYZER
#####################################################

class ComplexityAnalyzer:
    """
    Rule-based complexity estimator.
    In production, this can be replaced with an LLM classifier
    or a learned scoring model.
    """

    def __init__(self):
        self.low_keywords = [
            "what is", "define", "briefly", "summary", "list",
             ↪ "short note"]
        self.high_keywords = [
            "design", "architecture", "optimize", "analyze",
             ↪ "compare",
```

```
        "strategy", "multi-agent", "trade-off", "scalable",
          ↪ "production"]

    def detect(self, query: str) -> str:
        query_lower = query.lower()

        for keyword in self.high_keywords:
            if keyword in query_lower:
                return "high"
        for keyword in self.low_keywords:
            if keyword in query_lower:
                return "low"
        if len(query.split()) > 25:
            return "high"
        return "medium"
```

12.5 Managing Budget Constraints

Once the system understands the complexity of the request, the next important factor to consider is **budget availability**. In production environments, AI systems often operate under predefined cost limits. Each model invocation consumes tokens, and those tokens translate directly into operational cost.

If the routing system always selected the most powerful model, the cost of running the system could quickly become unsustainable. To prevent this, the routing agent incorporates a **Budget Manager** that tracks how much budget remains and determines whether a particular model can be used safely.

The Budget Manager performs three key responsibilities:

- **Tracking Total Budget** : At the start of the system, a total budget is defined. This represents the maximum amount that can be spent on model inference during a given session or operational period.
- **Monitoring Remaining Budget** : As requests are processed, the system continuously tracks how much budget has already been consumed and how much remains available.

- **Validating Model Costs** : Before executing a request, the routing system estimates the potential cost of the request and checks whether enough budget is available. If the estimated cost exceeds the remaining budget, the routing engine automatically selects a cheaper model.

This mechanism ensures that the AI system operates within its financial constraints while still delivering useful responses.

In large-scale AI deployments, similar budgeting mechanisms are used to ensure that systems remain **economically sustainable**, especially when processing large volumes of requests.

```
##########################################################
# BUDGET MANAGER
##########################################################

class BudgetManager:
    """
    Tracks total and remaining budget across requests.
    """
    def __init__(self, total_budget_usd: float):
        self.total_budget_usd = total_budget_usd
        self.spent_budget_usd = 0.0
    def get_remaining_budget(self) -> float:
        return round(self.total_budget_usd - self.spent_budget_usd,
         ↪ 6)
    def can_spend(self, estimated_cost: float) -> bool:
        return self.get_remaining_budget() >= estimated_cost
    def register_cost(self, actual_cost: float) -> None:
        self.spent_budget_usd += actual_cost
```

12.6 Estimating Request Cost

Before selecting a model, the routing system must estimate **how expensive the request might be**. Since language models charge based on token usage, the system needs a way to approximate the cost of executing a query before sending it to a model.

The estimation considers two factors:

- **Estimated Input Tokens** : An approximate count of tokens required to process the user query, derived from the length of the query.
- **Estimated Output Tokens** : An estimated size of the model's response. More complex queries are expected to produce longer outputs.

Using these estimates, the system calculates a **predicted cost for each candidate model** based on its token pricing profile. This allows the routing engine to determine whether the model can be used within the available budget.

After execution, the system also calculates the **actual cost** using the real token usage reported by the model. This ensures that the budget manager maintains accurate cost tracking for subsequent requests.

```
############################################################
# COST ESTIMATION
############################################################

def estimate_request_cost(model_profile: dict,
                          estimated_input_tokens: int,
                          estimated_output_tokens: int) -> float:
    input_cost = (estimated_input_tokens / 1000) *
↪   model_profile["input_cost_per_1k"]
    output_cost = (estimated_output_tokens / 1000) *
↪   model_profile["output_cost_per_1k"]
    return round(input_cost + output_cost, 6)


def calculate_actual_cost(model_profile: dict,
                          prompt_tokens: int,
                          completion_tokens: int) -> float:
    input_cost = (prompt_tokens / 1000) *
↪   model_profile["input_cost_per_1k"]
    output_cost = (completion_tokens / 1000) *
↪   model_profile["output_cost_per_1k"]
    return round(input_cost + output_cost, 6)
```

12.7 Designing the Routing Engine

With model profiles, complexity estimation, and budget management in place, the final step is to implement the **routing engine**. This component is responsible for selecting the most appropriate model for each request.

The routing engine evaluates several factors before making a decision:

- **Task Complexity** : The complexity label produced by the complexity analyzer determines which models are capable of handling the request.
- **Latency Preference** : Different applications have different performance requirements. Some systems prioritize fast responses, while others prioritize higher quality outputs. The routing engine ranks candidate models based on the selected latency preference.
- **Budget Availability** : Before selecting a model, the routing system estimates the cost of executing the request.

Using these factors, the routing engine evaluates all candidate models and selects the one that provides the best balance between **capability, latency, and cost**.

If no suitable model can be used within the available budget, the system falls back to the lowest-cost model to ensure the request can still be processed.

This routing logic forms the core decision-making layer of the system. It allows the agent to dynamically allocate computational resources while maintaining control over operational costs.

```
#####################################################
# ROUTING ENGINE
#####################################################

class RoutingEngine:
    """
    Selects the most appropriate model based on:
    - query complexity
    - remaining budget
    - latency preference
    """
```

```
def __init__(self, model_profiles: dict):
    self.model_profiles = model_profiles

def rank_models(self, complexity: str, latency_preference: str)
 ↪  -> list:
    candidates = []

    for profile in self.model_profiles.values():
        if complexity in profile["complexity_support"]:
            candidates.append(profile)

    if not candidates:
        candidates = [self.model_profiles["cheap_model"]]

    if latency_preference == "fast":
        latency_rank = {"fast": 0, "medium": 1, "slow": 2}
        candidates.sort(key=lambda x:
↪  latency_rank[x["latency"]])
    elif latency_preference == "balanced":
        latency_rank = {"medium": 0, "fast": 1, "slow": 2}
        candidates.sort(key=lambda x:
↪  latency_rank[x["latency"]])
    else:  # quality
        quality_rank = {"best": 0, "better": 1, "good": 2}
        candidates.sort(key=lambda x:
↪  quality_rank[x["quality"]])

    return candidates

def choose_model(self,
                 query: str,
                 complexity: str,
                 budget_manager: BudgetManager,
                 latency_preference: str) -> dict:

    estimated_input_tokens = max(len(query.split()) * 2, 50)
    estimated_output_tokens = 250 if complexity == "high" else
↪  120
```

```
        ranked_models = self.rank_models(complexity,
↪   latency_preference)

        for profile in ranked_models:
            estimated_cost = estimate_request_cost(
                profile,
                estimated_input_tokens,
                estimated_output_tokens
            )
            if budget_manager.can_spend(estimated_cost):
                selected = profile.copy()
                selected["estimated_cost"] = estimated_cost
                return selected

        fallback = self.model_profiles["cheap_model"].copy()
        fallback["estimated_cost"] = estimate_request_cost(
            fallback,
            estimated_input_tokens,
            estimated_output_tokens
        )
        return fallback
```

12.8 Executing the Selected Model

After the routing engine selects the most appropriate model, the next step is to **execute the request using the chosen model**. This stage is responsible for sending the user query to the language model and retrieving the generated response.

The execution layer performs three key tasks.

- Model Invocation
- Response Retrieval
- Token Usage Tracking

By separating the execution logic from the routing logic, the system maintains a clean design where the routing engine focuses on **decision making**, while the execution layer handles **model interaction and response generation**.

```
###########################################################
# LLM EXECUTION
###########################################################

def generate_response(query: str, model_profile: dict) -> tuple:
    response = client.chat.completions.create(
        model=model_profile["name"],
        messages=[
            {"role": "system",
                "content": (
                    "You are a helpful enterprise AI assistant. "
                    "Provide clear, structured, practical
                     ↪ answers.")},
            {"role": "user", "content": query}])

    message = response.choices[0].message.content
    usage = response.usage

    return (message,
        usage.prompt_tokens,
        usage.completion_tokens,
        usage.total_tokens)
```

12.9 Monitoring Routing Decisions

In addition to selecting models and executing requests, it is also important to **monitor how routing decisions are made**. When AI systems dynamically choose models based on cost and performance, developers need visibility into those decisions to ensure the system is behaving as expected.

To support this, the routing system includes a lightweight observability component called the **RoutingTracer**.

The purpose of this component is to record important routing events during execution. Instead of storing complex logs, the tracer maintains a simple structured list of events that describe how the routing process unfolded.

The tracer performs two primary functions.

- **Logging Routing Events** : During execution, the system records key events such as task complexity, model selected, estimated and actual costs, and remaining budget. Each event is stored along with a timestamp and relevant details. This provides a chronological record of the routing process.
- **Displaying the Routing Summary** : After the agent finishes processing the request, the tracer can display a summary of all recorded events. This summary provides a clear view of how the routing system made its decisions and how resources were consumed.

This observability layer makes the routing system more transparent. Developers can inspect routing behavior, verify that the correct models are being selected, and analyze system performance over time.

```
############################################################
# OBSERVABILITY
############################################################

class RoutingTracer:
    """
    Minimal observability for routing decisions.
    """

    def __init__(self):
        self.logs = []

    def log(self, event_name: str, payload: dict) -> None:
        self.logs.append({
            "event": event_name,
            "payload": payload,
            "timestamp": time.strftime("%Y-%m-%d %H:%M:%S")})
```

```
def show_summary(self) -> None:
    print("\n===== ROUTING TRACE =====")
    for entry in self.logs:
        print(f"[{entry['timestamp']}] {entry['event']}:
        ↪ {entry['payload']}")
```

12.10 Building the Cost-Aware Routing Agent

With all the individual components implemented, we now combine them into the **CostAwareRoutingAgent**, which acts as the central controller of the system. This agent orchestrates the entire routing workflow by coordinating complexity analysis, model selection, budget management, execution, and observability.

The agent integrates four key components:

- **Complexity Analyzer** – determines difficulty level of incoming request.
- **Routing Engine** – selects the most appropriate model.
- **Budget Manager** – tracks the budget spent and available.
- **Routing Tracer** – records routing decisions and execution metrics.

When the agent receives a query, the workflow proceeds through several stages.

First, the system analyzes the query to determine its **complexity level**. Next, the routing engine evaluates the available models and selects one that satisfies the complexity requirements while remaining within the available budget. The routing tracer records the selected model and the estimated cost of the request. Once a model has been selected, the system sends the query to the language model to generate a response. After the response is received, the system calculates the **actual cost of the request** using the token usage returned by the model. The budget manager then updates the remaining budget, ensuring that future requests remain within the defined cost limits. Finally, the routing tracer records important execution metrics such as token usage, latency, and remaining budget. These logs provide visibility into how the routing system behaves during operation.

By combining these components, the Cost-Aware Routing Agent provides a complete workflow for **intelligent model selection and cost optimization** in AI systems.

```
############################################################
# MAIN AGENT
############################################################

class CostAwareRoutingAgent:

    def __init__(self, total_budget_usd: float = 2.0):
        self.analyzer = ComplexityAnalyzer()
        self.budget_manager = BudgetManager(total_budget_usd)
        self.router = RoutingEngine(MODEL_PROFILES)
        self.tracer = RoutingTracer()

    def run(self, query: str, latency_preference: str = "balanced")
    ↪   -> str:
        start_time = time.time()

        complexity = self.analyzer.detect(query)
        self.tracer.log("complexity_detected", {"complexity":
         ↪  complexity})

        selected_model = self.router.choose_model(
            query=query,
            complexity=complexity,
            budget_manager=self.budget_manager,
            latency_preference=latency_preference)

        self.tracer.log(
            "model_selected",
            {
                "model": selected_model["name"],
                "latency": selected_model["latency"],
                "quality": selected_model["quality"],
                "estimated_cost": selected_model["estimated_cost"],
                "remaining_budget_before_call":
                 ↪  self.budget_manager.get_remaining_budget()})
```

```
        response_text, prompt_tokens, completion_tokens,
    ↪   total_tokens = generate_response(
            query,
            selected_model)

        actual_cost = calculate_actual_cost(
            selected_model,
            prompt_tokens,
            completion_tokens)

        self.budget_manager.register_cost(actual_cost)

        latency_seconds = round(time.time() - start_time, 3)

        self.tracer.log(
            "execution_metrics",
            {
                "prompt_tokens": prompt_tokens,
                "completion_tokens": completion_tokens,
                "total_tokens": total_tokens,
                "actual_cost_usd": actual_cost,
                "remaining_budget_after_call":
                 ↪  self.budget_manager.get_remaining_budget(),
                "latency_seconds": latency_seconds})

        return response_text
```

12.11 Running the Cost-Aware Routing Agent

With all components implemented, the final step is to execute the routing system and observe how it processes a request. This section acts as the **entry point of the application**, where the routing agent is initialized and provided with a query.

Once execution is complete, the generated response is displayed to the user.

In addition to the response, the routing tracer prints a **summary of routing events**, providing visibility into how the system made its decisions. This summary typically includes the detected complexity level, the selected model, estimated and actual costs, and the remaining budget.

This final step demonstrates how the system dynamically selects models while maintaining control over operational cost, latency, and resource usage.

```
#####################################################
# RUN PROJECT
#####################################################


if __name__ == "__main__":
    agent = CostAwareRoutingAgent(total_budget_usd=2.0)

    query = (
        "Design a scalable architecture for an enterprise
         ↪ multi-agent AI assistant "
        "that balances model quality, latency, and cost."
    )

    result = agent.run(query, latency_preference="balanced")

    print("\n===== AGENT RESPONSE =====\n")
    print(result)

    agent.tracer.show_summary()
```

```
===== AGENT RESPONSE =====

Certainly! Designing a scalable architecture for an
 ↪ enterprise multi-agent AI assistant involves balancing
 ↪ **model quality**, **latency**, and **cost** with
 ↪ modular components that enable flexibility, reliability,
 ↪ and efficient resource utilization. Below is a
 ↪ high-level architecture and design considerations:
```

---

1. Architectural Overview

```
+--------------+--------------+
|         Clients (UI)         |
| - Web / Mobile / Voice       |
+--------------+--------------+
               |
               v
+--------------+--------------+
|       API Gateway / LB       |
|   (Authentication, Routing) |
+--------------+--------------+
               |
               v
+--------------+--------------+
|     Orchestration Layer      |
|  (Agent Router / Manager)    |
+--------------+--------------+
               |
    +----------+-----------+
    |                      |
+---v---+              +---v---+
| Agent |              | Agent |
| (FAQ) |  ...         | (Sales)|
+-------+              +-------+
    |                      |
    v                      v
+--------------------------------+
|    Model Serving Layer /        |
|  Inference Engines (on-demand, |
|   cached, or lightweight)       |
+--------------------------------+
```

````
              |
              v
+-------------------------------+
|  Data / Context Store & Memory |
| (User profile, conversation    |
|  history, knowledge bases, etc)|
+-------------------------------+
              |
              v
+-------------------------------+
| Monitoring / Logging / Metrics |
+-------------------------------+
```

---

## 2. Component Details

### 2.1 Clients
- Multiple interfaces: Web apps, mobile apps, voice assistants.
- Handles input modalities, sends requests to API Gateway.

### 2.2 API Gateway / Load Balancer
- Handles authentication, authorization.
- Request throttling and routing.
- Provides a single point for interface scaling.

### 2.3 Orchestration Layer (Agent Router)
- Routes requests to the correct agent based on intent, domain.
- Can incorporate a lightweight primary NLU (Natural Language Understanding) component for routing.
- Supports fallback and escalation policies.
- Manages multi-agent conversations, context switching.
````
````

```
### 2.4 Agent Layer
- Each agent specializes in a domain (e.g., FAQ, sales, IT support).
- Agents can be separate microservices to scale independently.
- Agents implement dialogue flow, business rules.
- Can compose with LLMs or other models as needed.

### 2.5 Model Serving Layer
- **Model Quality:** Use a hybrid strategy combining:
  - Large foundation models (LLMs) for complex intents.
  - Smaller, domain-specific models or retrieval-augmented generation (RAG) for frequent or simple queries.
- **Latency Optimization:** Cache common queries and responses; use fast vector search for retrieval.
- Deploy models using scalable serving frameworks (e.g., Triton Inference Server, TorchServe).
- Autoscale inference nodes based on load.
- Consider edge deployments for low-latency needs.

### 2.6 Data / Context Store
- Store user profiles, conversation context, preferences for personalization.
- Use fast NoSQL stores (e.g., DynamoDB, Redis) with write durability.
- Store knowledge bases that agents query.
- Version and audit data for compliance.

### 2.7 Monitoring / Logging
- Track metrics: latency, error rates, user satisfaction.
- Use centralized monitoring platforms (e.g., Prometheus + Grafana).
- Alerting system for failures and SLA breaches.
```

```
- Logging for debugging and training data collection.

---

## 3. Balancing Model Quality, Latency, and Cost

| Aspect          | Approach                                                   |
|-----------------|------------------------------------------------------------|
| **Model Quality** | Hybrid approach: Use large LLMs only when needed; use smaller specialized models otherwise. Fine-tune domain-specific models periodically using feedback loops. |
| **Latency** | Cache frequent answers, run smaller models locally or on edge; asynchronous calls with user feedback for longer-running queries. Prioritize fast NLU for routing. |
| **Cost**        | Autoscaling inference resources; leveraging spot instances and serverless where possible; optimizing model size and input token length; offloading retrieval to vector DBs. |

---

## 4. Additional Considerations

- **Security:** Encrypt data in transit and at rest; secure access controls.
- **Privacy:** Support anonymization and compliance (GDPR, HIPAA).
- **Extensibility:** Microservice architecture promotes adding new agents/domains easily.
```

```
- **Feedback Loop:** Collect user feedback to retrain and improve models.
- **Disaster Recovery & High Availability:** Multi-region deployments, backups.

---

## 5. Example Technology Stack

| Component              | Possible Technologies                         |
|------------------------|-----------------------------------------------|
| API Gateway            | Kong, Amazon API Gateway, NGINX               |
| Orchestration Layer    | Kubernetes microservices, custom routing logic|
| Agent Services         | Python FastAPI, Node.js microservices         |
| Model Serving          | Azure ML, AWS SageMaker, Huggingface Inference Endpoints, Triton|
| Data Store             | Redis (for context), DynamoDB, PostgreSQL     |
| Vector Search          | Pinecone, FAISS, Elasticsearch                |
| Monitoring             | Prometheus, Grafana, ELK Stack                |

---

If you want, I can also provide a sample deployment diagram or help you tailor it to specific enterprise requirements. Would you like that?
```

```
===== ROUTING TRACE =====
[2026-03-06 18:03:14] complexity_detected: {'complexity':
↪  'high'}
[2026-03-06 18:03:14] model_selected: {'model':
↪  'gpt-4.1-mini', 'latency': 'medium', 'quality':
↪  'better', 'estimated_cost': 0.00042,
↪  'remaining_budget_before_call': 2.0}
[2026-03-06 18:03:35] execution_metrics: {'prompt_tokens':
↪  48, 'completion_tokens': 1118, 'total_tokens': 1166,
↪  'actual_cost_usd': 0.001808,
↪  'remaining_budget_after_call': 1.998192,
↪  'latency_seconds': 20.525}
```

12.12 Key Takeaways

In this project, we built a **Cost-Aware Routing Agent** capable of dynamically selecting the most appropriate language model for each request. Several important concepts were introduced in this chapter:

- **Model Profiles** that describe the capabilities, latency characteristics, and pricing of available models
- **Task Complexity Estimation** to determine the level of reasoning required for a request
- **Budget Management** to ensure that model usage remains within defined cost limits
- **Cost Estimation** to predict and track the financial impact of each request
- **Routing Logic** that selects the most appropriate model based on system constraints
- **Observability Mechanisms** to monitor routing decisions and execution metrics

Together, these components form a practical framework for **resource-aware AI systems**. By dynamically allocating models based on task requirements, organizations can significantly reduce operational costs while maintaining high-quality responses.

Project 10: Autonomous Enterprise Task Processing System

Key Objectives

- Autonomous Agents
- System Architecture
- Designing Agent Roles
- Knowledge Base for Context Retrieval
- Workflow Observability
- Shared LLM Execution Helper
- Implementing the Workflow Agents
- Building the Workflow Controller
- Running the Autonomous Workflow
- Key Takeaways

13.1 Autonomous Agents

Modern enterprises deal with large volumes of requests that require multiple steps of processing before a final response can be produced. A single request may require understanding the problem, retrieving relevant information, generating a solution, and verifying that the response is correct.

Traditionally, these steps are handled manually by teams of engineers or analysts. However, with advances in AI systems, it is now possible to automate these workflows by coordinating multiple specialized agents.

In this project, we build an **Autonomous Enterprise Task Processing System** that uses multiple AI agents to complete complex tasks through a structured workflow. Instead of relying on a single model to solve the entire problem, the system divides the task into multiple stages handled by dedicated agents. These agents collaborate within a controlled workflow to interpret the request, gather relevant context, generate solutions, and validate the final output.

Organizations often receive complex requests that require several steps before a final response can be produced. For example, consider the following request: "Prepare a technical summary of a recent system outage and recommend mitigation strategies."

To generate a reliable response, the system must perform multiple tasks:

1. Understand the intent of the request
2. Retrieve relevant background information
3. Generate a structured response
4. Validate the output before presenting it

Handling this process manually is time-consuming and inconsistent. A single AI call may also produce unreliable results because the task requires multiple reasoning stages. To address this challenge, we design an **autonomous workflow system** that coordinates several specialized agents, each responsible for a specific stage of the process.

13.2 System Architecture

The workflow is orchestrated by a **central workflow controller** that coordinates several agents. The architecture consists of the following components:

- **User Request** : The workflow begins when a user submits a request. This request acts as the trigger for the autonomous workflow.
- **Request Interpreter Agent** : This agent analyzes the request and converts it into a structured task description. The structured brief helps the system clearly define the objective and expected output.

- **Research Agent** : This agent retrieves relevant information from a knowledge base to provide context for the solution generation stage.
- **Solution Generator Agent** : Using the structured task brief and retrieved knowledge, this agent generates a clear and structured response suitable for enterprise environments.
- **Validator Agent** : Before presenting the response to the user, the validator agent reviews the output to ensure that it is complete, accurate, and aligned with the original request.
- **Workflow Tracer** : The system also records execution steps and performance metrics to provide visibility into how the workflow operates.

Together, these components form a **coordinated multi-agent workflow system** capable of solving complex enterprise tasks autonomously.

13.3 Designing Agent Roles

A core principle of multi-agent systems is **role specialization**. Instead of relying on a single agent to solve the entire task, the workflow assigns specific responsibilities to different agents. This makes the system more modular, reliable, and easier to extend.

The workflow is organized into four specialized agents.

- Request Interpreter Agent
- Research Agent
- Solution Generator Agent
- Validator Agent

By assigning clear responsibilities to each agent, the workflow becomes easier to manage while allowing the system to solve complex tasks through coordinated collaboration.

13.4 Knowledge Base for Context Retrieval

Before the workflow can generate a meaningful response, the system must have access to relevant background information. In many enterprise environments, responses should not rely purely on generative reasoning; instead, they should be supported by known operational knowledge.

To achieve this, the system includes a **small internal knowledge base** that stores concise explanations of common technical concepts such as system outages, latency spikes, memory leaks, and mitigation strategies. This knowledge base acts as a lightweight source of contextual information that the workflow can reference during execution.

The purpose of this component is to provide **grounding for the solution generation stage**. When the workflow receives a request, the research stage scans the knowledge base and retrieves information related to the task being processed. These research notes are then passed to the solution generator agent to help produce a more informed response.

This approach introduces an important concept used in real-world AI systems: **knowledge-assisted generation**. By combining retrieved context with generative reasoning, the system reduces the likelihood of incorrect or hallucinated responses.

In large-scale production systems, this type of knowledge source may come from structured databases, documentation repositories, or vector search systems. In this project, however, a simplified dictionary-based knowledge base is used to demonstrate the concept in a clear and accessible way.

```
import os
import json
import time
from datetime import datetime
from dotenv import load_dotenv
from openai import OpenAI

load_dotenv()

os.environ["OPENAI_API_KEY"] = OPENAI_API_KEY
client = OpenAI()

###########################################################
# KNOWLEDGE BASE
###########################################################
```

```
KNOWLEDGE_BASE = {
    "system outage": (
        "A system outage is a period when a service becomes
        ↪ unavailable. "
        "Common causes include infrastructure failure, database
        ↪ overload, "
        "network disruption, deployment issues, or third-party
        ↪ dependency failures."
    ),
    "latency spike": (
        "A latency spike refers to a sudden increase in response
        ↪ time. "
        "It is often caused by traffic surges, slow downstream
        ↪ services, "
        "resource contention, or inefficient queries."
    ),
    "memory leak": (
        "A memory leak occurs when an application continuously
        ↪ consumes memory "
        "without releasing it, eventually degrading performance or
        ↪ causing crashes."
    ),
    "mitigation strategies": (
        "Typical mitigation strategies include rollback, failover,
        ↪ traffic throttling, "
        "resource scaling, service restart, database tuning, and
        ↪ dependency isolation."
    ),
    "root cause analysis": (
        "Root cause analysis identifies the fundamental reason
        ↪ behind a failure "
        "instead of only addressing surface-level symptoms."
    ),
    "incident report": (
        "A good incident report includes summary, symptoms, impact,
        ↪ probable causes, "
```

```
        "recommended actions, and preventive measures."
    )}
```

13.5 Workflow Observability

As autonomous workflows become more complex, it becomes important to understand **how the system executes each step of the process**. To support this, the workflow includes a lightweight tracing component called the **Workflow Tracer**. The tracer captures information such as:

- the step being executed
- the input provided to the step
- the output produced by the agent
- the timestamp of the operation

It also records overall workflow metrics such as **execution latency and token usage**. All recorded information is stored in a structured trace file, allowing developers to inspect how the workflow behaved during execution. This visibility is especially valuable in production environments, where monitoring system behavior helps identify failures, optimize performance, and improve reliability.

```
##########################################################
# OBSERVABILITY
##########################################################


class WorkflowTracer:
    """
    Tracks the execution flow of the autonomous workflow.
    """
    def __init__(self):
        self.trace = {
            "steps": [],
            "metrics": {}}

    def log_step(self, step_name: str, input_data, output_data) ->
    ↪   None:
```

```
        self.trace["steps"].append({
            "step": step_name,
            "input": input_data,
            "output": output_data,
            "timestamp": str(datetime.utcnow())})

    def log_metrics(self, latency_seconds: float, total_tokens:
    ↪   int) -> None:
        self.trace["metrics"] = {
            "latency_seconds": latency_seconds,
            "token_usage": total_tokens}

    def save_trace(self, filename: str = "workflow_trace.json") ->
    ↪   None:
        with open(filename, "w") as f:
            json.dump(self.trace, f, indent=2)
```

13.6 Shared LLM Execution Helper

In a multi-agent workflow, several agents need to interact with a language model to perform their tasks. Instead of repeating the same model invocation logic in every agent, the system introduces a **shared helper function** that standardizes how the language model is called.

This helper function acts as a common interface between the agents and the language model. Each agent simply provides a system prompt and a user prompt, and the helper function handles the model invocation and response retrieval.

Using a shared helper provides several advantages like code reusability, consistent model interaction and token usage tracking.

By introducing this shared execution layer, the system maintains a clean separation between **agent logic** and **model interaction**, which simplifies both development and future improvements.

```
############################################################
# SHARED LLM HELPER
############################################################
```

```
def call_llm(system_prompt: str, user_prompt: str, model: str =
↪ "gpt-4o-mini"):
    response = client.chat.completions.create(
        model=model,
        messages=[
            {"role": "system", "content": system_prompt},
            {"role": "user", "content": user_prompt}])

    content = response.choices[0].message.content
    usage = response.usage.total_tokens
    return content, usage
```

13.7 Implementing the Workflow Agents

The core functionality of the system is carried out by four specialized agents.

- **Request Interpreter Agent** : This agent is responsible for understanding the user request. It analyzes the incoming query and converts it into a structured task brief that clearly defines the objective and expected output.
- **Research Agent** : The Research Agent retrieves relevant context from the internal knowledge base. This step ensures that the workflow is grounded in known information before generating a response.
- **Solution Generator Agent** : The Solution Generator Agent produces the final structured response. It combines the original request, the interpreted task brief, and the retrieved research context to generate a professional enterprise-ready output.
- **Validator Agent** : The Validator Agent performs a quality check on the generated output. It evaluates whether the response is complete, clearly structured, and aligned with the original request.

Together, these agents form the reasoning pipeline of the system, where each stage contributes to producing a reliable and well-structured final result.

```
##########################################################
# AGENT 1: REQUEST INTERPRETER
```

```
##########################################################

class RequestInterpreterAgent:
    """
    Understands the user request and rewrites it into a structured
↪   task brief.
    """
    def run(self, user_request: str):
        system_prompt = (
            "You are an enterprise workflow interpreter. "
            "Convert the user request into a structured task brief
             ↪ with: "
            "objective, task type, expected output, and key focus
             ↪ areas.")
        user_prompt = f"User request:\n{user_request}"
        return call_llm(system_prompt, user_prompt)

##########################################################
# AGENT 2: RESEARCH AGENT
##########################################################

class ResearchAgent:
    """
    Retrieves relevant knowledge from a small internal knowledge
↪   base.
    """
    def run(self, task_brief: str):
        task_lower = task_brief.lower()
        matched_knowledge = []
        for key, value in KNOWLEDGE_BASE.items():
            if key in task_lower:
                matched_knowledge.append(f"{key.title()}: {value}")
        if not matched_knowledge:
            matched_knowledge.append(
                "General Enterprise Guidance: For ambiguous
                 ↪ enterprise requests, "
                "collect context, summarize the issue, identify
                 ↪ impact, recommend "
```

```
                "actions, and validate the final output for clarity
                ↪ and completeness.")

        result = "\n\n".join(matched_knowledge)
        return result, 0  # deterministic tool, no LLM token usage

##############################################################
# AGENT 3: SOLUTION GENERATOR
##############################################################

class SolutionGeneratorAgent:
    """
    Produces the final enterprise-ready deliverable.
    """
    def run(self, original_request: str, task_brief: str,
     ↪ research_notes: str):
        system_prompt = (
            "You are an enterprise solution generation agent. "
            "Create a clear, structured, professional response. "
            "Use headings, concise explanations, and practical
             ↪ recommendations.")

        user_prompt = f"""
Original Request:
{original_request}
Structured Task Brief:
{task_brief}
Research Notes:
{research_notes}

Generate the final enterprise-ready output.
"""
        return call_llm(system_prompt, user_prompt)

##############################################################
# AGENT 4: VALIDATOR
##############################################################
```

```
class ValidatorAgent:
    """
    Reviews the generated output for completeness and clarity.
    """
    def run(self, original_request: str, generated_output: str):
        system_prompt = (
            "You are a validation agent. "
            "Evaluate whether the response is complete, clear,
            ↪ structured, and useful. "
            "Return JSON with keys: status, feedback. "
            "Status must be PASS or FAIL.")

        user_prompt = f"""
Original Request:
{original_request}
Generated Output:
{generated_output}
"""
        return call_llm(system_prompt, user_prompt)
```

13.8 Building the Workflow Controller

With the individual agents implemented, the next step is to coordinate them within a single execution pipeline. This responsibility is handled by the **Workflow Controller**, which orchestrates the interaction between all agents.

The workflow controller acts as the central coordinator of the system. Instead of allowing agents to operate independently, it defines a clear sequence of steps that the system must follow.

The workflow executes in four stages:

1. **Request Interpretation** – The system analyzes the incoming request and converts it into a structured task brief.
2. **Context Retrieval** – The research agent retrieves relevant knowledge from the internal knowledge base.

3. **Solution Generation** – The system generates the final response using the task brief and retrieved research notes.
4. **Output Validation** – The validator agent evaluates the generated response for clarity and completeness.

Throughout this process, the workflow tracer records execution steps and metrics, allowing the system to maintain visibility into how the workflow operates.

By centralizing the orchestration logic within a workflow controller, the system ensures that agents operate in a predictable and controlled manner. This design mirrors how many production AI systems coordinate multiple components to complete complex tasks.

```
##########################################################
# WORKFLOW CONTROLLER
##########################################################

class AutonomousWorkflowSystem:
    """
    Orchestrates all agents in sequence:
    1. Interpret request
    2. Research context
    3. Generate final output
    4. Validate output
    """

    def __init__(self):
        self.interpreter = RequestInterpreterAgent()
        self.researcher = ResearchAgent()
        self.generator = SolutionGeneratorAgent()
        self.validator = ValidatorAgent()
        self.tracer = WorkflowTracer()

    def run(self, user_request: str) -> dict:
        start_time = time.time()
        total_tokens = 0

        # Step 1: Interpret the request
```

```
task_brief, tokens = self.interpreter.run(user_request)
total_tokens += tokens
self.tracer.log_step(
    "request_interpretation",
    user_request,
    task_brief)

# Step 2: Research relevant knowledge
research_notes, tokens = self.researcher.run(task_brief)
total_tokens += tokens
self.tracer.log_step(
    "research_context_retrieval",
    task_brief,
    research_notes)

# Step 3: Generate final output
generated_output, tokens = self.generator.run(
    user_request,
    task_brief,
    research_notes)
total_tokens += tokens
self.tracer.log_step(
    "solution_generation",
    {
        "original_request": user_request,
        "task_brief": task_brief,
        "research_notes": research_notes},
    generated_output)

# Step 4: Validate output
validation_result, tokens = self.validator.run(
    user_request,
    generated_output)
total_tokens += tokens
self.tracer.log_step(
    "output_validation",
    generated_output,
```

```
            validation_result)

        latency_seconds = round(time.time() - start_time, 3)
        self.tracer.log_metrics(latency_seconds, total_tokens)
        self.tracer.save_trace()

        return {
            "task_brief": task_brief,
            "research_notes": research_notes,
            "final_output": generated_output,
            "validation": validation_result,
            "latency_seconds": latency_seconds,
            "token_usage": total_tokens}
```

13.9 Running the Autonomous Workflow

With all components implemented, the final step is to execute the workflow and observe how the system processes a request from start to finish.

The execution begins by creating an instance of the **AutonomousWorkflowSystem**, which initializes all agents and the workflow tracer. Once the system is ready, a user request is provided as input. In this example, the request asks the system to prepare a technical summary of a system outage and recommend mitigation strategies.

After the workflow finishes executing, the system displays several outputs including the structured task brief, retrieved research notes, the final generated response, and the validation result. It also prints execution metrics such as latency and token usage.

This final step demonstrates how multiple agents can collaborate within a controlled pipeline to complete complex enterprise tasks autonomously.

```
############################################################
# RUN PROJECT
############################################################

if __name__ == "__main__":
```

```
workflow = AutonomousWorkflowSystem()

request = (
    "Prepare a technical summary of a recent system outage,
     ↪ identify likely causes, "
    "and recommend mitigation strategies in a structured
     ↪ enterprise-ready format."
)

result = workflow.run(request)

print("\n===== STRUCTURED TASK BRIEF =====\n")
print(result["task_brief"])

print("\n===== RESEARCH NOTES =====\n")
print(result["research_notes"])

print("\n===== FINAL OUTPUT =====\n")
print(result["final_output"])

print("\n===== VALIDATION RESULT =====\n")
print(result["validation"])

print("\n===== WORKFLOW METRICS =====\n")
print({
    "latency_seconds": result["latency_seconds"],
    "token_usage": result["token_usage"]
})
```

```
===== STRUCTURED TASK BRIEF =====

### Task Brief

**Objective:**
```

```
To create a comprehensive technical summary of a recent system outage that includes an analysis of potential causes and actionable mitigation strategies.

**Task Type:**
Technical Documentation

**Expected Output:**
A structured report detailing the summary of the outage, identified causes, and proposed solutions for future prevention, presented in a professional format suitable for enterprise communication.

**Key Focus Areas:**
1. **Outage Overview**
   - Duration of the outage
   - Affected systems and services
   - Impact on users and operations

2. **Investigation and Analysis**
   - Initial diagnosis of the problem
   - Data and logs review
   - Stakeholder interviews

3. **Identified Likely Causes**
   - Hardware failures
   - Software bugs or configuration errors
   - Network issues
   - External factors (e.g., DDoS attacks, power outages)

4. **Mitigation Strategies**
   - Immediate corrective actions taken
   - Long-term improvements (e.g., system upgrades, redundancy enhancements)
   - Monitoring and alerting improvements
```

```
5. **Summary and Recommendations**
   - Consolidated findings
   - Proposed timeline for implementations
   - Ongoing evaluation metrics

6. **Appendices (if necessary)**
   - Technical diagrams
   - Incident log details
   - Contact information for follow-up

This structured report will facilitate understanding of the outage events, promote transparency, and guide future actions to enhance system reliability.

===== RESEARCH NOTES =====

System Outage: A system outage is a period when a service becomes unavailable. Common causes include infrastructure failure, database overload, network disruption, deployment issues, or third-party dependency failures.

Mitigation Strategies: Typical mitigation strategies include rollback, failover, traffic throttling, resource scaling, service restart, database tuning, and dependency isolation.

===== FINAL OUTPUT =====

# Technical Summary of Recent System Outage

## 1. Outage Overview
```

```
**Duration of the Outage:**
The system experienced an outage lasting approximately 3 hours, from 10:00 AM to 1:00 PM (UTC) on October 5, 2023.

**Affected Systems and Services:**
- User Authentication Service
- Payment Processing Gateway
- User Dashboard and Reporting Tools

**Impact on Users and Operations:**
- Approximately 35% of daily active users were unable to log in, affecting customer transactions and service access.
- A revenue decline estimated at 20% during the outage window due to halted transactions.
- Negative user experience reported through customer service channels.

## 2. Investigation and Analysis

**Initial Diagnosis of the Problem:**
The outage was initially diagnosed as a potential server failure leading to degraded service performance.

**Data and Logs Review:**
- System logs indicated a spike in error messages regarding database connectivity.
- Network traffic logs displayed unusual patterns suggesting excessive load during peak hours.

**Stakeholder Interviews:**
Interviews with IT staff revealed that a recent database update coincided with the outage, prompting further investigation into potential misconfigurations.
```

```
## 3. Identified Likely Causes

- **Hardware Failures:**
  Timeout errors in cloud server reports indicated that one
  ↪ of the primary application servers was non-responsive
  ↪ leading to service degradation.

- **Software Bugs or Configuration Errors:**
  Identified a misconfiguration in the database connection
  ↪ pool settings which was contributing to overload.

- **Network Issues:**
  While traffic patterns were monitored, a brief internal
  ↪ network glitch was noted, further exacerbating the
  ↪ situation.

- **External Factors:**
  No external attacks such as DDoS or power outages were
  ↪ detected during the timeframe of the incident.

## 4. Mitigation Strategies

**Immediate Corrective Actions Taken:**
- The non-responsive server was rebooted, allowing
↪ restoration of services.
- Adjustments to the database connection pool configuration
↪ were made to alleviate the load on the database.

**Long-Term Improvements:**
- Implementation of automated failover mechanisms to reduce
↪ downtime.
- Upgrading server capacity to handle peak traffic more
↪ effectively.
```

```
- Increased redundancy by duplicating critical components.

**Monitoring and Alerting Improvements:**
- Enhanced monitoring solutions have been deployed to track system performance metrics in real-time, enabling quicker response times.
- Implementing automated incident alerts communicated directly to the technical team.

## 5. Summary and Recommendations

**Consolidated Findings:**
The outage was primarily caused by a combination of hardware issues and software misconfigurations, compounded by a previous database update.

**Proposed Timeline for Implementations:**
- Immediate adjustments and monitoring installations: by October 15, 2023.
- Long-term infrastructure upgrades to be completed by December 2023.
- Regular quarterly reviews of system performance and incident responses starting January 2024.

**Ongoing Evaluation Metrics:**
- System uptime percentage
- Response times for user logins
- Number of support tickets related to system accessibility

## 6. Appendices

**Appendix A: Technical Diagrams**
- Diagram of system architecture during normal and peak load operations.
```

```
**Appendix B: Incident Log Details**
- Detailed timeline of events leading up to, during, and
 ↪ after the outage.

**Appendix C: Contact Information for Follow-Up**
- IT Support: it-support@example.com
- Incident Manager: incident.manager@example.com
- Head of IT Operations: head.itops@example.com

This structured report provides a clear understanding of the
 ↪ outage events, promotes transparency regarding its
 ↪ impact, and sets actionable steps to enhance overall
 ↪ system reliability in the future.

===== VALIDATION RESULT =====

{
  "status": "PASS",
  "feedback": "The response is complete, clear, structured,
   ↪ and useful. It includes detailed sections that address
   ↪ each aspect of the technical summary requested, such
   ↪ as the outage overview, analysis, identified causes,
   ↪ mitigation strategies, summary, recommendations, and
   ↪ appendices. Each section is well-organized and
   ↪ provides actionable information, making it suitable
   ↪ for an enterprise-ready format."
}

===== WORKFLOW METRICS =====

{'latency_seconds': 45.844, 'token_usage': 2477}
```

13.10 Key Takeaways

In this final project, we built an **Autonomous Enterprise Task Processing System** that demonstrates how multiple AI agents can collaborate to solve complex tasks through a structured workflow. Instead of relying on a single model call, the system breaks the problem into stages such as task interpretation, context retrieval, solution generation, and validation.

Throughout this book, we explored how to design intelligent agents, implement planning and execution mechanisms, incorporate observability, optimize model usage, and orchestrate multi-agent systems. These concepts represent the core building blocks of modern **Agentic AI systems**.

By combining these ideas, developers can build AI systems that are more reliable, scalable, and capable of handling real-world enterprise workflows. The projects in this book are intended to provide a practical foundation that you can extend to build your own **production-ready AI agents and autonomous systems**.

14. Agentic Frameworks: From Patterns to Implementation

Key Objectives of This Chapter

- Why Agent Frameworks Exist
- What Agent Frameworks Actually Do
- LangChain — The General-Purpose Agent Framework
- LangGraph — Building Stateful Agent Workflows
- CrewAI — Role-Based Multi-Agent Collaboration
- AutoGen - Conversational Multi-Agent Systems
- Comparing Agent Frameworks
- Frameworks vs Custom Agent Systems
- The Future of Agent Infrastructure

14.1 Why Agent Frameworks Exist

As AI systems evolved from simple prompt-based interactions to multi-step reasoning systems, building agents began to require much more than sending prompts to a language model.

Modern AI agents often need to:

- reason through problems step by step

- interact with external tools or APIs
- retrieve information from databases
- maintain memory across interactions
- coordinate multiple tasks or agents

Managing these capabilities directly in application code quickly becomes complex. Developers must handle reasoning loops, tool execution, state tracking, retries, and safety constraints.

To simplify this growing complexity, **agentic frameworks** began to emerge.

Frameworks provide reusable infrastructure for common agent behaviors such as:

- orchestrating reasoning loops
- managing agent state and memory
- integrating tools and external systems
- controlling workflows and task execution
- tracing and debugging agent decisions

Popular frameworks such as LangChain, LangGraph, CrewAI, and AutoGen attempt to standardize these capabilities.

However, it is important to understand that frameworks **do not define how agents think**. They simply provide structured ways to implement the architectures and patterns discussed earlier in this book.

The real intelligence of an agent system still comes from:

- the model
- the architecture
- the system design
- the reasoning strategy

Frameworks are therefore best understood as **implementation layers for agent patterns**, not replacements for sound system design.

14.2 What Agent Frameworks Actually Do

Agent frameworks are often described as tools for building AI agents, but this can be misleading. Frameworks do not create intelligence themselves. Instead, they provide the **infrastructure that allows agent systems to run reliably**.

Most frameworks support a similar set of responsibilities that enable agents to operate effectively.

Managing Reasoning Loops

Many agents rely on iterative reasoning rather than producing a single response. The agent repeatedly reasons, takes an action, observes the result, and continues until a solution is reached.

A typical loop looks like:

Thought → Action → Observation → Thought → Action → Observation

Frameworks manage this cycle by executing each step, determining when tools should be called, feeding results back into the reasoning process, and stopping the loop when a final answer is produced.

Tool Execution

Agents often interact with external systems such as APIs, databases, search engines, or internal services. Frameworks provide structured ways to register tools, format inputs, execute them safely, and return outputs to the agent.

State and Memory Management

Agents frequently need to maintain context across multiple steps, including conversation history, intermediate reasoning, retrieved documents, or task progress. Frameworks help manage this state so agents can continue operating across interactions.

Workflow Orchestration

In more advanced systems, agents perform sequences of dependent tasks such as breaking problems into subtasks, coordinating agents, retrying failed actions, or handling conditional steps. Frameworks provide mechanisms to manage these workflows.

Observability

Because agents operate through multiple reasoning steps, debugging can be difficult. Frameworks often include execution traces, tool call logs, and monitoring capabilities that help developers understand and evaluate agent behavior.

The Core Idea

Most frameworks manage five key elements:

- reasoning loops
- tool execution
- state and memory
- workflow orchestration
- observability

Once these responsibilities are understood, frameworks become much less mysterious. They are simply **structured environments for running agent systems effectively.**

14.3 LangChain — The General-Purpose Agent Framework

Among the many frameworks that have emerged in the agent ecosystem, **LangChain** has become one of the most widely used tools for building LLM-powered applications.

LangChain was originally designed to simplify the process of connecting large language models with external systems such as databases, APIs, and knowledge sources. Over time, it evolved into a broader framework for building **chains, agents, and retrieval systems**. Today, LangChain serves as an entry point for many developers exploring agent-based systems.

The Philosophy Behind LangChain

LangChain is built on a simple idea:

LLM applications are rarely a single prompt.

Instead, real-world systems typically involve multiple steps such as retrieving external information, transforming inputs, calling tools or APIs, processing intermediate outputs and generating structured responses. LangChain attempts to make these multi-step workflows easier to construct by providing reusable abstractions.

Rather than writing large amounts of orchestration logic, developers can assemble building blocks provided by the framework.These building blocks form the foundation of the LangChain ecosystem.

Core Components of LangChain

LangChain organizes LLM applications around several core abstractions.

Models

At the center of every LangChain system is a language model. The framework supports many model providers and allows developers to interact with them through a unified interface. This abstraction allows systems to switch models without rewriting application logic

Prompts

Prompt management is a major focus in LangChain. Instead of hardcoding prompts directly into application code, LangChain provides **prompt templates** that allow dynamic variables to be inserted into prompts.

Example concept:

Prompt Template: "You are a data analyst. Answer the question using the dataset summary below.

Dataset Summary: {dataset_summary}

Question: {user_question}"

Prompt templates help enforce structure and make prompts reusable across different workflows.

Chains

Chains represent sequences of operations executed in order. For example, a chain might perform the following steps:

1. Retrieve relevant documents from a vector database
2. Insert retrieved content into a prompt
3. Send the prompt to the model
4. Parse the model output

This concept allows developers to construct **LLM pipelines** where the output of one step becomes the input of the next. Chains were the original organizing concept behind LangChain before agent systems became popular.

Tools

Agents frequently need to interact with external systems. LangChain provides a standardized interface for defining **tools** that agents can call.

Examples of tools include:

- database queries
- calculators
- search APIs
- code execution environments
- internal services

Each tool typically contains:

- a name
- a description of what the tool does
- a function that executes the tool's logic

The model can then decide when to invoke the tool during reasoning.

Memory

Many AI applications require some form of memory. LangChain provides memory modules that allow systems to store and retrieve contextual information such as conversation history, previous responses and summarized interactions. These memory systems enable more coherent multi-turn conversations and persistent context.

Agents in LangChain

While LangChain originally focused on chains, it later introduced **agent abstractions** that allow models to dynamically choose actions. In an agent workflow, the model is given access to a list of tools and must determine:

- whether a tool should be used
- which tool to call
- what input should be provided to the tool

The agent then observes the result and continues reasoning until a final answer is produced. A simplified reasoning cycle looks like:

Thought → Choose Tool → Execute Tool → Observe Result → Continue Reasoning

LangChain provides agent templates that implement variations of this reasoning loop.

Retrieval-Augmented Generation in LangChain

One of LangChain's most widely used capabilities is support for **retrieval-augmented generation (RAG)** systems. RAG systems allow models to access external knowledge stored in vector databases. LangChain provides integrations with many vector databases and embedding providers, making it relatively straightforward to build RAG systems.

Strengths of LangChain

LangChain became popular largely because of its flexibility and ecosystem. Some of its key strengths include:

- **Extensive integrations** : LangChain integrates with many model providers, vector databases, and external tools.
- **Rapid prototyping** : Developers can quickly assemble applications using built-in components.

- **Large community** : The framework benefits from a large developer community and extensive documentation.
- **Modular architecture** : Components such as prompts, tools, chains, and memory can be reused across projects.

Limitations and Challenges

Despite its popularity, LangChain has also faced criticism from engineers building large-scale systems. Some common challenges include:

- **Abstraction complexity** : As applications grow, the abstraction layers can become difficult to reason about.
- **Debugging difficulty** : Tracing execution across multiple chains and components can be challenging.
- **Control flow limitations** : Complex workflows involving loops, conditional branches, or persistent state can be difficult to express using simple chains.

14.4 LangGraph — Building Stateful Agent Workflows

As developers began building more sophisticated agent systems, a limitation of traditional LLM pipelines quickly became apparent. Many early AI applications were built as **linear sequences of steps**:

Prompt → Retrieve Context → Call Model → Produce Output

This pipeline works well for simple applications such as chatbots or retrieval-based question answering. However, real-world agent systems rarely behave like linear pipelines. Consider a practical scenario. Suppose we want to build an agent that can:

- analyze a user request
- break the task into smaller steps
- retrieve relevant information
- call external tools when needed

- retry failed actions
- refine intermediate outputs
- produce a final structured response

In such systems, the next step depends heavily on what happened in previous steps. The agent may need to loop, retry, branch into different paths, or update its understanding of the problem as it progresses. To address this challenge, the LangChain ecosystem introduced **LangGraph**.

LangGraph provides a framework for designing **stateful agent workflows using graph-based execution models**. Instead of organizing operations as fixed pipelines, LangGraph treats agent systems as **graphs of interconnected steps that operate on shared state**.

This approach allows developers to build agents that can reason, act, observe results, and adapt their behavior over time.

Why LangGraph Exists

The core motivation behind LangGraph can be summarized in a simple observation:

Agents are not pipelines. They are stateful systems.

In real-world agent workflows, the system must constantly evaluate its current situation before deciding what to do next. The decision may depend on:

- previous reasoning steps
- outputs produced by external tools
- retrieved knowledge
- intermediate task progress
- success or failure of earlier actions

Without explicit state management, implementing these behaviors becomes extremely difficult. LangGraph addresses this challenge by introducing **state as a first-class concept in agent orchestration**.

Instead of passing outputs directly between steps, the entire system operates on a shared state object that evolves as the workflow progresses. Each step reads from this state, performs its computation, and updates the state before passing control to the next step.

The Graph-Based Mental Model

LangGraph organizes agent systems as **graphs of operations connected by control flow transitions**. Rather than executing a fixed sequence of operations, the system moves between nodes depending on the current state of the workflow.

Each node in the graph represents a unit of work such as reasoning about the current task, deciding whether a tool should be used or executing an external tool. Control then moves to another node depending on the outcome of that step. This structure allows agent systems to behave much more like real decision-making processes.

Because the workflow operates on persistent state, the system can revisit earlier steps as needed. This allows the agent to iterate through reasoning cycles until the task is completed.

Reasoning Loops in Agent Systems

Many of the agent architectures discussed earlier in this book rely on **iterative reasoning loops**. LangGraph is particularly well suited for implementing these kinds of reasoning cycles.

Instead of embedding loops inside prompts or ad-hoc application logic, LangGraph allows loops to be represented explicitly in the workflow graph. The system continues executing until a termination condition is reached.

This design provides greater transparency and control over agent behavior.

State as the Core of the System

The most important concept in LangGraph is **state**.

State represents the evolving context of the agent as it works through a task. Rather than passing intermediate outputs between functions, the entire system reads from and writes to a shared state object.

This state might include information such as:

- the original user request
- intermediate reasoning traces
- retrieved documents
- outputs produced by tools

- evaluation results
- partial solution

Because state persists across steps, LangGraph can support **long-running workflows and complex reasoning processes**. This approach also makes it easier to implement advanced behaviors such as task decomposition, iterative refinement, error recovery and collaboration between multiple agents.

LangGraph and Multi-Agent Systems

Another powerful capability of LangGraph is its ability to coordinate **multiple agents within the same workflow**. Instead of designing a single agent responsible for all tasks, developers can create specialized agents that handle different responsibilities.

Because all agents operate on the same shared state, they can collaborate effectively while maintaining a consistent view of the task. This makes LangGraph a strong foundation for building **structured multi-agent systems**.

Strengths of LangGraph

LangGraph introduces several advantages for building advanced agent systems.

- **Explicit control flow** : Developers can define how execution moves through the system rather than relying on hidden prompt logic.
- **Persistent system state** : Workflows can maintain context across multiple reasoning steps.
- **Structured reasoning loops** : Iterative reasoning can be implemented safely with clear stopping conditions.
- **Improved system transparency** : The graph structure makes it easier to inspect how the agent reached a decision.

These capabilities make LangGraph particularly attractive for engineers designing **complex or long-running agent workflows**.

When LangGraph Is the Right Choice

LangGraph becomes valuable when agent systems require more sophisticated orchestration than simple pipelines can provide.

It is particularly useful for:

- agents that perform multi-step reasoning
- systems that rely on tool usage and retries
- workflows involving conditional branching
- long-running tasks that maintain persistent state
- multi-agent collaboration systems

In these situations, graph-based orchestration provides a level of flexibility that linear pipelines cannot easily achieve.

When LangGraph May Be Unnecessary

Despite its strengths, LangGraph is not always the right tool. For simpler applications, a graph-based architecture may introduce unnecessary complexity.

Examples where LangGraph may be excessive include:

- simple chatbots
- single-step tool calling agents
- basic retrieval-augmented generation systems
- straightforward LLM pipelines

In these cases, a simpler framework or direct model interaction may be more appropriate. Understanding this distinction helps engineers avoid **overengineering agent systems**.

14.5 CrewAI — Role-Based Multi-Agent Collaboration

While some agent frameworks focus on workflow orchestration and state management, another design philosophy has gained attention in the agent ecosystem: **multi-agent collaboration**.

Instead of designing a single agent responsible for solving an entire problem, this approach distributes responsibilities across several specialized agents that work together to complete a task. This idea forms the foundation of **CrewAI**.

CrewAI provides a framework for building **teams of agents**, where each agent is assigned a specific role and collaborates with others to achieve a shared objective.

The Core Idea: Agents as a Team

CrewAI draws inspiration from how human teams solve complex problems.

In many professional environments, tasks are rarely handled by a single individual. Instead, different specialists contribute their expertise. A researcher gathers information, an analyst interprets findings, a writer produces a report, and a reviewer checks the final output.

CrewAI applies this same principle to AI systems. Rather than relying on one agent to perform every task, developers create multiple agents with clearly defined roles. Each agent focuses on a narrower responsibility, contributing to a larger workflow.

This approach can lead to more structured reasoning and clearer task boundaries.

Defining Agent Roles

In CrewAI, each agent is typically defined using three core elements: role, goal and tools.

- **Role** : The role describes the responsibility of the agent within the system. For example: Research Specialist, Data Analyst or Content Writer. The role helps guide the reasoning behavior of the agent.
- **Goal** : The goal describes what the agent is trying to achieve. It defines the outcome the agent should produce based on its role. For example, a research agent might have the goal of identifying relevant information sources, while a writer agent may focus on producing a well-structured summary.

- **Tools** : Agents may also have access to tools that help them accomplish their tasks. These tools might include: search APIs, document retrieval systems, data analysis utilities or external knowledge bases. The available tools influence how the agent approaches its assigned role.

Task Delegation in a Crew

CrewAI systems typically operate through **task delegation**.

A task is assigned to the crew, and different agents contribute to the task based on their roles. The output produced by one agent may become the input for another agent. Each agent contributes a specific capability, allowing the system to gradually refine the final result.

This structured collaboration can help break complex problems into manageable steps.

Strengths of the CrewAI Approach

The role-based design of CrewAI offers several advantages.

- **Specialized reasoning** : Agents can focus on narrower responsibilities, which often improves the clarity of their reasoning.
- **Modular system design** : Because each agent has a defined role, workflows can be extended by adding new agents without redesigning the entire system.
- **Structured collaboration** : The framework encourages developers to think about agent systems as collaborative processes rather than single monolithic agents.

These characteristics make CrewAI useful for workflows involving research, analysis, content generation, and decision support.

Practical Considerations

Despite its advantages, multi-agent systems also introduce additional complexity.

More agents typically means:

- increased communication between components
- higher token usage
- greater latency in producing final outputs

Designing effective agent roles also requires careful planning. If responsibilities overlap too much, agents may repeat work or produce inconsistent results.

For this reason, multi-agent systems should be used when collaboration genuinely improves the workflow rather than simply adding complexity.

When CrewAI Is Most Useful

CrewAI works best in systems where tasks naturally divide into specialized responsibilities. In such cases, distributing responsibilities across multiple agents can make the system easier to design and reason about.

However, for simpler applications, a single well-designed agent may be sufficient.

14.6 AutoGen - Conversational Multi-Agent Systems

Another approach to building collaborative agent systems focuses on **conversation between agents rather than predefined task pipelines**. This idea is explored in **AutoGen**, a framework developed by Microsoft Research.

AutoGen models agent systems as **structured conversations between multiple agents**, where each agent represents a different capability. Instead of strictly defining workflow steps, agents exchange messages and gradually refine a solution through dialogue.

The Core Idea: Agents That Talk to Each Other

In AutoGen, agents interact by sending messages back and forth, much like participants in a discussion.

Each agent may represent a different function, such as a planner, a coding assistant, a tool agent, a critic and so on. Through iterative communication, the agents collaboratively work toward a solution. This conversational model allows agents to improve their responses over multiple iterations.

How AutoGen Coordinates Agents

Instead of defining a strict workflow graph, AutoGen relies on **conversation protocols**.

Agents communicate through structured messages that contain instructions, responses, and feedback. These messages guide the overall process and determine which agent acts next.

Because communication is central to the framework, AutoGen systems often resemble **collaborative discussions between agents** rather than fixed execution pipelines.

Strengths of the AutoGen Approach

AutoGen offers several advantages for building collaborative systems.

- **Flexible collaboration** : Agents can dynamically exchange information and refine outputs through conversation.
- **Iterative problem solving** : Agents can critique and improve each other's work across multiple rounds.
- **Natural modeling of complex tasks** : Some problems benefit from discussion-like reasoning rather than rigid workflows.

These capabilities make AutoGen particularly useful in experimental systems involving coding agents, planning assistants, and iterative reasoning tasks.

Practical Considerations

While conversational multi-agent systems are powerful, they can also introduce challenges.

Because agents communicate through multiple message exchanges, systems may experience increase latency, higher token consumption and less predictable execution paths.

For this reason, AutoGen is often used in **research-oriented or exploratory agent systems**, where flexibility and experimentation are more important than strict workflow control.

When AutoGen Is Useful

AutoGen is well suited for scenarios involving **iterative collaboration between agents**, such as:

- coding assistants that generate and test code
- systems that refine solutions through critique
- exploratory problem-solving environments

However, for production systems that require strong control over execution flows, frameworks such as LangGraph may provide more predictable orchestration.

14.7 Comparing Agent Frameworks

By this point we have explored several agent frameworks, each designed around a different philosophy of building AI systems. This section provides a quick comparison to help engineers decide **which framework best fits the architecture of their system.**

Framework Focus

Framework	Core Idea	Best Use Cases
LangChain	General LLM framework	RAG systems, tool agents, prompt pipelines
LangGraph	Stateful agent workflows	Complex agents, reasoning loops
CrewAI	Role-based agent teams	Research and analysis workflows
AutoGen	Conversational agent collaboration	Coding agents, iterative reasoning

Engineering Characteristics

Framework	Workflow Control	Multi-Agent Support	Complexity
LangChain	Moderate	Limited	Moderate
LangGraph	High	Yes	Higher
CrewAI	Moderate	Yes	Moderate
AutoGen	Lower	Yes	Moderate

Quick Decision Guide

If your system needs…	Consider
LLM pipelines with tools and retrieval	LangChain
Complex agent workflows with explicit control flow	LangGraph
Teams of specialized agents collaborating	CrewAI
Agents refining solutions through conversation	AutoGen

In practice, many real systems combine ideas from multiple frameworks. The right choice depends less on popularity and more on **the architecture and complexity of the agent system being built.**

14.8 Frameworks vs Custom Agent Systems

Throughout this book, we built ten agent systems from the ground up without relying on agent frameworks. This was a deliberate choice.

Frameworks can accelerate development, but they also introduce layers of abstraction that can hide how agent systems actually work. When developers begin their journey with frameworks, it is easy to assemble working systems without fully understanding the mechanics behind them.

By building agents from first principles, we were able to explore the **core building blocks** of agent systems:

- reasoning loops
- tool integration
- memory and state management

- workflow orchestration
- error handling and guardrails

Understanding these components makes it easier to design reliable systems and evaluate frameworks critically.

Building agents directly provides several advantages for engineers. - Deeper system understanding - Greater architectural control - Clearer performance optimization - Better framework evaluation

Once developers understand how agents work internally, frameworks become easier to evaluate and use appropriately. Frameworks become increasingly useful as systems grow in complexity.

Frameworks help manage common engineering challenges such as:

- tool orchestration
- workflow coordination
- agent communication
- logging and observability
- integration with model providers and vector databases

Instead of reimplementing these capabilities repeatedly, frameworks provide reusable infrastructure that speeds up development.

The most effective approach is often a combination of both strategies. Early in development, building agents directly helps engineers understand the architecture and behavior of their systems. As systems mature and grow more complex, frameworks can help standardize infrastructure and reduce engineering overhead.

14.9 The Future of Agent Infrastructure

Agent systems are still in an early stage of development. Today, many teams are experimenting with agents through frameworks and prototypes. Over the next few years, however, the ecosystem will likely move toward **structured infrastructure designed specifically for agent-based systems**.

Just as web applications eventually evolved from simple scripts into full platforms with standardized tools, agent systems are beginning to develop their own infrastructure layers. Understanding these emerging layers helps engineers anticipate how agent systems will be built and deployed in the near future.

Emerging Infrastructure Layers

Several categories of infrastructure are already beginning to appear in the agent ecosystem.

- **Agent orchestration systems** : As agents become more complex, orchestration platforms will manage workflows, task routing, and multi-agent coordination. These systems will handle long-running processes and structured reasoning loops.
- **Observability and debugging tools** : Agents make decisions across many steps, often involving tools, memory, and external data sources. Observability platforms will allow engineers to trace reasoning steps, inspect tool usage, and diagnose unexpected behavior.
- **Evaluation and benchmarking systems** : Testing agent systems is significantly harder than testing traditional software. New evaluation frameworks will help measure reliability, accuracy, and cost across complex agent workflows.
- **Persistent memory infrastructure** : Future agents will operate over longer time horizons and will require mechanisms for storing knowledge, summarizing interactions, and retrieving relevant past information.

Together, these layers will gradually transform agents from experimental prototypes into reliable production systems.

What This Means for Engineers

As the ecosystem evolves, the most valuable skill will not be simply knowing how to use a particular framework. Instead, engineers will need to understand **how agent systems are designed**. Frameworks will continue to change, but these underlying patterns will remain consistent.

Final Takeaway

This book began with a simple goal: moving from prompts to practical AI agents.

Across the chapters, we explored the architectures, patterns, and engineering principles that make agent systems work. The projects demonstrated how agents can reason through problems, use tools, manage memory, and collaborate with other agents.

Frameworks will evolve and new infrastructure will emerge, but the foundations of agent design remain the same.

Models provide intelligence.
Agents provide action.
Engineering provides reliability.

The next generation of AI systems will not be defined solely by better models, but by better **systems built around those models**.

And the engineers who understand how to design those systems will shape the future of agentic AI.

Access to Code and Resources

All projects, implementations, and supporting materials from this book are available through controlled access. This ensures that the code remains structured, up-to-date, and aligned with the concepts explained throughout the chapters.

How to Get Access

To request access, please send an email to:

□ amritapanjwani@gmail.com

Include the following details: - Your name - Where you are reading this book (KDP / Notion Press / other)

What You Will Receive

You will receive a downloadable package containing all project code and resources

Notes

- The code is intended for learning and experimentation
- Readers are encouraged to modify and extend the implementations locally
- Updates and improvements may be shared periodically

Thank you for being part of this journey into building agentic systems.

Conclusion — The Shift Has Already Begun

You began this journey learning how to use AI; you now understand how to build it. The shift from prompts to systems is the most important takeaway from this book. You have worked through reasoning loops, memory, planning, and multi-agent orchestration — but more importantly, you have learned how to think in terms of state, control flow, tools, and feedback. That mindset is durable. Models will evolve, frameworks will change, and tools will improve, but the ability to design systems that act with intent will remain. Not everything will work — agents will fail, outputs will be imperfect, and plans will break — but that is inherent to building intelligent systems. Progress comes through iteration, refinement, and structured problem solving. The next step is simple: apply this thinking to real problems, build systems, observe where they fail, and improve them.

Key Takeaways - Think in systems, not prompts
- Design around state, control, and feedback
- Expect failure — engineer for iteration
- Focus on real problems, not demos
- Build, test, refine, and scale

www.ingramcontent.com/pod-product-compliance
Lightning Source LLC
LaVergne TN
LVHW050908210926
848482LV00012B/375